Ji

JANE RENOUF was b
a convent education, she graduated from the University of Kent to train as a newspaper reporter in south London. After two years of marriage, she and her husband Paul, who is a photographer, decided to leave city life behind, and moved north to the Lake District, where they have lived for the past twenty years, and where Jimmy, the eldest of their three sons, was born in 1981. Jane's first book, a manual for hill walkers, was published by Penguin Books in 1977; her work as a writer over many years has covered a wide spectrum including biography, local history and newspaper journalism.

# Jimmy

─────────❖◇❖─────────

## No Time to Die

## JANE RENOUF

Fontana
*An Imprint of HarperCollinsPublishers*

A royalty of 2 percent of the published price of each copy of *Jimmy* sold (approximately 12p per book) will be donated to the Cancer Relief Macmillan Fund, to be used specifically for the funding of more Macmillan paediatric nurses in all parts of the UK.

Fontana
An Imprint of HarperCollins*Publishers*,
77–85 Fulham Palace Road,
Hammersmith, London W6 8JB

A Fontana Original 1993

9 8 7 6 5 4 3 2 1

A catalogue record for the book is
available from the British Library

ISBN 0 00 637853 6

Set in Galliard

Printed in Great Britain by
HarperCollins Manufacturing, Glasgow

In memory of Jimmy:
that his light may never go out;
for all who loved and cared for him;
and for all children living or dying with cancer,
in celebration of their infinite courage.

'Not for myself, God knows, I grieve; but for him the young life, so gleeful . . . so ready to embrace all that life gave, to go so early, so swift away, letting go all he so passionately wished to hold.'

SEAN O'CASEY of his son Niall, who died of leukaemia in 1956. Taken from *Niall: A Lament*, Calder Publications, © Eileen O'Casey 1991

# CONTENTS

# INTRODUCTION

'How are you feeling today?' I asked my son. It was a warm, sunny morning, late in March, as he lay on his back to one side of our double bed. The curtains at the only window in the room were still partly closed to protect him from the bright sunshine, and smelt softly of freesias. His head was supported awkwardly on the pillow by his thin, painful neck, and his emaciated little eight-year-old body hardly made a shape under the duvet, except where his swollen spleen had distended his stomach and made a slight bulge visible. His face was paler than white, his deep blue eyes sunk in his lined forehead, the lids hardly able to stay open wide enough for his tired eyes to see me. His lips were dry, and it required several seconds of calculated effort to whisper the faint reply.

'I feel brill, Mum. I'm fine,' he answered, and smiled his sweet, sad smile.

Less than two days later his heart finally stopped beating under my hand as I held him, and he died in my arms.

Why write a book about our son Jimmy? Despite advances in curing childhood cancers, many children still lose the battle and die, so there was nothing unusual in his death. Yet these lost children are very special people. They die with their bravery unsung and unrewarded, their fight for life through painful and unpleasant treatment wasted and in vain. Each death is an outrage in an age when medicine has almost eradicated infant mortality; each death leaves behind broken, tired families, grief-stricken parents and lonely brothers and sisters. Jimmy's death was no exception. His tragedy was no greater nor less than any other dying child's and his story no more brave or pathetic than any of the two or three hundred children who died of cancer this year. Why should Jimmy deserve an entire book to be written all about him when the bravery and courage of his fellow sufferers and losers remains quietly and modestly unrecognized except by those close enough to have shared their lives?

After all, Jimmy was ill for only twenty months, a relatively short time compared with many child cancer victims, who often live through several tense and anxious years to find out whether treatment has been successful or not.

When a child is diagnosed as suffering from acute lymphoblastic or myeloid leukaemia, intensive treatment starts immediately and almost all can expect to go into remission within weeks or months, when the disease is brought under control and cancer cells are eradicated from the bone marrow. After the initial treatment, a two-year period of maintenance chemotherapy begins, during which some 95 per cent of the patients will not only survive, but feel quite well. Unfortunately for some children a relapse occurs, most commonly after the first two years of treatment, and chemotherapy has to start again. Chances of long-term survival are seriously reduced, but all is by no means lost, and a bone marrow transplant may be the best chance available.

Doctors predicted that Jimmy's treatment would have a 60 per cent chance of effecting a complete cure. The idea that he would relapse while still on maintenance treatment within the first two years was not even considered; the consequences were too grim and the possibility of this happening a mere 5 per cent.

But Jimmy was destined to be part of this tiny minority. His cancer returned in the middle of treatment, only fourteen months after diagnosis. Within another six months, he was dead.

A year before he died, when he still had every hope of beating leukaemia, and was so fit and well that he had returned to school, he stopped me one night as I kissed him goodnight.

He shared a bedroom with his five-year-old brother, Martin. Jimmy slept on the top one of their bunk beds. It was quite difficult to reach him to touch his cheek as he lay quietly above me. Below, Martin was already asleep.

Jimmy suddenly said, 'Mummy, while you're there, my light will never go out,' and he squeezed my hand, pleased to see my approval. He repeated the sentence before closing his eyes to sleep and I was left wondering what he meant. Was it a vow of confidence in my ability to keep him alive and well?

I treasured the words, even wrote them down. I enjoyed the imagery and sheer poetry of seeing his life as a candle burning in the night as much as I basked in his trust. But the morning that he died, I recalled his hopeful prophecy and I felt that I had let him down very badly, having been powerless to prevent his brave light from going out. His trust in me had been misplaced. I had let the light be extinguished.

Several days later, as I walked down the street in that state of numbness that occasionally relieves extreme grief, I suddenly heard his words again, but with a new meaning.

'While you're there, my light will never go out,' he had said. Although he had been dead a week or so, we had noticed that the warmth of his being still surrounded everything that we did, and influenced our thinking. His light did, indeed, continue to shine and would do so as long as we had minds to remember him. In time, maybe in two or three generations from now, when his immediate family are dead, his short existence will be lost in obscurity. But while we are here to remember Jimmy and carry his light in our own everyday lives, its brightness will never be dimmed. I can think of no better way of ensuring this than by writing down as much as I can remember about him.

The writing of this book became a commitment, so that old age and failing memory would never rob us completely of his eight precious years, from 1981 till 1990. Within these pages are preserved more of his strong spirit than we can ever find standing in the churchyard beside his quiet, sad little grave.

Although the book is about Jimmy, it is also a memorial to the hundreds of other children living and dying with cancer, deprived of so much of the energy and fun of childhood. May Jimmy's story give added impetus to all those working to find both a cause and a cure for this terrible disease.

It is a tribute too to those who care for them at every level of hospital life. Doctors and nurses in charge of these children care also for the entire family and its problems; but we parents never forget the comfortable, loving homeliness of the auxiliary and domestic staff, familiar cheery faces to each child. Their helpfulness and patience often put the whole ward in good spirits and their contribution to hospital life can never be overestimated.

There was nothing out of the ordinary about Jimmy and despite his bravery he was certainly no saint on earth. His story is partly our story too, the effect that his leukaemia had on our family relationships, the strains it imposed on all of us, and the way in which illness changed his character.

As the months pass by, carrying us further and further away from Jimmy's life, we find that our love for him has intensified and is starting to idealize our image of him. We remember all the good things about him, and start to forget his bad points.

In fact, illness meant that irritability and frustration often replaced his characteristic reasonableness; unable to compete physically in life, material values sometimes replaced the more important personal ones, and his spending power became one of the few things he could exercise any control over. As he became weaker and more ineffective physically, he needed to wield power in trivial ways, and when a Monopoly board represented the four corners of his shrinking world, winning became essential. He rarely showed anger or resentment over his illness to anyone except his brother Martin, who often bore the brunt of Jimmy's sick, bad temper. One lasting sadness and regret we will always feel was our failure to effect a reconciliation between the two brothers before Jimmy died. It is only honest to say that to his dying moments, Jimmy never forgave Martin for not having leukaemia. He could never see Martin's robust good health without expressing his anger in hurtful ways. But he spared his parents this anger; instead, he would ask the same question over and over again: 'Why does it always have to be me that gets the bad luck?'

Perhaps one day the last vivid memories of a sick and dying child will fade sufficiently to remember only the healthy boy we once loved so much, a child who loved life, whose understanding and maturity often outstripped ours, and whose articulate, affectionate nature endeared him to children and grown-ups alike.

# ONE

### ✳

# Birth and Beginnings

Paul and I were married in 1970, and spent the first two years of our marriage living in a large and pleasant company flat in Surrey. We had met whilst I was at the University of Kent, and Paul had been taking one of his more interesting times out from a career initially in insurance.

This particular break from his nine-to-five city routine found him driving minibus parties of students to Greece and Russia during the summer months. I was a student on one of his trips to the USSR, and he acted as driver and courier over thousands of miles and dozens of countries as I cooked for the party. From the moment we shook hands on Belgian soil in Ostende, we were friends. The friendship grew quickly and blossomed into love by the time we reached Vienna, and held firm as we passed through Prague, witnessing the Russian invasion of 1968, continued through Hungary, over the Carpathians into Lvov, through Kiev to Moscow and back home via Leningrad, Finland, Sweden and Denmark. A nine-year age gap hardly seemed to matter and two years later, after my graduation, we were married.

The first years were busy as we established the ground rules of marriage and I worked as a junior reporter for the local paper while Paul returned to a desk and the claims forms, more in order to secure a cheap flat for us than to satisfy his enthusiasm for catching the 8.23 to London Bridge Station and another day spent considering the risk factors of industrial boilers.

The year was 1972 when we first read dire predictions of inner city breakdown and decay, race riots and overcrowding. We decided a city was no place to bring up the family we eventually planned to have, and looked for an escape before sudden parenthood might force us into a cheap company mortgage and a commitment for life to a dead-end office job. It was a time when self-sufficiency had crept into the language, and we dreamed of country cottages, a vegetable garden, and complete freedom and independence from being wage slaves.

The reality of self-employment was somewhat different. With little money and no obvious way of earning a living, we opted for a partnership and by pure process of elimination reached the conclusion that we could run either a post office and shop, or a guesthouse.

While on holiday walking in the Lake District we did a little house-hunting in Westmorland, and finally found a tall, narrow house mainly composed of steep stairs and small rooms, on the side of a main road in one of the area's principal tourist towns. With no time to attend catering courses before the beginning of our first season, I turned the Vacancies sign round one cold Easter with as much idea of how to cook an evening meal for twelve as any Joint Honours in Philosophy and English and a Proficiency in Journalism could teach me. Within hours the house had filled up, the No Vacancies sign was almost permanently in place and we became guesthouse proprietors.

Year after year, we cooked our way through the 1970s as we served up platefuls of roast beef or steak and kidney puddings. Our business was most successful and our visitors were for the most part kind, thoughtful guests whose company we enjoyed in the evenings, and whose bedrooms we faithfully cleaned every morning. Many of them remain friends to this day.

Vietnam came and went; value-added tax, Watergate and Nixon, it mattered little as we steamed, boiled and fried, hoovered and dusted. In those days there was no winter tourist season and our visitors went home in October, not to return until Easter. So for eight months of each year, we worked seven-day weeks, but the remaining four months were jobless and free.

We were quite contented, even though no babies arrived to complete our happiness. There were near misses, failures, disappointments and tests, but still no children after ten years of marriage.

Determined that the disappointment of childlessness would not blight our lives, we accepted it as unfortunate but unalterable, and chose instead to capitalize on the freedom that we still enjoyed without the tie of young children.

I supplemented our income by working as a district reporter for our local paper, and in 1977 I became a paperback writer when Penguin Books published a book I had written on mountain common sense and first aid, in conjunction with the leader of our local mountain rescue team. Paul took photography very seriously, especially wild life and landscape.

We travelled each winter, twice overland to the Sahara and High Atlas in North Africa, taking groups of friends camping with us by minibus. When the mood took us, we booked flights and holidays to Greece or Spain or Italy. One winter we took the Greyhound bus from New York all the way south to the Gulf of Mexico and back. 'Forget about having children,' the experts had told us, 'because there just aren't going to be any.' We never doubted their words for an instant.

It was only after accepting that childlessness really wouldn't blight my life as a woman, or make me feel less than biologically complete, that I became quite convinced that I was pregnant, a view not shared by anybody else especially as tests proved negative. But I was right, and they were wrong, and sadly our first baby died and I miscarried.

The only analogy I could use at the time to explain my feelings was that of somebody who wins the Pools, only to find that nobody posted the coupon. I wandered wearily round the fields near our house that July, watching the hay-making in progress and other people's children playing in the bleached stubble. Humiliated again, I faced this new loss by looking for success in other directions. Another pregnancy seemed unlikely after the infection and illness caused by the first miscarriage; yet two years later, returning from a short holiday feeling sick and tired, we both knew almost instinctively that we had another baby on the way.

Delighted, I awaited official notification of the pregnancy test. It came one day in May, the same day a mad assassin had attempted to kill the Pope. I was cooking dinner for ten, preoccupied with my news, when the kitchen door opened a fraction and an old and very irreligious friend poked his head round the door to tell us with excitement about the murder attempt on the Pope.

'To hell with the Pope, I'm pregnant!' came my reply. Jimmy was on the way.

I am certain beyond doubt that Jimmy was conceived on Boat Race Day, and ironically enough, it was on Boat Race Day nine years later that he died.

The pregnancy progressed through morning sickness to eventual high blood pressure and toxaemia, and by November things were not looking healthy for the baby, due on Christmas Day. By mid-November I was in hospital, which was the safest place for both of us to be in the event of an early labour. Eleven years of waiting made the baby a particularly precious one, and every precaution was taken to ensure a safe delivery and a live, healthy baby.

The second of December dawned cold and frosty and, with little else to do, I settled down to another energetic day of crossword solving, when I suddenly realized I couldn't see the clues any more, and the room had filled with bright flashbulbs and popping stars. My blood pressure was too high, and the baby had to be induced immediately.

Four hours later, Jimmy's head appeared to the assembled company, and to hurry things up and stop his foetal distress, he was hauled out with forceps. The very first thing he did in life was to drench the waiting paediatrician with an arc of wee, a fact which later delighted him and a story he never tired of telling. Paul, who was present at one side of my head as far away from the action as he could be, had brought his Thermos of coffee and packet of chocolate digestives and was quite unprepared for a birth which reminded him more of a heavy rock concert with clashing metal, expletives and blood than the natural, gentle birth we had prepared for at antenatal classes.

The excitement over, the staff disappeared, leaving Paul and me alone with our tiny, beautiful and perfect baby boy. His eyes were the darkest blue set in an angelic face, every feature perfectly in proportion. I lay on my side staring at him in the little incubator by the delivery bed, and he stared back at me, his eyes wide open. It was as if he needed to observe and record all the details of my face, his expression wise and wondering. We continued to stare for over a quarter of an hour before his features relaxed and he became a peaceful sleeping baby and the strange maturity faded.

I later read of the existence of a period of intense mother/baby interaction and mutual observation which sometimes occurs just after birth and I think we were fortunate to enjoy this heightened awareness of each other.

Weighing in at just over five pounds, James Thomas was taken to the Special Care Baby Unit and put inside an incubator, and I spent my first night apart from my baby hugging a Polaroid photograph of him, longing for him to be beside me in a little cot, just like all the ordinary and less problematic full-term babies around me.

It was afternoon of the next day before I could visit him, and I suffered very real distress that night as I thought about my clumsy attempts at breast-feeding, which the staff had implied were overtiring Jimmy, so that by the time we had finished he was too weary even to suck a bottle. It wasn't easy, sitting on stitches so tight I felt as though I had been laced up; the unit insisted that all visitors, including feeding mothers, should wear a slippery polythene pinafore which made it even harder for a first-time mother unaccustomed to handling a tiny baby to get a firm hold, tempt a reluctant, sleepy baby to breast-feed through layers of pinafore and nightdress in temperatures that would have melted chocolate, and all this under the supervision of a watching nurse or midwife.

Add to this the fact that all the experts gave different, conflicting advice, and that a test weigh before and after a feed often revealed that Jimmy's efforts to suck actually reduced his weight during the feed, and it seemed a miracle we persevered at all. When all the milk dried up, and Jimmy's neonatal jaundice made him even sleepier, the breast pump kept a tiny trickle flowing; but it was a losing battle, and the tears of disappointment amounted to more fluid than the breast pump produced during some feeds.

Eventually, after ten days or so, it was decided that we could go home, provided there was adequate supervision. Paul and I left Lancaster and headed up the M6 one cold Thursday afternoon, unable to believe that now we really were three, and in the carrycot in the back lay our precious little cargo. Word had spread round the village about our 'miracle' baby after an eleven-year wait, and we arrived home to piles of cards and knitted matinée jackets.

The problem of feeding Jimmy remained. Despite all efforts, there was virtually no breast milk, and although soya milk was a fair substitute, it wasn't thought to be as good as the home-made stuff for a premature, low-birth-weight baby. The health visitor was quite adamant. Stop complementing breast feeds by topping up with soya milk, chuck the bottles away, let Jim go hungry for a couple of days, and with enough stimulation and hungry sucking, the problem would solve itself, she said. She was right. Within three days, I could have fed quins, and Jimmy ruled his supply and demand until some nine months later when he tested his sharp, new little teeth with a vicious bite, and declared himself not interested in breast milk any more.

However good many antenatal classes are, no mother, midwife or health visitor could ever describe the exhaustion, frustration and confusion of those first few weeks with a first baby when night and day become one indecipherable jumble. Relationships and routines have to be redefined and mothers expecting to be overwhelmed with baby love often find themselves feeling cold and even resentful as they try to get acquainted with a selfish stranger whose demands are unending.

So it was at first with Jimmy. His jaundice was slow to improve, and it made him sleepy and reluctant to feed. At about three weeks old, he developed colic so badly that within a minute or two of starting to feed, he would draw his little legs up to his tummy, throw his head back and roar. Fortunately his colic was limited to day rather than night-time, but he thought nothing of screaming for up to twelve daylight hours at a time. We took it in turns to pace the floor with him, and after a month I began to think that Jimmy not only didn't love me, but was fundamentally unhappy, and would grow up into a miserable child. He fretted and fussed, and so, no doubt, did we.

Added to this, everybody remarked in turn how lucky we were and what a little miracle Jimmy was, and it made us feel even guiltier that so far his life had brought us nothing but conflict and exhaustion.

It was about six weeks after he was born that Jimmy stopped being a noisy stranger and started to be our baby. Our love was rewarded with a smile, and from that moment on we were bonded to each other as though with superglue.

His first year passed very quickly as his endearing baby behaviour captivated us and delighted all who saw him. He was most beautiful to look at, with serene, perfectly proportioned features, and a great maturity of expression. At six months, he would lie on his stomach in his cot and suddenly he would arch his strong back, push his head up high and turn to grin at us. He loved to be carried high up in the papoose carrier when we went for a walk, though by eleven months he could walk by himself, managing five wobbly steps in a row before his knees would buckle underneath him and he would land with a thump on the carpet, still laughing.

One of his favourite toys was a cheap, wooden push-along trolley, which Paul filled with wooden bricks he had made for Jimmy. He had a little blue toy rabbit, and a dog which sucked its thumb by sticking its velcro paw to its velcro tongue. He was as happy as a baby could be, surrounded night and day by both his mother and his father, and he was quick, responsive, bright and beautiful.

The fear of a silent, unpreventable cot death was always a threat lurking in the back of our minds. How ironic it would be to lose Jimmy inexplicably and tragically after waiting so long for his arrival. But because such deaths have no known cause, there was nothing we could do to prevent it and instead of worrying about such a remote possibility it would have been wiser to look more carefully at his cot itself where a much more immediate threat to his life lay hanging about eight inches above his head and neck.

Jimmy was nearly nine months old, able to pull himself up to peer over the top of his cot, when I left him one morning to have his rest alone in his room. The guesthouse continued to thrive, and I worked on as I had before in the kitchen and the dining room and the bedrooms, cooking, waiting on and cleaning. It was a busy life, but by working together at home we shared Jimmy's babyhood together and he was always at the centre of everything we did, watching as we served the breakfasts, or made the beds.

This particular Friday, instead of taking the washing out to hang it in the garden, a job which took me at least ten minutes, I stopped instead to glance quickly through the second-hand car column of the local paper. There was no reason why I suddenly felt I must run up to Jimmy's room; he didn't shout or cry. He couldn't have done, because he was dangling in his cot, suffering a rapid strangulation.

Round his neck, wound very tightly, was a length of thin tape on which were sewn some tiny little elephants. The tape had been tied round the bars of his cot, but one end had come undone and Jimmy had somehow managed to pull himself up to a standing position, and wind the tape round his neck. The more he had struggled to free himself, the tighter the noose became, and as I rushed into his room, his head was pushed back, his face completely grey without any colour, and his eyes bulging.

It felt as if my entire life was passing before my eyes in slow motion as I fumbled to free him, yet it can only have taken a few seconds. I thought he was dead; but as I released his neck, the colour flowed back to his cheeks and he started to howl loudly. His eyes continued to bulge for some time, and I wondered if he might be brain-damaged. The tape had pulled round his neck so tightly that friction had grazed his skin. But he was alive, noisily so, and within five minutes he managed a drink, a rusk, and a shaky smile. I knew he would have been dead within a few seconds if I hadn't run upstairs.

It was a long time, some years, before I finally stopped feeling guilty at what had almost happened. If Jimmy had died, his death would have been rated as accidental, but we could never have accepted that verdict. The fact that we had left something tied to his cot bars with the potential to strangle our baby would have made his death due to unforgivable negligence. I still check cots for unsafe toys or dangling tapes whenever we visit friends with babies.

When Jimmy was very ill and dying, I used to wonder whether it would have been better for him if he had died with the elephants round his neck in that freak baby accident, knowing very little and suffering for less than a few seconds. But it wasn't an option open to us, and even if it had been and we had asked Jimmy to choose what he would have preferred, the reply would have been, 'Oh, Mum, what d'ya think, course I wanted my life.'

Paul and I gave Jimmy a little brass model steam engine for his first birthday, an unsuitable present that he could only damage, but one which started his life-long fascination for trains and engines. The train, which produced a wisp of greasy smoke from an infusion of oil in its inner workings, clambered round the kitchen floor, hooting its lonesome moan every fifteen seconds, in weak imitation of a Union Pacific engine crossing the great prairie grasslands in the Old West. At first frightened of its eerie hooting, Jimmy soon loved it. He always looked after his treasures.

Throughout his second year, he was dearer to us both than we could ever have imagined possible in our childless days. He saw as much of his father as he did of his mother and his life was uncomplicated and extremely happy.

Every day throughout that second summer, he and Paul would go off together, hand in hand, Paul bending down to reach Jimmy as he toddled along the rough path down to the river, then through the park and to the shops. He wore a little white cap sometimes to shade his eyes, and a pair of blue shorts and dusty, open sandals. Often he would trip over the end of one sandal, and some walks down to the river ended with a sore knee or a bruised elbow. Sometimes they took Jimmy's pushchair, when he would either stand up and face backwards, or push the chair himself when it would travel downhill faster than he could run, leaving him flat on his face, knees grazed yet again. To watch a father and his little son having such fun together was a moving sight; how fortunate we could not see into the future and what lay ahead for us all.

There was not a cloud on Jimmy's horizon in those days. He was small for his age, with blond hair and fine, delicate features. His eyes were dark blue, so dark they sometimes appeared black. Despite the fragility of his looks, he was strong, fit and healthy, never ill, hardly ever caught colds, and the only childhood illness he encountered was chicken pox.

He enjoyed our working life, and loved to meet the guests, though his daring raids on their toast racks at breakfast time, cute though people thought he was, had to stop. He learned at a very early age about awareness of other people, and he understood the reasoning and sense behind the few rules imposed, and responded with maturity, as he did throughout his life.

We lived by a main road bustling all day with heavy traffic. We couldn't shut a gate to keep him in the garden because guests would have been unable to come and go, and we would have lost business; but Jimmy never disobeyed and would never have attempted to stray away from safety because he understood why it would have been dangerous to do so. Even then, we appreciated how fortunate we were to have a child as sensible as he was.

Jimmy's first experiences of the seaside were along the Cumbrian coast when he was about fifteen months old. We took him on the beach one cold February day, and he sat down on the gravelly ground to feel the sand, even taste it in his haste to discover new sensations. We collected shells, avoiding the characteristic litter that always seems to cling to beaches. There were punctured, rusting cans of antifreeze, plastic shampoo bottles and swathes of torn polythene sheets washed ashore from passing ships.

About this time we visited the beaches at St Bees, Seascale and Ravenglass, Silecroft and Haverigg. It was 1983, and although we'd heard of the arguments regarding nuclear safety presented at the Parker Inquiry in 1978 which debated the safety and feasibility of reprocessing at nearby Sellafield, or Windscale as it was known then, we were not deterred from visiting the coast. We had yet to hear of the worryingly high incidence of childhood leukaemia in Seascale during the years immediately before.

The arguments surrounding nuclear safety rumbled on – each report of unacceptably high levels of radiation from one set of experts was immediately countered with assurances from others that such levels fell well within safety limits. When the experts themselves could not agree on what constituted nuclear safety, we had little chance as ordinary individuals of assessing the risks accurately. Although we were not particularly concerned at the time, this didn't stop us asking some very searching questions in the years that followed as we agonized over the

causes of Jimmy's cancer, questions which even now remain unanswered.

Could it really have been true that small amounts of highly
radioactive material lay undecayed along the beaches, and inland too?
Had the suspected link between childhood leukaemias and exposure
to even small amounts of radiation ever really been proved? And could
it be possible that just one tiny particle of plutonium in a little fistful
of sand, ingested by means of a licked finger, or breathed in by a
curious toddler, might cause cancer in later years – or was it all just
anti-nuclear propaganda?

Even if those beaches had ever been declared unsafe, the chances
that these occasional visits alone might have resulted in Jimmy's illness
and death are extremely remote. But perhaps together they form just
one minute piece in a much bigger puzzle – one in which a small
minority of children fall victim to some form of cancer, while hundreds
of others live and play daily within yards of suspected cancer-causing
agents, displaying no ill effects whatsoever.

As we had little understanding of these issues, we never really
considered nuclear safety on the beach where I sat in the sun so
contentedly during my pregnancy, and where later Jimmy played;
instead, we were more concerned at the obvious signs of raw sewage
from outlet pipes running down the beaches, and it was the threat of
illness from these which stopped us from returning to that coast. Jimmy
enjoyed his first experiences of the seaside and went home with
pocketfuls of shells, and wellingtons loaded with gritty sand, and we
brought back precious rolls of film showing a small, bright little boy,
dressed in a big blue duvet suit and red wellingtons, smiling with
excitement at his first glimpses of the sea. Rightly or wrongly, we would
never even contemplate taking our surviving children to those beaches
now.

Jimmy's life remained stable and unchanging during his first two
years. By sixteen months he could communicate in sentences, which
opened the door to books and his love of words and stories. His
concentration never flagged as we explored the lives of Postman Pat
or Thomas the Tank Engine. He joined the local library as soon as he
could reach the shelves, and his fascination with books far outweighed
the casual interest he gave to television.

By his second birthday, he had noticed the growing bump which
came between us as he snuggled up to me, but was quite unaware

what impact such an innocent bulge would have on his whole life. When my pregnancy was confirmed the autumn before, we were only too ready to leave our old way of life; so we put the guesthouse up for sale and bought an old and virtually derelict stables and workshop, in which we would all live and Paul would work as a photographer. Suddenly everything in Jimmy's world was changing all at once.

Martin's birth was as casual and relaxed as Jimmy's had been problematic and tense. My sister, Cate, came to stay to keep Jimmy company, and the two of them spent several happy days and nights together. They shared Jimmy's bedroom and he would hang over the edge of his cot in the early morning, chatting freely and widely about the important things in his life, delighted at her attentiveness. When he came to visit us in the maternity hospital, he hardly had time to peep at big, red-haired Martin in his cot, or give me a cuddle. I had, after all, left him on his own, and now I had introduced somebody else into our perfect lives. He probably felt very neglected and angry.

Just three weeks later, one wet and dreary Thursday, Jimmy watched with tears streaming down his face as the removal men emptied his home of every familiar landmark.

His new home was a two-hundred-year-old building at the end of a blind alley in the centre of the town, which had enough space to make both photographic studios and darkrooms, with living accommodation upstairs. The building had been the stables where coach horses serving the nearby hotels were accommodated for the night in stalls downstairs. The upper part of the long, narrow building was used for storing hay, and provided a dry, warm place for the ostlers to sleep. Four little mangers in the wall, connected originally by chutes to the stalls below, allowed the horses to be fed directly from the hay loft, and the thick and solid old walls of this friendly place kept us cool and quiet in summer and well insulated in winter.

The building was being used as a light engineering workshop before we bought it but was now redundant, so we qualified for a grant from the Council for Small Industries in Rural Areas to convert the old workshop into a new business.

But however radical the work required for conversion was downstairs, it was infinitely worse upstairs. The accommodation was little more than a space, with rough-cast walls, high beamed ceilings, and a makeshift kitchen and bathroom. The prospect of living in it seemed like a bad dream, but we were determined to make the best of it until such time as we could afford to buy a house separate from the business.

Much as I tried to like it, my first impression was that of claustrophobia. The building was bounded on three sides by tall, featureless walls, and the fourth side overlooked the back of a busy fish-and-chip shop kitchen. There was no garden to speak of, just a strip of land used as a rubbish dump behind the building. Nothing grew there – or so we thought.

But we were wrong. A deadly nightshade had forced its head up through the compressed rubbish. This rare reminder of living, growing things so impressed Jimmy that he felt impelled to sample the berries, something he had never been daft enough to do ever before despite the laburnum tree in our old garden. He was found with purple juice staining his lips, but not his tongue. Fortunately he had stopped short of eating the berries and had swallowed nothing.

In its favour, the building was well away from traffic and noise. The rough old plaster looked mellow in the afternoon sun, and with the addition of three bedrooms, a new kitchen, bathroom, central heating and windows overlooking the chip shop rather than the wall, it became pleasantly habitable. We were always happy there. Sitting within its solid old walls was a little like browsing in a quiet library in the centre of a busy town. The noises are offstage, distant, and never intrusive.

Our priority had been to convert the ground floor first so that we could open for business and produce an income. For some eight months, we lived entirely without earning anything, while we watched with horror as the cost of converting the building doubled. The upstairs living accommodation took second place, and consequently work was hardly started at all by the time we had to leave the guesthouse to let the new owners move in. Martin was just three weeks old when we faced our temporary homelessness. Kind friends took us in and we stored our belongings at our unfinished new home.

Throughout moving day, Jimmy watched glumly as teddies and toys all disappeared into crates and cardboard boxes, but it wasn't until evening that he discovered the removal men had packed his Ra-ra. This was a piece of cloth that he held in his hand when he needed a little confidence, and that helped him go to sleep as he sucked his thumb. The cloth changed shape and feel over the years. Once upon a time it had been a pink duster, but that was washed out to sea after Jimmy left it on a beach in Dorset as the tide came in. The current Ra-ra was a fragment of old cot sheet, and life in a strange house was insupportable without it. His old Doggy had also been packed up in the same crate, and when Paul went to find them, tired, hungry, dispirited and despairing, he was met with tea chests piled high to the ceiling, and no notion which one to look in. Hard thinking and a good memory finally helped locate the Ra-ra and Doggy, and Jimmy agreed to go to bed in his cot which took up residence for the next few weeks wherever we were staying.

Poor Jimmy became increasingly insecure, insisting on wearing a nappy again, and trailing miserably round from each strange bedroom to his unfinished new home. One wet lunchtime, a stiff, unusable duplicate key refused to open the front door of the house where we were currently staying, and Jimmy and I had to sit in the rain on the doorstep as I fed Martin until we could find another key.

On another occasion, as I crossed the busy main road at one of its widest points, pushing Martin in his ricketty old pram, and holding on to Jimmy's hand in the traffic, one wheel rolled off the pram and the frame collapsed, spilling carrycot and baby into the road. Before Martin could be picked up and rescued, Jimmy darted off in front of a car to retrieve the runaway wheel, while both traffic and pedestrians came to a standstill to enjoy the drama.

The end of that week, another wet and chilly one in May in a house with no heating or drying facilities, we prepared to move yet again, but with nowhere to go to that night. Jimmy had crept into our bed that morning and spilt a full mug of orange juice, which had soaked through to the mattress. The one-bar electric fire proved useless to dry it, and the next guests were arriving to use the house within hours. A solution had to be found, so we went shopping for a change of scenery and some inspirational problem-solving.

It was only after we had walked twice round the little supermarket and I reached for my shopping bag and purse that I noticed it was Martin's empty plastic nappy bucket I had over one arm instead of a bag.

But however dire things were, eventually help always arrived in some form or another, and we finally moved into our new home in the early summer of 1984.

Work continued throughout the long, hot summer and the bills homed in like the swifts that year, early rather than late. Our earned income was still nothing, as Paul worked day and night to finish painting and plastering downstairs. Until this was complete, there would be no business and no income.

It must have been a dull summer for Jimmy. Anxiety made us silent and withdrawn. There were no days out, no Daddy to play in the daytime, no garden, and if it hadn't been for Dawn, Jimmy's world would have been even duller in those stressful months.

Dawn was just 17 when, as a trainee nursery nurse from college, she came to our family to complete a six-week placement to learn about the practical nature of childcare. She is cheerful and pretty, resourceful and uncomplaining and Jimmy loved his temporary nanny. She bathed and fed, played and mopped up, changed nappies for Martin or made play dough for Jimmy. We spent hours in the park, or having picnics by rivers, and although she became very fond of Jimmy, she was sharply perceptive and accurate about his character and jealousies as she recorded each day in her project file. Her own place as the youngest in a family of three girls gave her a clear insight into sibling jealousy. We were delighted to be given the file recording life with two-year-old Jimmy after he died. Dawn eventually moved on from being a nanny and is currently an Education Welfare Officer.

That autumn, with family life gradually settling into a new pattern, and our new business starting to pay us a wage at last, Jimmy took the first tiny step away from us and joined the village playgroup, which was run from a room on the top floor of a college of education.

Although the room was quite big, it was far too small for the two dozen children and toys which were crammed into it twice a week. Self-closing fire doors and a steep flight of stairs made a trip to the toilets a hazardous adventure for the toddlers, and we took them in convoys of three or four. Jimmy was slow to enjoy the experience of playgroup. He disliked being left by both his parents and would often cry for a while. But we persisted and gradually he became more at ease.

One of the children that he played with had no hair, and not many of us actually knew why. The answer was, of course, that this little boy had recently been diagnosed as having leukaemia and was just recovering after his first intensive treatments of chemotherapy and radiotherapy. His beautiful face and the maturity with which he discussed things with his mother were very noticeable. He died four years later, in 1988.

Infant school nursery followed playgroup, the first real taste of school. The youngest children attended each afternoon for just a couple of hours, and suddenly our little boy had become a school child. Jimmy took his treasures and Ra-ra to nursery each day in a little Paddington Bear bag, later replaced by a Thomas the Tank Engine bag.

At the end of each afternoon, he would watch for my arrival, sitting on the sofa in the book corner, or even hiding behind it, and he loved to hurl himself into my open arms and have a quick hug before we packed up his things to go home. He would tell us what storytime had been about and was especially pleased if a favourite book he had taken to school had been read aloud to the other children.

The nursery class was housed in an extension a little apart from the noisy bustle of the bigger children, and the nursery playground, green, leafy and pleasant, gave the little ones a gentle start before they made their own way into the jungle of the big playground.

The classroom itself was, and still is, a small paradise for the children. The inspiration of the nursery teacher and her assistant has created a place of scope and style, colour and warmth, excitement and security. If the season is autumn, parents have to stoop low to avoid the autumnal bows festooning ceilings and walls; Christmas makes the room a sparkling cave, and the only day when the nursery seems to show its bare bones is the last day of term when walls and ceilings have to be stripped.

Jimmy loved his first experience of school. Shy and timid though most of them were at the beginning, the confidence that such a special atmosphere gave all the children helped them to face school in the future. The nursery teachers thought of every small detail to help each child, and before the older ones left they were taken on short visits to the big school. Jimmy hated the prospect of leaving his beloved, safe nursery and refused to go on visits. This was hardly surprising; the nursery was a difficult place to leave behind for ever.

In the last term before leaving, the children became 'all-day' pupils and stayed for lunch. This used to be served in the nursery at little round tables, where each child had made his or her own placemat, and the children took it in turns to choose a favourite song or hymn to sing instead of saying grace. Hungry little faces would turn towards the dinner ladies and the smell of food as they quavered through 'All Things Bright and Beautiful', and at the end of each long school day, feet dragging, bag sagging as he kicked his way home holding on to Martin's pushchair, Jimmy would relate in detail what they'd had for lunch, how much he'd not eaten and whether he'd cried at school that day. Nursery shaped Jimmy for life; it showed him how good school could be and encouraged his enthusiasm and enjoyment of education and finding out about life.

This desire to find out about things often led to the shelves of the local library, crawling round looking for books to expand whatever project was current in the nursery. It could be anything from frogs to lighthouses, and once a suitably simple book was found to illustrate the theme, Jimmy would proudly carry it to school next morning to throw more light on the subject in hand. He must have been an ideal little pupil to teach, so willing to learn.

The subject was pond life on one occasion when Martin, newly walking and very accustomed to library visits, disappeared. His push-chair was empty, and I ran out through the foyer and the stiff swing doors to search out in the street. The search revealed nothing, but by the time I returned the library staff, always the nicest, most patient, friendly people one could hope to find anywhere, were laughing loudly at the sight of Martin sitting on the staff room floor, with his hand in the biscuit tin. He had trotted off, opened the cupboard and helped himself to his favourite digestives. Jimmy was somewhat mortified, probably because he hadn't thought of doing it first.

Just as he could find books, especially overdue ones down the back of the sofa, Jimmy was very clever at tracing anything lost. His memory was crystal clear and we always called him Finder In Chief. He could locate anything from lost keys to mislaid hats, though once we purposely 'lost' a blue cap belonging to Paul. We both noticed that whenever Paul wore this particular cap, within a short time he always became very grumpy and cross. So we hid it for over six months, enjoying the joke together every time we 'looked' for it.

Jim had a quick wit which helped him understand jokes and humour and we rarely explained anything twice. With a knowing glance, or a secret smile, he would appreciate most comedy from slapstick to shaggy dog stories. His favourite comedians were Lenny Henry and David Jason, but his humour was diverse enough to enjoy the cultish *Young Ones* every bit as much as *The Last of the Summer Wine*, which he loved to share each week with his Granny Anna, as they sat contentedly together giggling.

As Jim progressed from nursery to reception class, his confidence grew daily. His new teacher was young and pretty, and he always noticed and commented on the clothes that she wore.

It is the tradition at Jimmy's school to welcome parents with their children each morning in the classroom. Mums and Dads take their children into the room, which gives them the chance to see what work is being done, what projects decorate the walls and how well each child is getting on. The teacher is available to talk to parents every morning, and we soon realized that the transition from nursery, with most of his friends, had gone very smoothly and he was happy and active in class.

Life felt very much more settled at home. Martin was growing from baby to toddler and it was becoming very clear that not only did the boys look quite unlike each other, but they were also quite different temperamentally.

Jimmy was conscientious and dutiful, with a firm desire to do well; he was careful with his possessions and toys, systematic and tidy, but not particularly generous about sharing anything with anyone. He respected authority, and understood the reasoning of rule-making. Martin, by contrast, was clumsy, untidy and chaotic, but easily generous and never jealous or vindictive.

At weekends we often walked on the hills, or hired a rowing boat on one of the lakes or took the children to local events. We took picnics and chose walks near water so that the children could paddle and play, though Jimmy never enjoyed getting wet and cold quite as much as Martin did. Winter weather, unless it was very severe or wet, didn't change our preferred weekend activity and we walked and wandered the whole year round.

It was Jimmy, not his father, who always remembered to take our little 'family' camera, and record the day on film. The camera was not simply for picture-taking; it also helped him to play at being Daddy, and he gradually adopted Paul as his role model and hero. It was early days, but we looked far ahead and dreamed of a time when Jimmy might take over the studio and photography from Paul, and continue to run the family business. It certainly looked a possibility as Jimmy struggled to focus, or talked knowledgeably about the light being 'too contrasty' or the film being overexposed.

About this period, we took the children for a spring holiday over to the Isles of Scilly. It was a place I first visited as a child, but its special significance for us was spending our honeymoon there in 1970.

The children soon shared our affection for the beautiful islands, and we spent an idyllic ten days staying in a holiday home. The house itself was damp, with broken beds and a bath which took an hour to empty, but nothing spoilt the fun we all had throughout that happy, brilliantly sunny holiday.

The long May evenings were spent watching and waiting for the darkness, when the great beams of light from lighthouses all around the dangerous, rocky islands, scene of many a famous shipwreck, would sweep the sky and sea.

To us, the Scillies were, and are, the last little bit of England, pure, virtually unspoilt and extremely beautiful.

When we got home, the children found Smarties in their wellingtons and KitKats down their beds. My sister, Cate, had been to call while we were away. She is one of those people that children love to love, and she loves them, too. Prevented from doing many ordinary things in life by severe rheumatoid arthritis, she never allows it for one moment to interfere with her love of life. She and Jimmy loved each other dearly.

I took the children to visit Cate in Dorset as often as I could, and if we set off by train from home at around six in the morning, with a fair wind and a good tube connection across London, we could reach her house in time for lunch.

She had everything that our boys most wanted in the world; a video with Thomas the Tank Engine films; a big garden with rabbits and a summerhouse; a Soda Stream drinks maker and burgers by the dozen in her freezer. Her two boys, accustomed to caring for Cate and her special needs, were already very good at thinking about other people, and would take charge of Jimmy and Martin during the entire visit to give the grown-ups a break.

The four cousins loved being together; my big nephews looked after their little cousins unselfishly. They often paired up by their initials – J and J, Jimmy and Jonathan, and M and M, Martin and Matthew. Jimmy was delighted at his physical likeness to both Cate and Jonathan.

The trips to see Cate compensated for the lack of family holidays; despite the length of journey, I always felt it was worthwhile crossing London by Underground, wheeling the boys in a double buggy, carrying our luggage on my back in a rucksack. On one occasion, when Martin was a baby still in nappies, the train was very crowded. There was nowhere to change a dirty nappy except in the lavatory, where the floor was awash with urine and the 110 m.p.h. Intercity caused us all to lurch helplessly, hanging on to the basin and the towel.

Somehow I changed Martin's nappy, and, nervous about my handbag containing all our holiday money in cash, I gave it to Jimmy to hold rather than putting it down on the filthy floor. Priding myself on the juggling and balancing act that had been necessary to change the nappy, I swayed down the train clutching Martin, and hanging on to Jimmy.

It wasn't until about half an hour later that I looked up from the book we were attempting to read, and saw a young man walking down the train holding a black shoulder bag. I thought he looked a little odd, especially as he seemed to be stopping at every seat and talking to every passenger; then, as it slowly dawned on me that it was my bag he was holding, I realized that Jimmy must have left it in the toilet and I had failed to notice its absence. But what to do?

Supposing some dishonest passenger should claim it before he reached us? With no identification except what was in the bag, I couldn't prove it was mine. Or suppose he reached me and I rightfully claimed it – would it look insulting if I searched it immediately to check the money hadn't been removed? And what if it had? The person who found it first might have pocketed my £200 and left the bag empty for a second person to discover.

Jimmy looked innocent and interested as I grabbed the bag and tried to look convincingly like the real owner. He knew nothing of its importance, my feelings of panic, or the relief to find the money intact.

The kind finder had to be trusted and all temptations to open the purse and count the money had to be resisted. This moderate behaviour paid off because fortunately all the money was there untouched.

The story of the missing bag in the toilet never failed to make Jimmy laugh, and he was very proud to be the small boy on the train, looking after his mother, her money and everybody's general welfare.

There was only one small regret as we looked with such pride at our little family. Neither Paul's father nor mine was alive to see and enjoy his grandchildren, and Paul's sensitive, intelligent and loving mother no longer recognized anyone, reduced to an existence with neither speech nor memory by senile dementia. The only grandparent our boys ever knew was my mother, Anna. She came to live in our town when Martin was still a baby, and she has never ceased to provide the same gentle stability and security to their lives as she gave to mine, without ever seeking to influence or interfere with the way we chose to bring them up.

*

# TWO

# Diagnosis

As their childhood unfolded, and our two babies became little boys, and then bigger boys, it was hard to believe that life could be so happy. There was great affection and closeness within our family, and few occasions of real conflict between ourselves or the boys.

That was not to say that there were never any arguments between Jimmy and Martin, but their antagonism to each other was typical of brothers close in age, with a gap of just twenty-seven months separating their births.

The first time we ever noticed Jimmy being especially mean or unpleasant to Martin occurred when Martin was about a year old. He was a very large baby, and crawled slowly and laboriously one day behind a sofa. Jimmy quietly pursued him, thinking nobody had noticed, and as Martin brought his neck up to look round, like a sleepy tortoise stretching a head up and out of its shell, Jimmy was ready with a swift blow to the back of Martin's neck, which sent him screaming and sprawling on his back. Jimmy's meanness was dealt with so swiftly that he was in bed without his supper before he even had time to apologize, which we always insisted on. He never repeated the assault.

Jimmy was possessive about his toys, and he craved individual attention from Paul, his hero. Martin could be unreasonable and occasionally tempestuous, but always quick to recover his good temper and never one to bear grudges. Jimmy liked nothing better than to gain some private time on his own with Paul, excluding Martin, who was more than generous in the way he gave in to Jimmy's dominance. Martin wanted nothing more than to be good friends with his older brother, and his pleasure and delight when Jimmy chose to be his playmate were transparent. When Jimmy refused, Martin learned to play alone and develop self-sufficiency, a gift which helps him now to face life without Jimmy.

One Saturday afternoon in early May, 1986, the weather was so unusually warm that I took our two boys and a little girl from Jimmy's class to play on the fell near the village. We walked a mile or so up-hill, then decided to go no further because all three children wanted to play in the stream, building dams and paddling.

The sky clouded over, and heavy black clouds rolled nearer, hiding the sun, but the weather remained so warm, nobody wanted to return home.

Then suddenly a thunderstorm broke not far off, and we moved immediately away from the exposed and dangerous hillside. As we ran towards home and safety, the rain lashed down, and the children laughed with excitement as our clothes became wet through. It was still warm enough not to mind the soaking we received, and we slowed from a run to a trot through the park as there seemed no point in hurrying any more. We could not have been wetter.

The storm passed, and we went home to rub ourselves dry with towels. Nobody wanted a bath or shower, and the afternoon ended reading and playing indoors.

We didn't know it at the time, but the rain that fell that afternoon over the South Lakes area of Cumbria during the thunderstorm drenched us with radioactivity from the Chernobyl nuclear disaster in the Soviet Union.

Only two days before, after high levels of radioactivity had been picked up by monitors in Sweden, it had been revealed in the world's press that a nuclear power station in the Western Ukraine, at Chernobyl, had suffered a melt-down, releasing dangerous amounts of radioactivity into the atmosphere over Europe. There were predictions that if it rained over the South-East of Britain during the weekend, there might be some small amounts of fallout.

But the wind changed, and nothing could have prepared us in the North-West for that Saturday afternoon storm, the after effects of which brought ruin to some upland sheep farmers, and severely restricted others. Caesium-137 in sheep, which renders them unsafe to eat, is, so far, the only known damage that the accident caused our area. Levels of radioactivity in grassland in two areas still remain too high to lift the ban on sheep even now.

But, as the levels of childhood leukaemias and other blood cancers reach epidemic proportions in the area round Chernobyl, we can only wonder whether Jimmy's drenching in the polluted rain had any part to play in the development of his own leukaemia. Many scientists would deny this, yet levels of radioactivity were found to have concentrated particularly in the silt at the bottom of small tarns; just the sort of shallow pools Jimmy bathed in frequently that year – along with hundreds of children in our district who did not subsequently develop !eukaemia, it has to be said.

Ironically, it was Martin we were most concerned about at the time. There was no official advice except a ban on locally produced lamb which was issued about four weeks after the event. Unofficial advice warned mothers not to give cows' milk to babies under two years old.

There was neither time nor money for taking holidays with the children that year, but the big tent that we bought second-hand gave us a new freedom to enjoy our own beautiful surroundings, while never being very far from home.

Jimmy was five the following summer, and Martin just three when we pitched the tent at Coniston Water and took our first holiday in the Lakes, just ten miles from home. Camping with friends who had a dinghy provided us with exciting sails across the lake, and the boys loved life under canvas so much that they would have been happy to stay all summer, whatever the weather, and never go back home to bathrooms and beds.

Living in a tent was like playing Wendy-houses to the boys, who invented all sorts of games with their friends Tim and Alice, and a crafty little schemer called Charlie from a tent nearby. His husky little voice with a strange accent pitched midway between Belfast and the Bronx made such a deep impression on us all that whenever Jimmy and Martin planned some impossible plot to a new game, they always adopted Charlie's strange, compelling accent.

Towards the end of the school summer holidays, we pitched the tent at a large site at the far end of Ullswater and stayed for ten days. The children rode their bikes round the site in perfect safety, there were hot showers, a shop, and even chips and a disco for wet nights.

Jimmy was still very timid whenever asked to run an errand or do something practical on his own. The campsite was a perfect place to encourage his confidence, and after several days he finally managed to go alone to the little shop to buy Fat Frog ice lollies.

Paul returned home to work, visiting every couple of days, but life was far from dull. As we waited for a boat trip one morning, we watched helplessly as a nonswimmer nearby waded into the water, lost his footing and disappeared. He was dragged out as though dead about five minutes later but was revived by a passing scoutmaster and survived.

The next day, the boys saw a calf born in a field nearby, which was even more exciting to them than a near-drowning.

The camping trips that summer are particularly memorable because they were the last holidays we experienced with two healthy children. Life as we knew it was soon to change for ever, but not before we enjoyed a last soft, warm, sunny autumn, filled with walks and picnics. There were two wonderful Sundays spent on the fells near Keswick in September 1987. We looked at clouds and fungi, ant hills and birds. With some inexplicable premonition, it seemed as though life were so perfect, such happiness couldn't last. Something, sometime soon, was bound to go wrong. The very fact that there was nothing out of place in our lives made us more vulnerable somehow. Such contentment seemed fragile, as if some avenging god would notice we had more than our share, and seek to redress the balance. Such superstition might allow for an accident or small mishap but hardly the string of disasters which ended just over two years later by extinguishing our brightest light.

The first clouds to blot out the sun overshadowed our lives late that September. We had spent a warm day in early autumn walking through woods near Derwentwater, Keswick. Paul was his normal self, interested in everything we could see, making lengthy stops while he took photographs.

Both boys needed a little encouragement to tackle some of the hills on this particular walk, so I made up a story about a character they had invented called Jock Bear, whose activities and pet hates were somewhat similar to their own. We trailed along while I made up a story, and as the walk ended in a wood near a river, the children were delighted to smell, then find, a foul, stinking fungus growing by the side of the path. The stinkhorn was crawling with flies attracted by its characteristic odour of rotting meat, and the sight of it was as repulsive as the smell.

The fungus was like some sort of ill omen, but the children were fascinated by its sheer nastiness and reluctant to walk on. Later that day, after Sunday dinner at home with Granny Anna and two old friends, Paul complained of extreme tiredness, ignored our guests and went to sleep.

Next morning he woke up with sore, red eyes, and for two days we thought he had conjunctivitis, or even some rare reaction as a result of touching the stinkhorn. On the third day, his face was swollen and his neck stiff. The doctor thought he must have mumps. By the fourth day, he had stopped all pretence of trying to carry on working, and by the weekend he was in bed, with such a fever that the mumps theory looked unlikely.

On Sunday morning, I noticed his skin was looking sallow; by afternoon he had turned yellow and a quick urine test revealed that he had developed jaundice.

We watched with growing anxiety as Paul's illness worsened each day. His fever at night was so bad that he would alternate between dripping sweats and shivering, teeth-chattering chills, during which he would pile on blankets and thick socks.

For the next five nights, his mind wandered as his temperature swooped up and down, and on more than one occasion he imagined he was crawling through the crypt of a tiny little church he had visited recently to photograph a sculpture. To reach it, he had to crawl through his tunnel of bedclothes, ending up on the floor pulling his mountain socks on as the shivers would start again.

By day he was quieter, too weak to need much attention, not that there was anyone constantly at his bed to nurse him. Instead, it was business as usual in the studio downstairs where I had to stall the impatient customers, and conceal how ill Paul was, and how long he would need to recover, in case clients took work elsewhere.

Nothing could have been worse for the business. There was a list of twenty-four commercial jobs awaiting completion, work piling up in the darkroom, and his accounting system known only to himself and his computer spreadsheet.

Jimmy went to school all day, but Martin attended nursery in the morning only. For the first time, the first of many, we relied on kind friends to help look after the children by fetching from school, or having them to play, but even this was complicated by the fact that nobody could identify Paul's illness and whether it imposed a threat to anyone else.

No amount of sophisticated tests ever revealed exactly what the illness was, but guesses ranged from glandular fever, a strong favourite, to Weil's disease, often caught from rats or dirty water. The blood tests were never conclusive. A mystery disease is even worse than a nasty one that people know about. The risk of catching it was ever-present and one could hardly blame parents at school who were worried that their children played with ours.

Four weeks went by before Paul was well enough to sit up and watch a little snooker on television while toying with some dry bread, but within a fortnight, he had returned to work, to save the business from collapsing, and salvage what work was left. Had he not been self-employed, his convalescence would have been at least a month.

His illness returned at intervals over the next eighteen months; and although the children appeared to be unaffected, I eventually contracted a weaker, less serious version of the mystery bug.

The illness left the family tired and depleted for the next six months, and depressed at the disruption still being caused by the unknown virus.

It was not until after Christmas that we felt fit enough to start enjoying normal life again and in February we travelled south to visit both our families in Surrey, Kent and Dorset. We visited aunts and uncles, cousins and second cousins and brothers and sisters, and both the children enjoyed the novelty of meeting relations they hadn't seen for some time, or were meeting for the first time.

Some of the older relatives were so aged and infirm, we felt as though we were saying farewell to them. Little could we imagine the irony that our own seemingly healthy little son would be dead within two years while Paul's frail mother, in a psycho-geriatric ward, unable to recognize her sons or even feed herself, actually outlived her grandson; as did my fragile uncle, now aged ninety-one. Yet Paul's lively and vivacious aunt, who complained of a slight cough as she entertained us, had died of lung cancer within eight weeks of our visit.

Life had returned to normal at home. With great relief we put Paul's illness behind us and looked forward to less troubled times after such a hard winter.

We have no exact record of the very first day on which we noticed that Jimmy was looking unusually pale and tired. It probably happened in such a gradual, insidious way that instead of noticing his strange appearance, perhaps we became accustomed to it slowly so that for a while it seemed normal.

By the beginning of May, it was such a struggle to persuade Jimmy to eat sometimes, that we almost had to feed him like a baby. But eating had never been of great interest to him, so perhaps we didn't remark that mealtimes were becoming more of a battlefield than usual.

The weather in the spring of 1988 was glorious; the trees came into bud early, the bluebells transformed hillsides into swathes of azure, and the new leaves looked greener and more translucent than ever before.

There were eight weeks of long, warm, sunny days and we often took a picnic supper out in the evening to Rydal, Windermere or Coniston. One brilliant Sunday Paul spent the day photographing mountain bikers on Loughrigg Fell, above Rydal and Grasmere. The pictures were to form the basis of a cinema advertisement. Not to be outdone, Jimmy took his camera too, and shadowed Paul capturing action shots over rocky fell ground or through water. Jimmy's results were very professional.

Once a year, the village Civic Trust organize a litter sweep in which the children can help with their families. Jimmy took his rubber gloves and black plastic sack and headed with Martin to the river, where they helped fish out the cans and bottles. This annual exposure to rubbish made such an impression on him that Jimmy never dropped litter himself, and hated seeing anyone else do it.

Although his fatigue and paleness were sometimes noticeable by the time of the litter sweep, they never actually prevented Jimmy from participating in anything that was important to him. Worried though we were, there was always great relief in seeing him rush off as usual to do the things he really wanted to do. His zest for life made it even harder to believe that it was anything really serious that made him look so white and feel so worn out.

There was another remarkable example of Jimmy's strength and stamina in the middle of May, only a month before his cancer was diagnosed.

One Sunday we set off with Jimmy's best friend, Jonathan Gorrigan, his sister, Becky, and their mother, Karen, to climb Skiddaw, one of Lakeland's 3,000-foot peaks. The two boys had been close friends at school since Jonathan and his family came to Ambleside about eighteen months before. By now, all four children were frequent companions, especially after they had spent much time together during Paul's illness when the Gorrigans gave us constant practical help.

It was a warm day in the valley when we started up Skiddaw; fooled by the blue skies, I failed to take adequate warm clothing for Jimmy and Martin, and by the time we came in sight of the summit, the clouds had covered the sun and a cold, sharp wind was blowing.

Reluctant to give up a summit attempt when we had got so far, we continued the walk after Paul made a wind-proof vest for Martin out of a plastic carrier bag. Jonathan offered to give his cagoule to warm Jimmy up, and we divided what clothing we had between the children.

Jimmy and Jonathan romped and played all day and skipped up the steepest parts of the hill with ease. The summit was cold and extremely windy, and we huddled in the stone shelter for a rest.

On our return down the steep sides of Skiddaw, the four children roly-polyed down the grassy slopes as if we were just setting out, fresh and energetic, rather than returning exhausted after a challenging day.

Jimmy looked as fit and well as any six-year-old who had just tackled a mountain walk that would defeat many adults.

But his paleness returned, and became constant instead of frequent. At this point, I began to have such a strong feeling of unease about his white face that it hurt me to see it. The anxiety I felt made me mention Jimmy's paleness to everybody we met, but people were endlessly reassuring, and their stories convinced me that most children are inexplicably pale at some time in childhood.

Jimmy had been such a healthy child, he hadn't needed to see a doctor for three years; but when his hands suddenly became covered with itchy eczema a couple of weeks before, I had taken him to one of our doctors. I mentioned the paleness, but it wasn't one of the days when Jimmy looked especially white, so the doctor didn't comment, and once again I was reassured.

The paleness continued; but so too did the hot weather, and lots of children looked pale in the heat. But the eczema, although improved on his hands, spread to Jimmy's buttocks, where it became infected very quickly and began to look more like thrush. We returned to the Health Centre, and saw another doctor. He prescribed an antibiotic for the infected rash, but when I asked to be referred with Jimmy to the Paediatric Consultant about his paleness, the doctor thought it was unnecessary. My suggestion that a blood test be done was also rejected as unnecessarily upsetting for Jimmy, and not easy to do.

I crept away, feeling half humiliated for having made such an ungrounded fuss, and half reassured. How overanxious we were being; of course children get headaches in the sunshine and breathless in hot weather. How silly of us to be so worried. When Jimmy's illness was finally diagnosed, about three weeks later, we learnt how the vast majority of children wait weeks, often months, before doctors recognize there is a problem at all, and what it might be. Leukaemia is, indeed, the biggest killer of children after accidents; but it still remains a rarity, so rare that most doctors can only expect to see one case during an entire career in general practice. Some children even spend two or three weeks in their general hospital before the disease is suspected and they can finally be sent to a regional treatment centre for child cancer.

Jimmy's rash responded to the antibiotics immediately. Karen took the children on a picnic despite doubts about Jimmy's fitness, but he was first to splash into the cold lake, playing in the water like any normal little boy. Soon the rash had almost gone, but Jimmy's paleness had not. Our feelings of uneasiness returned, and I no longer felt confident in all the reassurances we had been given by friends and doctors alike.

There was nothing about his behaviour generally when he was with other children which suggested he was unwell. He managed to keep up with his friends, but the effort involved by this time must have been enormous, and his tiredness began to make him extremely irritable at home. Only later did he tell us about the headaches he suffered in the playground at school. One day, Granny Anna passed the school at playtime and noticed Jimmy sitting exhausted on the ground, hanging on to the railings like some hunted animal. But we knew nothing of this and nobody at school noticed any problems.

The thing that Jimmy liked doing best of all on warm, sunny evenings was riding his bike with Paul. A circular route took them along a beautiful, quiet lane with a stream running alongside, crossed at one point by stepping stones. But the route included a hill to puff up, and by the middle of June, Jimmy was finding it difficult to get to the top, and eventually impossible.

His breathlessness was also noticable as he tried to race round the park on his bike and by the third week, he seemed stiff in his legs when walking. I knew I had to convince the doctors that Jimmy really was unwell.

Something rather odd happened the following Saturday. Jimmy suddenly asked if Paul would take a portrait photograph of him, a strange request from a little boy who preferred taking photos to posing for them.

His surprising request was well-timed because there were a few shots left on the end of a roll of colour film that Paul had used that day to photograph a wedding.

Jimmy took the whole affair very seriously and changed into his best shirt, then sat in the studio smiling his sweet, gentle smile. His eyes looked weary and resigned, as if he couldn't fight the fatigue he felt any more.

In that face we see now the man our little son might have been one day. He was gentle, loving and kind, a strong force for good in a bad world. There was only one other time in his life he ever requested Paul to take his portrait. It happened just fifteen months later, only two days before his relapse was diagnosed, at a time when everybody thought that he was fit and well. It was as if in some uncanny way, he sensed when he was in danger, and having a photograph of himself was the only sure way any part of him would survive.

After the photographic session, we went to a barbecue at the house of friends nearby, and the chance finally came to persuade the doctors who happened to be there that Jimmy desperately needed help. His white face, with thin little blue lines round his mouth, coupled with his general irritation and exhaustion proved more powerful and convincing than anything we had said during the past month. Action was taken immediately, and by Monday afternoon Jimmy and I were waiting to see the Consultant Paediatrician at the local district hospital.

Sunday was our very last day together as a normal family. I got up at six o'clock and worked in the office downstairs, writing my local history newspaper column for the next four weeks ahead. I was describing the rise and fall of the country house, and the working lives of those in service before the last war. I enjoyed my work, and the column almost wrote itself as ideas tumbled onto the screen of the word processor. Jimmy, with his habitual kindness, brought me down coffee and toast which he had made for me, and by midday I had completed the four weekly instalments.

We spent the next few hours planting out our flower baskets and boxes, so that our balcony would bloom throughout the summer, and we could pretend we had a real garden. Granny Anna came to dinner in the evening as usual, after which both boys disappeared into the bathroom and spent three-quarters of an hour laughing and splashing in the bath. The floor was awash when they finally agreed to get out and go to bed, but it was reassuring to hear Jimmy making such a noise and enjoying so much fun. Once again the fear of his paleness being something more than just a little anaemia receded. How could he be very poorly when he could still play like that?

Monday was fine. Paul left very early to work over in Cockermouth, where he was photographing a hotel, and Jimmy and I looked forward to a day together in our nearby town, and the twelve-mile bus journey we would both enjoy travelling there. We arrived in plenty of time, and went to the park for a picnic. Jimmy hardly ate at all. His appetite was tiny, and I gave him a piggyback up the hill in the hot sun as we walked towards the hospital.

With time still left, we dropped in to see Karen in the flat where they were temporarily living, and as we discussed Jimmy's appointment, I suddenly knew, beyond doubt, that Jimmy was very ill. But with only the very haziest knowledge of leukaemia or anaemia, I had no idea what to expect, and never for one moment even considered cancer as a possibility.

The interview with the quiet, gentle doctor was fairly short. He took a blood test, and examined Jimmy, mentioning points that he noticed as he went along, but points which meant very little to me. Jimmy's spleen was enlarged; there were tiny little pin-prick bruises on his legs, almost too small to see; and he was extremely pale and anaemic. I realized the doctor already knew with certainty what was wrong, and only needed to confirm his suspicions, because he warned me that Jimmy might need to stay in hospital away from home for a while to put things right, and that I would need to be with him. The expression on his face communicated his anxiety. He promised that we would have the results of the blood test within a couple of hours, that evening, by phone.

My only thought as we went home was to act as normally as I could so that Jimmy would not be afraid. I carried him along the pavement so that he could peep over the wall and see the town below us, and I sat him down on the dusty path as he wilted in the sun, grumbling gently about the lateness of the bus home. There was nothing I could do but carry on as usual, and we were all sitting down to sausages for supper as the phone rang.

Fortunately it had been moved out of the kitchen into our little spare room where I normally worked at night, so I answered the call on my own with the door shut. The doctor said very quietly and solemnly that I would have to be prepared to take Jimmy to Manchester the next morning and stay with him for several weeks.

'What is it, then?' I asked.

'I think you already know, and I think you suspected it when you came to see me this afternoon,' he said. 'Are you going to say the word, or shall I?'

'Leukaemia,' I said, suddenly thinking of the worst possible thing it could be.

'It's a very good thing Jimmy has a younger brother because he'll probably need a bone marrow transplant,' he continued. 'I hope you've got a tracksuit, or something you can get into quickly during the night, because he's going to need you constantly, night and day, and you'll have to put everything else aside, and arrange for other people to look after your family,' he predicted.

I called Paul in, and told him, and we clung to each other, sobbing, promising that we would be strong in our love and face whatever lay ahead together. Then we returned to the children and finished supper, continuing as if nothing had happened. We had agreed that our last evening as a family should finish as it had been planned before, and after supper Paul took the boys to the park as promised, while I made emotional phone calls round the family, breaking the news. It was only after bathtime as I sat on the top bunk with one boy each side of me, reading Beatrix Potter aloud, that I told them what would happen the next day. I tried to make it sound as exciting as I could – a trip to Manchester, something special for each child, lots of time for Martin with his loving Granny, and lots of interesting toys and games in hospital for Jimmy while the doctors and nurses made his headaches and tiredness better.

Friends came and went throughout the evening and next morning as I tried to pack for a month. Suddenly Karen was there, quietly piling up clothes, sorting out washing and ironing. Throughout the next month she was there each morning, unobtrusive but vital, doing all the household jobs and leaving a meal prepared for Paul and Martin before she left.

I thought the idea of Jimmy having his own toilet bag would please him very much, so we went together to the chemist and bought a bright red and yellow flannel with 'Good Morning, Sunshine' emblazoned on it to put in the bag with his new toothbrush. The dye in the flannel ran scarlet like blood every time we used it, a good trick for Jimmy to play on his nurses early in the morning when they came to help him wash.

We left for Manchester at lunchtime, calling in to see the paediatrician en route to collect the letter which would be Jimmy's passport to admission. Martin came with us, excited at having a day off school. The network of motorways seemed so unfamiliar that first journey, but within a week we knew every inch of the ninety-mile trip.

One of the very best things we discovered on arrival was that the children's cancer ward at the Royal Manchester Children's Hospital, Pendlebury, which is normally one of the most cramped and noisy places imaginable, was closed for decorating and we were directed up to the new Bone Marrow Transplant Unit, which was temporarily housing all cancer patients until the ward reopened.

So, instead of the traditional open ward, reverberating with noise and dotted with the flickering screens of a dozen unwatched televisions, all left on conflicting channels, we were introduced into the peace and quiet of a room sleeping a maximum of only three children. Throughout the afternoon various staff came and told us their names, and what they would be doing for Jimmy. There were too many faces to remember, and after a confusing hour or two with a fractious Martin, Paul decided that the time had come to leave us, and we all kissed goodbye for a couple of days.

I understood from the beginning by the way Jimmy watched my face so intently that his tolerance of anything painful or unpleasant would depend on my reactions. If I accepted what was being done, he would, too; and his eyes never left my face as I talked to the various doctors and prepared Jimmy for his first transfusion, injections and intravenous drip.

Everything about hospital life was new and strange. He had never before had to take a tablet, and his first attempt ended up with his breakfast and lunch on the floor. It took him two weeks to learn how to toss them back with a quick gulp of juice, and he never lacked practice, with as many as twenty to take some days during the next year.

We walked to the treatment room for the first time carrying one of Jimmy's favourite books, a collection of poems about school called *Please Mrs Butler*. A little distraction might help the needle go more easily into the vein. The Senior House Officer was a doctor called Karl, in his mid-twenties, looking dark and foreign but with a perfect English accent.

Karl was so young himself that he hadn't forgotten what it felt like to be a child, and it was his ability to treat children without patronizing them which helped many newcomers accept the unpleasant things that he had to do to them. The children played tricks on him, stealing his coat and stethoscope to conduct bogus ward rounds; the nurses loved his chaotic forgetfulness, and bought him cream cakes when he passed his exams. He was only with us a month before moving on to his next job, but that was long enough to help Jimmy become accustomed to a regime of injections and drips.

That first night in hospital, I curled up on the bed with Jimmy, now attached to a drip, and stroked his hair until he went to sleep. Although he wanted me to stay all night, I knew how impractical this would be and unless I left him alone with the nursing staff at the very beginning, it would be more difficult to make the break later on, day or night.

The parents' accommodation was across the unlit hospital grounds, and we were advised to ask a porter to accompany us. But it was impossible to find one most evenings, and I always walked alone without mishap.

The new parents' block had been built just four years previously with kitchen, laundry and drying room. The kettle in the kitchen was chained to the wall and the laundry was empty of machines. Everything that could have been stolen had gone, and even the duvets on the bunk beds had been taken that year. I shared a room with three other mothers, never knowing from one night to the next who my neighbours would be. Some snored, others smoked illicitly, one was removed after three dramatic panic attacks.

We could leave nothing of any value anywhere. The stealing went on in every corner of the hospital. Leaving food in the parents' fridge was an open invitation to anyone to help themselves. Public conscience and morality were nonexistent. It was everyone for themselves. We all expected the food left in the parents' fridge to disappear within hours, but one afternoon the thieves went one step further and the entire fridge disappeared forever, with the food still inside. The thieves beat combination locks, broke open windows, stole purses and toilet paper; once they even walked in through a French window, disconnected the television being watched at the time by a young cancer patient and walked off with the set in broad daylight.

Living in the parents' accommodation was gruelling, and even seven years in a bleak convent dormitory had done little to prepare me for the lack of privacy and peace at a time when I needed it so desperately. There was nowhere to go and cry, something which all oncology department parents need to do to release the stress of the situation and express a little of the anguish. There were only two public toilets serving the entire hospital and neither was the sort of place anyone would linger in for more than the necessary minute or two. Toilet paper was nonexistent, because of the thieves, and the toilets were floating with cigarette ends. It was the sort of environment, I felt, more likely to cultivate a good outbreak of cholera or plague than to encourage the high standards of hygiene needed to guard against infection on a cancer ward.

The first few days were spent scanning and taking X-rays to detect any tumours not immediately obvious. We were asked if we would participate in an experiment to test the effectiveness of magnetic resonance scanning. To do this meant delaying Jimmy's treatment by two days, which I agreed to because the staff assured us that he would lose nothing by doing so.

The day after we arrived, Jimmy had the first of many bone marrow tests. As we waited outside the little theatre where he would be put to sleep, and have the marrow extracted from his back, a familiar face suddenly appeared, and an old friend, Maureen, sat down beside me, with a carrier bag stuffed with food, comics and books.

In the first five minutes, she had spotted a kink in Jimmy's drip line, read him the *Beano* and found us a drink. Although Maureen and her husband, Roger, were originally our friends from home, they had moved, and now live quite near Manchester. By happy coincidence, Maureen had worked as Sister on a ward at Pendlebury for several years, where she met and eventually married Roger Pool, a doctor, and we first knew them both in Cumbria when their eldest child, Tim, was a toddler with Jimmy.

Heads turned as she walked briskly through the door, and although it was eight years since she had left, many of the staff welcomed her as though she were coming on duty after a weekend away. She knew every inch of the hospital and where to find everything, and she spent many days with us, helping to nurse Jimmy and allowing me time for short rest breaks away from the ward. Life would have been infinitely harder without Maureen and Roger.

Bone marrow test Wednesdays were all much the same. When it was Jimmy's turn, we walked into the theatre and I had to stay with him as he went to sleep, sometimes by injection and other times using gas and a face mask. I soon learned to talk very quietly to him, persuading him to relax and not resist the sleepiness.

I never felt easy being party to something that he hated so much; he would wake up a quarter of an hour later, feeling sick and dizzy, his back sore where the marrow had been extracted, and often stiff and bruised nearby on his lower back where doctors had performed a lumbar puncture, and put drugs into his spinal fluid to block the cancer cells' path to his brain. We always hated bone marrow Wednesdays; and the only compensation for me as I waited anxiously in the recovery room for his trolley to be wheeled in was the fresh coffee left percolating for parents and staff to help themselves. This was a small but precious bonus for us all in recognition of the stress everyone suffers, waiting for the important bone marrow test results.

On future bone marrow days, I could usually spot waiting parents who were new to this particular ordeal; and on that first Wednesday, I stood alone, facing the wall, feeling very frightened and hoping nobody would speak to me in case all control slipped. People all around chatted casually, nobody else was crying.

It is amazing how soon most parents learn to live with the stress and fear which underlies every single day, able even to joke and gossip whilst never forgetting for one moment the significance of the disease our children fight. Perhaps, in a sense, we onlookers become almost brutalized by what is happening to our children; the toxic, unpleasant treatment is the only option open to us in order to give them a chance to beat cancer, and to sympathize too much with the suffering child might make it harder for both child and parent. There comes a time when both sides just have to get on with it all.

That first bone marrow day was before we both learned to 'get on with it', and I felt emotional and so very sad. My grief was at the loss of my healthy child; after an illness like leukaemia, it was hard to think he would ever be really healthy again. There would always be doubts and fears.

Jimmy's tranquil face looked so vulnerable as he slept off his anaesthetic and, stroking his hair, I imagined the cancer cells running riot throughout his body, unchecked and untreated. I had known every tiny little mole on the surface of that small body, every finger and toe; I had made it from my cells, given birth to it, fed and nurtured it, loved and cuddled it and now it felt somehow alien, as if some foreign force unfamiliar to me had taken control of it, and I felt almost afraid to touch it. It was like a country under a brutal army of occupation.

Maureen was still there at midday, ever practical with sandwiches

and flask, and early in the afternoon I was summoned to hear the
official diagnosis and find out which type of leukaemia Jimmy had. An
explanatory booklet thoughtfully provided by staff had given enough
information to know that Acute Lymphoblastic Leukaemia was a better
bet than Acute Myeloid Leukaemia, and I hoped the verdict would be
ALL.

The diagnosis was given in a very formal setting. I was accompanied
by a staff nurse, and the sitting room where we met seemed very small
as we sat in a semicircle, with the consultant, social worker, nurse,
student nurse observer, myself and Maureen. The walls seemed to be
closing in on us and I wanted Paul to be there with me. He would
have been if we had been able to close the business, or leave it running
with staff. We could do neither, and unless he stayed at home and
worked while I looked after Jimmy in hospital, we would have no
income to live on as well as a son with leukaemia.

The good news, if 'good' was the right word, was that Jimmy had
ALL, not AML; but the news was not as 'good' as it might have been
because Jimmy's white cell count had shown a sizeable leap upwards
over the 24-hour period it was tested, which indicated, with the
knowledge they had at the time, that his prognosis would be less
optimistic than it might have been. Normally an ALL patient such as
Jimmy, bearing in mind his age and sex, could expect a 70 per cent
chance of complete cure. Jimmy's was put at 60 per cent.

Once we had discussed the diagnosis, the next subject to tackle was
Jimmy's treatment programme. One of the first facts to grasp is that
each child, in order to be treated at all in this country, has to be a
guinea pig. Unless the scientists experiment continually with dosages,
no progress can be made towards improving results. Treatment of
childhood leukaemia relies on the current UKALL programme.
UKALL, or the United Kingdom Acute Lymphoblastic Leukaemia
programme, is controlled by a computer which receives information
about each child, selects at random one of four treatment protocols,
and then assesses the effectiveness of all treatments over the next couple
of years.

The results are examined every four years, and the protocols are then
modified to include the most successful regimes of the last UKALL
programme to form the basis of the new one, and the whole operation
starts all over again.

The computer had selected an A protocol for Jimmy, one which gave the least possible treatment especially in the early stages, when the Induction month would not be followed up by Intensification nor a repeat of the initial treatment which children on the B, C and D protocols had.

We were in no position to argue with the selection. Not even the doctors themselves could really say whether greater amounts of the toxic and damaging chemotherapy drugs represented a higher likelihood of a cure. More treatment doesn't necessarily add up to better results, and as some of the drugs used are carcinogenic in themselves and destroy vast numbers of healthy cells, a heavier treatment protocol might lead to even more problems in the future. So what can bring about a cure now can cause serious long-term problems.

The moral dilemma we as parents faced was whether we should submit our child to a randomized choice of protocol which might not turn out to be the optimum treatment for his particular leukaemia. But it was only a moral dilemma in the academic sense and not a real choice; the UKALL trials offered parents no options at the time.

Just supposing there were a choice, and we were to select a level of treatment which ultimately failed, would we not blame ourselves for ever? And if the doctors chose for us, would we not blame them? And if the computer selection system contributes to the current research, without which no improvements can be made for the future, wasn't this really the only sensible way a decision could be made?

It is only with hindsight that I think that the computer decision to give Jimmy as little treatment as possible was wrong; and that the morality of random selection is questionable, however much it lets everyone off the hook by taking a decision nobody wants to be responsible for.

Since Jimmy's death, the randomized selection has been narrowed to take far greater account of the level of white cell count with which a child arrives. There are currently two lighter treatment programmes for those under a certain limit, and two heavier ones for those over that limit, so the choice the computer has is one of two possibilities rather than one of four. Jimmy's count was very high, at the upper end of the higher limit. The lowest treatment category which was randomly selected would not have been considered at all within the current UKALL trials, which now include one, two and sometimes even three intensifications. Jimmy had no intensifications at all – however, his sensitivity to even small amounts of chemotherapy might always have posed big problems, whatever the treatment programme.

I would also, in retrospect, question the true value of giving parents predictions for the future, in the form of percentage cure chance forecasts. The magic number is sometimes all that parents have to cling on to through the grim weeks and years ahead.

Pondering sometimes for days at a time about the possibility of our son being in the 60 per cent cure category or the 40 per cent failure group was all a complete waste of time anyway. It never even occurred to us that Jimmy would be in neither of these categories, but instead in the tiny minority of 5 per cent who never even make it through the first two years' treatment. However positive one's approach in combating this dreadful disease, however motivated one is to fight the bad cells, survival in cancer is very much a lottery. Until all the pieces of this complex jigsaw puzzle are fitted together, survival remains unpredictable.

The diagnosis interview was distressing and tense. It felt most uncomfortable to be in the centre of a circle of faces watching me intently, trying to gauge my reactions. Staff are well trained to answer questions and repeat information at any time, and most parents are too shocked at first to be able to make much sense of the complicated treatment schedules.

I remember the social worker asking if Jimmy were religious and if he understood about death. It didn't seem very helpful to talk about death so soon, but the point was made that not all children respond to treatment, and that Jimmy might never recover, even for a short time. That won't happen to us, I thought. It can't.

One of the hardest moments of the day was to return to Jimmy's bedside immediately after the diagnosis had been given, looking as I normally did – calm, unworried and as though nothing too bad was happening. Jimmy objected strongly to my having left him for an hour, and I had no time to wash my face or disguise the blotchy red eyes.

This was my first lesson of many in control of emotions. I was determined that Jimmy would never see me in tears. Crying was not something I did frequently at home; to see Mummy crying now would frighten him so much, it could seriously affect his mental state and the way in which he would accept his treatment. I knew it was vital that I should show confidence, so that he would learn to feel confident too.

To give vent to anxiety and fear became a luxury that neither of us could afford. Crying was rather like illicit smoking – a snatched sob or two in the lavatory, or a good silent howl under the bedclothes at night, hoping the other three strangers sharing bunk beds close by wouldn't be disturbed.

How do parents feel when told that their child has a very serious illness which may cause him to die and that the treatment itself is damaging?

Some parents refuse to face the possibility of death. With an illness like leukaemia, there is no grey area in the middle; either the child is cured and lives, or is not cured and dies. I knew Jimmy would never be fairly well; he would either be very well or dying. But the notion of his having cancer was so shocking and painful, it made death completely unthinkable.

My first few days at Manchester were spent grappling with shock and disbelief, grief and anxiety, but only when the solitude of a short meal break or trip to the kitchen to make a drink for Jimmy allowed me to relax the cheerful face for just a brief time and feel the emotions which had to be so firmly supressed when we were together.

Most of the time we spent playing card games, reading, talking, coaxing Jimmy to take his tablets or let the thumb-prick lady from the Path Lab take a small sample of blood from his thumb. It required maximum ingenuity to make every new experience into an interesting adventure, whether it was having an X-ray or learning to take his tee shirt off over the arm permanently connected to his drip.

We explored the hospital corridors together, transporting the drip stand with us, visiting numerous tanks of tropical fish daily. We attended the twice-weekly midday feeding of Gnasher, the piranha fish, as advertised – and never once arrived at precisely the right moment. We fed money into mechanical rocking trains in the main corridor, we fed even more money into public telephones talking to Paul and Martin.

Jimmy soon saw through my weak attempts at making hospital life fun and we agreed how boring the fish were, even the species in X-ray that seemed to kiss each other all day with gummy, sucking mouths, and the piranha, renowned for its fierceness but always to be seen swimming peacefully round in a little tank floating with bits of old bacon.

On the morning of 1 July, just before Jimmy's treatment was due to start with a blood transfusion, we were taken by taxi to the

Department of Diagnostic Radiology, which was part of the Department of Medical Physics at the University. We had agreed to let him be the subject of a magnetic resonance scan. It was hoped that if these scans proved accurate in pinpointing tumours and clusters of tumour cells, they might eventually replace the bone marrow testing which had to be done on each child every three months.

This would remove the need for the general anaesthetics and all the risks these involve. But in order to check the accuracy of this type of scan it was necessary to use it in conjunction with conventional bone marrow tests to see if the two results matched up.

A scan, we thought, would involve little more than a few minutes' lying still, and an interesting ride through the city both ways to provide a change of scene and a little diversion from Jimmy's hospital bed. But we were wrong.

Jimmy was very weak by this time, and had to be carried nearly everywhere including up the two flights of stairs in the building when we arrived. A friendly nurse came with us, but she was new to oncology and had been sent as part of her training rather than to help us.

We waited nearly an hour before we were called in to the scanning room. The space was taken up by an enormous structure in the middle of the room looking like a space capsule, and the patient had to be slid into it on a narrow sort of stretcher, then lie absolutely still inside for as long as it took to build up a good picture, while unable to communicate with anyone outside. The staff worked from behind a console in a screened-off area.

The sight of the huge metal capsule was too much for Jimmy. His fear surfaced for the first time, and he shouted and screamed. He didn't want to go inside it, and was terrified of being isolated from me.

The staff appeared unused to dealing with frightened children, and unprepared to calm Jimmy's terror. With hindsight, we should have walked out there and then. Instead I struggled to pacify him so the test could start, and although he finally allowed himself to be put inside the machine, he couldn't lie still because he was too upset.

To a casual observer, Jimmy might have appeared to be a little boy who was wasting precious time fussing about something that wouldn't hurt him. To me, he was a child who, up until four days before, had never even experienced a blood test before, let alone illness, hospitalization and separation.

The noise of the magnets bumping and banging inside the structure made matters worse and, having reminded the staff how weak and ill he was, I lifted the back of the capsule and climbed in with him. We both decided that the scan would only continue if I stayed with him, so we held hands, head to head in our narrow tunnel while I told him stories and pretended we were clothes tumbling round in a spin dryer.

The staff were not happy because the quality of their computer pictures was poor, but it was either that, or nothing.

I had understood our participation in the experiment would mean one scan only, but after we'd finished, stiff and cold, and crawled out, the staff told us we would have to attend every few months.

On future occasions I insisted on mild sedation for Jimmy which he took willingly; he then crawled into the capsule without anxiety, went to sleep and gave staff perfect, still pictures in a fraction of the time it took that first visit. Many adult patients needing MR scans are already very ill, some in pain, and others suffering from nausea. Often they need a little sedation so that they can remain quite still in the narrow space, and it seems sensible that children should be offered similar help to that the adults have as a matter of course.

If we had fully understood what the MR scan would entail, we would never have allowed Jimmy to be part of this trial. He gained nothing from it, but we hope his small contribution to science has benefited other children.

Jimmy's treatment started as soon as we got back to the hospital. The first part of treatment, Induction, entails giving the children very toxic drugs by intravenous drips, by lumbar puncture, by injection and by mouth. The children generally become very sick, weak and poorly before they can start to get better, but within a few weeks, the treatment usually brings the disease under control and inhibits the growth of new cancer cells.

Once a control is established, and tests show no more than a very low percentage of residual cancer cells left, the children are said to have gone into remission. If the cancer cells later return, patients have suffered a relapse. Jimmy's body responded so speedily to that first burst of treatment, that his remission was achieved in just two weeks.

# THREE

# Remission

If life had ever demanded of me that I should visit a children's cancer ward prior to Jimmy's illness, I would either have dreaded the experience and regarded it as an ordeal, been profoundly moved by it and thought about it at length afterwards – or, more likely, I would never have even managed to walk through the ward door.

It came as a complete surprise to discover that even a children's cancer ward has its own everyday routine largely made up of cheerful pleasantries, jokes with the staff and a hundred other trivialities as far removed from pain and death as possible.

If treatment fails, most children die at home, and very few actually slip away while in hospital. This means that the children on the ward are still undergoing treatment, and parents are always hopeful about the outcome whatever the odds. Where there's treatment, there's some hope, however small, and the ward was never usually a despairing sort of place unless one particular event had suddenly upset the fine balance of control.

But our first hospital experience was not on a ward, but in the privacy of the Bone Marrow Transplant Unit. Staff said they disliked nursing children in these small units of one, two or three. They thought the children missed the spectacle of life going on around them all the time on the ward, and became bored more easily, while parents missed the companionship and support of other parents.

It was also harder for nurses to keep an eye on each child, and locate in an instant each bleeping drip which needed topping up. But from a parent's point of view, I was most relieved that our first introduction to children with cancer was in the semi-privacy of a smaller room where it was easier to be close, more like home, and less like an institution.

The day when redecorating work on Borchardt Ward was complete and we moved to the public noise and bustle was memorable. The new children were anxious and silent as they looked at each other en masse for the first time. Their space and privacy was gone, the beds were pushed very close together, and the ward was completely full seven days a week.

The first glimpse of such a busy ward can be unavoidably disturbing. Children cry with fear and homesickness night and day; there are screams from the treatment room and wails from the playroom; and the televisions thoughtfully provided for every child are often left on unwatched, adding to the cacophony and confusion. The lights are bright, and with the amount of expert nursing that chemotherapy requires, Borchardt Ward can seem just as busy at night as in the daytime.

If that had been my first taste of hospital life with Jimmy, I know it would have made us very miserable. Fortunately, the Bone Marrow Transplant Unit gave us time to adjust to a new way of life more gently, and time to get accustomed to seeing other children who were very ill.

Nicky shared Jimmy's room. He was three years old, and never said a word for three weeks. His white count was extremely high, and he did not go into remission for weeks. We feared greatly for his future. But cancer is so unpredictable that it is Nicky who is alive today after a successful bone marrow transplant, and Jimmy who is dead, having never been offered the chance of one.

I soon realized how very deeply I felt for all the sick children. Most of us loved and cared for each other's children as well as our own. Only one thing affected me as profoundly as the fate of my own child, and that was hearing bad news of another child.

Whatever the nurses felt privately about caring for children with cancer, staff attitudes were cheerful and brisk. They were sympathetic without becoming too closely involved, and their concern included care of parents too. Nurses would be ready at any time to explain, discuss or just comfort as families questioned or wept.

It requires great skill and vigilance to administer chemotherapy drugs; drips have to be monitored constantly, individual problems solved and children kept occupied and content however limited their energies. Great importance was placed on the role of education in the ward's daily routine. Just because children were in hospital, staff said, was no good reason for missing school completely. If they couldn't go to school, school would go to them.

There was a very sound reason for this. It is recognized that children undergoing certain drug treatments and radiotherapy lose some powers of memory and concentration and their IQs often drop a little. So, to minimize the intellectual damage, education continues in hospital.

Mrs Smith was a calm, smiling teacher who encouraged and praised all her sick little pupils and found value in all that they did. She welcomed the children's enthusiasm for anything at all and rewarded each interest with a plentiful supply of materials. When she discovered Jimmy liked drawing birds, she returned next day with an enormous bird book, sheets of quality drawing paper and good colouring pencils.

At first Jimmy enjoyed a couple of hours' work a day, sometimes on his own with the teacher; he galloped through his work books, and read fluently. But the novelty of private tuition soon faded when he missed having other children to fool around and giggle with, and he became adept as a hospital truant, hiding in the toilets or feigning sleep. Hospital was for playing, not working, he thought.

Paul and Martin came to visit every three or four days. Martin would run into my arms, hug me, then find a reason why he was cross with me.

We hardly knew how to re-establish our relationship during such short, unsatisfactory visits. I had no idea what Martin's life was like at home without me and he had no idea what hospital was really like. The end of each visit brought tears for us both. He would cry with little sound but much grief as we kissed goodbye, and he was still crying as I watched him leave, alone in the back of the car, strapped in his child seat.

I knew the hurt he felt, the damage being done; but he and Paul seemed happy enough together when we phoned, and Jimmy's needs at the time were so great, there was very little I could do to help Martin. He survived my absence very well, protected by Paul's strength and the security of strong family relationships. When Granny moved in temporarily with us at home, she even brought her own bed, where Martin snuggled up each morning while she read *Postman Pat* or *Thomas the Tank Engine*.

My first escape from the hospital was to a pub for a meal and a drink, but the outside world, where children had hair and weren't suffering or even dying, seemed unreal. My own reality had shifted, and was confined inside the hospital perimeter fence. Anything outside that seemed unsafe, and I always hurried back to Jimmy, anxious and a little guilty for my absence.

The next Sunday, Jimmy was allowed out for the day. But he was vomiting continually, and the following morning we were moved into isolation in case he had an infection which might spread to the other children.

We were both upset at the prospect of moving, and tried to persuade the doctor to let us stay where we were, but she was adamant. For me, it was a move away from the small support systems I had built up and the kind staff I had got to know and for Jimmy, it was loneliness and isolation and more srange faces. The nurses promised he could have his old bed back when we returned.

The now defunct isolation ward was a single-storey red-brick building in the grounds, smelling strongly of raw disinfectant. The smell was so pervasive that the packs of cards and games that we used that week continued to smell of disinfectant for months afterwards, and clothing still smelled even after numerous washes.

Th first person I met was a man dressed in navy overalls carrying a can with a large spray who asked me if I knew where Sister was.

'I'm the pest officer and I've come to deal with the infestation of ants,' he informed me.

For the following two hours I was stranded alone with Jimmy because I couldn't leave his room and risk cross-infection, so I was unable to go and look for help. We were confined to a room with no bedpan and Jimmy, by this time, had diarrhoea every half hour. Once a nurse had been found, presumably on the ant trail, she waved in the general direction of a few cupboards and told us to take what we needed. Out of sight felt like out of mind, and I soon imagined Jimmy and his treatment had been conveniently forgotten by everybody.

It was important that he didn't pass on any infections to other children with cancer, but equally important that he wasn't put in danger of contracting anything himself. The little baby next door had measles very severely, yet staff seemed to pass between her room and Jimmy's quite freely.

The parents' room had only one broken chair in it, but because the ward was due for closure no money could be spent to improve conditions.

After three days, Jimmy's sickness and diarrhoea had stopped, but he lay tired and floppy, looking listlessly through red-rimmed eyes, and I was certain he had another type of slow infection. His temperature wobbled up and down, and it was decided finally that he needed intravenous antibiotics.

Unfortunately, the site of the drip in Jimmy's hand had become infected and very sore, and it took all day and several attempts to try and find a new vein that would take the needle. After this had been finally achieved, Jimmy suddenly requested a ham sandwich after his ordeal. But the canteen, open for only half an hour each evening to parents, was closed. The junior doctor, who had been on duty for many hours, and the off-duty nurse, who happened to be passing and stopped to help, both disappeared, and the ham sandwich arrived five minutes later with a big hug for Jimmy.

It is very difficult to stand by as a parent, unable to help, and see the suffering and unhappiness one's child is experiencing. Escape is impossible because the child needs a parent's constant leadership, confidence and strength; but the strain of witnessing suffering in somebody you love very much leaves parents depressed, guilty, and very weary. The commonest wish amongst us all must be, 'If only it was me, and not my child.'

The next day Paul and Martin arrived, and by some special dispensation granted by the hospital management and engineered by the wonderful Family Care ladies, who supervised parent accommodation, every rule was broken to allow Martin and Paul to sleep on the old isolation ward with Jimmy.

Martin brought Cheesy, his soft toy mouse, and we made him up a bed on the floor of the empty room next to Jimmy. It was a very wet afternoon, and Martin had brought his bike to ride round the hospital's disused tennis court, but the weather kept us indoors, playing cards and board games.

Jimmy had responded well to the antibiotics, and only needed one dose in his drip every six hours. But the drip had to remain up, because of the time and effort involved in replacing it in the blocked-off cannula every few hours. This restricted Jimmy's freedom of movement, and we couldn't take him out anywhere.

Jimmy had been given £5 by one of our friends, and with an impetuous burst of generosity, he decided to take us all out for a fish-and-chip tea. But what to do about the drip? He worked on the problem all afternoon. He consulted, negotiated, argued and won. After his six o'clock drugs, his ham sandwich friend capitulated, disconnected the drip and released him for a couple of hours, provided that we didn't go in a public place anywhere that Jimmy could pick up another infection.

Try finding a chip shop on a wet Saturday night with a private dining room available at a moment's notice! It wasn't just raining, it was pouring in rivers down the streets of Salford. Pavements were awash and most of the chippies were closed anyway.

But an open chip shop had to be found so that Jimmy could exercise his generosity. At last we spotted one, and once we had explained the problem, a backroom with a table in it was found. The floor was slippery with grease, the walls dingy and stained but our host hardly noticed as he bought Coca-Cola for his brother, fish and chips and mushy peas all round and settled back to enjoy his treat.

It was still too soon as yet to know whether Jimmy's treatment was proving successful and whether he was going into remission. The important bone marrow test in a few days would reveal all this, and to help ease the tension of waiting I went to town one day for a short break, and bought a smart pair of red sandals.

Red seemed far too bright and frivolous a colour to wear while Jimmy was so ill, so I put the shoes away and promised myself that I would wear them only when Jimmy went into remission.

The bone marrow test took place a few days later, and the results normally came by early afternoon. I heard the consultant outside discussing Jimmy and he sounded cheerful and very optimistic. 'I think we've got this one,' he said.

Jimmy had indeed gone into remission and out came the celebratory red sandals. It seems sadly ironic that those trivial symbols of hope failed to wear out, but lasted long after Jimmy died.

After a week or so, Jimmy was allowed back to his old room in the Bone Marrow Transplant Unit, much to his delight. I used to stay with him until late in the evening, and when he was asleep, the kind night staff let me use Sister's office to try and keep up with my work and produce my weekly newspaper column on local history. This meant getting hold of regular supplies of research material from home, but everybody helped endlessly to keep our lives running as smoothly as possible. Both family and friends got to know I was on the Unit at that time of the evening, and staff took numerous phone calls until one day when a staff nurse came flouncing in and announced: 'You don't need a nurse, you need a social secretary!' I burst into tears, cried on her shoulder and imagined what would be said at the nurses' report time: 'Jimmy's mother distressed and unable to cope.'

Just before we were due to go home after a month in hospital, we moved yet again, this time back to the newly decorated Borchardt Ward. That last evening, we heard that another child from our town, a girl six months older than Jimmy, had arrived with a cancer yet to be identified in detail. Although her family lived near us, Elin and her sister, Holly, went to different schools and we hadn't actually met them before.

Elin's mother, Pam, had also spent some weeks trying to get doctors to take her worries about Elin seriously. We talked for some time when the children were asleep. It all seemed very strange. Suddenly there were two cases of child cancer in our small town in four weeks.

There was a coincidence in our meeting that was even stranger, and one that it took months to discover. Later that year, while having tea together at Pam's home, I noticed an obscure book of poetry which had been on my university reading list. It took us only a few seconds to realize that we had both been humanities students living in Rutherford College, University of Kent, during 1967-8, and although we had never consciously met we had shared mutual friends and had both been present at various events on several occasions. Our shared past has often given us much to talk about and much in common far beyond sharing the common tragedy of cancer in both our children.

Jimmy finished his Induction treatment as Elin began hers, and Jimmy and I arrived home next day to a big welcome from Martin and Paul and even a 'Welcome Home' banner across our big living room. The first place we visited was the bathroom, to wash the hospital smell away, and Jimmy, Martin and I sat all three in the bath together, hugging each other with the novelty of being reunited at last.

Safe and ordinary as home appeared to be, I couldn't put out of my mind the scenes I had left behind of pain, suffering, and grief. The sounds of children crying echoed through my mind and I could find no peace. During the first few hours at home, I lived as though sleepwalking, unable to concentrate, and unable to relate to the myriad of trivial problems awaiting my return. Nothing seemed of any significance at all in the face of Jimmy's illness.

Our first day at home coincided with the town's gala day. Jimmy was eager to go and see the carnival procession as usual but I knew I wasn't ready to face the world yet with the face of optimism that friends needed to see in us.

Instead I stayed at home and spent the afternoon releasing all my pent-up grief, anger, frustration, and despair. It was all swept away on a great tide of emotion by the time the children came home to tea, and after this outburst I was able to readjust to life back at home.

We had two weeks' respite before the next intensive course of treatment at the Christie, the world-famous cancer hospital in south Manchester, where Jimmy was to undergo cranial irradiation to eradicate any cancer cells which might have crept up in the cerebral spinal fluid to his brain. All the evidence showed that the fluid was clear, but cells sometimes escaped detection, and it was considered essential to irradiate his brain despite strong evidence that it would not only reduce Jimmy's IQ by a few points, but also interfere with his concentration and memory. The mental picture of cranial irradiation I built up in anticipation made it seem very frightening.

The week before he was due to start his stint at Christie's, Jimmy had experienced particular problems after his regular lumbar puncture. He had complained of pain that night in his back, and had vomited constantly over the next few days. His head ached, his neck hurt, and within four days he was too weak and nauseous to walk any more. He lay on the sofa at home throughout a hot summer Sunday while Paul made him cardboard models of Thomas Tank Engines.

By the time we had arrived at Christie's the next day, Jimmy was too ill to appreciate the spacious ground-floor children's ward, the garden and playground outside, and the relaxed attitude of the nursing staff. The atmosphere was like a holiday camp in comparison with Borchardt, which often felt like a front-line field battle station straight out of *M.A.S.H.*

Treatment at Christie's was usually not continual and the daily sessions of radiotherapy lasted only a few minutes after which the children were free to play.

Not so Jimmy, who was far from free to do anything except lie in his bed attached to yet another drip as he continued to vomit repeatedly for five days. The toy tractor on which he would have trundled up and down the wide ward and out into the pleasant garden lay idle. Unable to escape his bed, Jimmy watched a 12-year-old boy who lay opposite, his mind slowly crumbling under the grip of a rare sheath tumour which had wrapped itself round his brain. His mother and grandmother spent each day by his bed like two heroines from Greek tragedy, beautiful, strong and elegant women, refusing to give up hope as they read him all the sports reports from newspapers. Their child had always wanted to be a sports reporter, and by reading to him about football matches, they hoped to keep his tired, sick brain functioning. But he could no longer speak coherently and the noises that he made were confusing and distressing.

Jimmy lay and watched. He didn't need to ask anything because he already knew most of the answers. Further down the corridor, Kylie Minogue sang 'I Should Be So Lucky', and the catchy song echoed round the courtyard garden, while a sad, unlucky eighteen-year-old sat in bed trying on wigs and the pink silk pyjamas her friends had given her. The low wooden building, specially designed and recently built for the children, smelt of wood preservative in the hot August sun, and the new Senior House Officer giggled with the staff nurses to pass the time because nobody urgently needed anybody.

A long, long passage linked the children's unit with the main hospital, where there were carpets on the ward and corridor floors, wallpaper and tasteful rubber plants. In the Outpatients waiting area sat nervous couples awaiting test results, their relationships tested through sickness now instead of health; and despite a recent hold-up and robbery, there was even a bank provided to serve both staff and patients.

Each long ward faced the garden through French windows, and on every garden patio, whatever time of the day or night, the smokers, unable to kick the habit even in the face of death, enjoyed a quick drag out in the fresh air to help relieve the stress. Back on the children's ward it was ironic that the parents' kitchen and sitting room were used for smoking by the domestic staff.

The first day at Christie's I had accompanied Jimmy down to a special room where his head was measured with implements which looked like wire coat hangers. They were bent into the shape of his skull and accurate measurements were taken to plot exactly where the radiation was to be targeted. Using indelible blue pens, lines were drawn to show the radiotherapists where to aim. We called them Jimmy's space marks, and he became so attached to them, he was happy that they took two weeks to fade.

Measuring Jimmy's head meant taking a series of X-rays of his skull, a frightening thing for a little boy who had no idea what to expect when everyone was sent from the room and he was left alone, strapped to a table in the dark. He cried loudly. The doctor became very impatient that Jimmy couldn't keep still and threatened that if he didn't stop crying, his mother would be sent away. This was too much for me, and I walked out from behind the protective screen and told Jimmy I had no intention of leaving him, but that if he kept still and quiet it would all be over more quickly. He responded immediately.

I was told this same doctor had decreed that no mother could accompany her child for the daily doses of radiation, and none of the staff were in a position to overrule him. It took Jimmy two or three days before he relaxed enough to be able to get some small enjoyment out of his ride through the hospital corridors with one of the cheerful band of nurses who ran the children's ward. Although the radiation didn't hurt, the room in which he lay alone was dark and full of imposing technology, and when I asked him to draw a picture of it so that I could actually imagine what was happening to him each morning, he drew a detailed sketch of the lights on the ceiling above him, because it was all he could see lying flat on his back.

On the final day of his treatment, as an enormous concession to us and in view of Jimmy's calmness and maturity, I was allowed to accompany him for his treatment, so long as I pretended I was not his mother if the dictatorial doctor should happen to spy us. Jimmy had formed firm friendships with all the radiotherapy staff, and had chatted freely about his home and family. His articulate and friendly nature had made quite an impression on the three attractive ladies who worked there, and there was genuine sadness when they said goodbye.

Jimmy and I observed life around us together as we always did in hospital and shared our usual likes and dislikes. We giggled like naughty children in our mutual loathing for one of the staff we thought patronized the mothers and children alike and called all the toddlers by silly names. She insisted all the parents left by eight o'clock each evening, which I felt interfered with the evening routine of settling Jimmy down to sleep which we had developed so closely and securely during the first weeks of his illness.

The parents were accommodated some distance away, through the vast hospital, across a busy road, through the grounds of a large old house, along by a wood until we reached the nurses' home where every door seemed to be double-locked to keep prowlers out, though the nearby wood gave excellent cover for muggers and flashers. The first week I shared a twin-bedded room with a kind, comfortable lady whose only son had a brain tumour. Her belief in God was very strong, and I envied her trust in His ability to make everything whole again.

Whenever people talked to me about God as though I shared their close relationship with him, I was always overcome with feelings of hypocrisy and guilt that God and I did not share a closeness, especially since I had discovered how children suffer and die despite a merciful God who loves little children.

My sister, Cate, expressed it in her usual succinct way when she said that God must have turned away and blinked momentarily when Jimmy developed leukaemia. The events that unfolded over the next twenty months in our family made it feel as if God had not only blinked but had gone to sleep wearing a blindfold as far as we were concerned.

Jimmy was attached to his drip and vomiting continually throughout his first week at Christie's, but by Friday he had recovered sufficiently to spend the weekend with the Pools. Their house, on a Pennine hilltop, often provided a sanctuary of normality, temporarily relieving our stress. The geese honked a noisy welcome as we arrived to find delicious meals waiting, clean clothes, cakes baking; Tim and Alice shared toys and games with Jimmy and Martin while Roger and Maureen allowed us the freedom to relax by going for walks, sleeping or just sitting quietly reading. Their unexcited, solid good sense coupled with their loving concern calmed and comforted us frequently.

Life cheered up the following week as Jimmy's condition had improved and he took full advantage of Christie's playground and toys. He was even selfish enough to take the toy tractor he wanted to play with so much into the bathroom every time he needed to go to the toilet, to prevent anyone else from snatching it away.

He made friends with an older boy opposite whose opening gambit never faltered. 'I've had two brain tumours, and three relapses and they don't know what to do about me now,' Stuart told all newcomers. His scatty hyperactivity created problems for the nurses, and although he knew how carefully he had to look after his poor head, he often bumped it or gashed it, and even got patches of bad sunburn on the area of his head being treated with radiotherapy. The children are warned not to go out in the sun without wearing a hat, and not to use perfumed soap or shampoo to prevent skin reactions.

We were sent to Christie's theatre twice for lumbar punctures and doses of drugs which had to be given intrathecally, into Jimmy's spinal fluid. This required the usual general anaesthetic and Jimmy was very apprehensive in case Christie's should do anything differently from Pendlebury.

He needn't have worried because the Spanish lady anaesthetist with her musical laugh and chunky necklaces almost hypnotized Jimmy to sleep with her extrovert personality, and he was allowed to wake up back in his bed instead of on a chair in the recovery room, or being walked up and down the corridor outside, which was normal in the cramped conditions back at Pendlebury.

The weather was fine and warm, and the surrounding suburbs near the hospital were pleasant and well provided with shops. There was a big park about a mile away, with plenty of ducks to feed and a small farm animals' zoo to while away the sunny afternoons.

Each fine day after his treatment, we headed off up the road with Jimmy in an old buggy to explore every corner of the large park with its shrubs and flowerbeds and big open spaces.

It was with growing confidence that I realized that despite the uncertainty of Jimmy's future always hanging over us, it was still possible to find enjoyment in life. The contrast between the harrowing scenes of sadness and suffering we witnessed daily, and the tranquillity of a beautiful park on a sunny day emphasized the simplest of joys, and this small glimpse of ordinary life heightened our sense of enjoyment.

Another simple trick of survival through these anxious weeks both at Pendlebury and Christie's with Jimmy involved spending a small amount of time just once a day by myself. Such enjoyment was rationed, so that even the most unsophisticated of pleasures became highly enjoyable. The daily treat was either ten minutes reading a newspaper, or eating a chocolate bar, or maybe half an hour spent while he was having a sleep taking a luxurious shower with some exotic shower mousse.

Jimmy and I talked throughout each day about anything and everything, about home and school, or what people we knew might be doing. Our regular local visitors included Sonja, Cate's sister-in-law, from York, who brought with her not only her serenity but delicious chocolate cake as well. A close friend of Sonja's children often came too. Katy, who was a dentist at the University, had already known Jimmy for three years, and when she found how near we were in Manchester would come nearly every evening, bringing lots of inventive fun and energy to play with him.

One day she took us back to her tiny flat to meet her friends. She made Jimmy her favourite snack, Marmite toast, which he ate greedily.

She was so pleased to see him eating, that she made some more. We got lost on the way back to Christie's and were anxious not to get locked out; the car journey made Jimmy sick, and the Marmite toast ended up splattered over a wide area of the courtyard outside the entrance. Luckily it rained in the night.

When Sonja came to visit at Pendlebury in the evening, it was at the end of a busy day teaching the flute in schools all round Manchester and York. Sonja often read to Jimmy while I had a quick meal in the canteen.

Although staff had done an excellent job explaining to Jimmy initially about his illness, he didn't express much interest in it after that, and rarely asked questions of me in the first few days. Now, he chose Sonja to help him understand it more fully.

On the day we arrived in hospital, Jimmy had been given an excellent small book, illustrated in the style of the popular 'Mr Men' series which explained leukaemia in language the average six-year-old could under-stand. It was frank without being frightening, and it made no false promises or fairy-story predictions that all the patients would live happily every after when treatment was over and they went home.

It described the treatment and injections, the anaesthetics and clinic visits that Jimmy would have to face. I had suggested reading the book to him, but he rejected it as 'boring' and I dropped the subject. But as soon as I went off to the canteen at suppertime, leaving him alone with Sonja, he asked her to read him the book twice, and again the following evening.

Jimmy was very pleased when Becky and Jonathan came to visit him at Christie's, so that he could share with them the novelty of all the unfamiliar toys. The family were on their way to stay with their relatives, and we sat out in the garden in the hot sun talking about Jimmy and all his problems.

I loved to be with Jimmy at all times but it was a great relief when close friends visited; while Jimmy was occupied, I could drop the mask and let slip the confident, calm exterior and indulge in a little despair and frustration.

Karen, John and I stood in the car park at Christie's, waving goodbye to Katy, arms round each other, when Karen suddenly announced: 'Whatever happens, we'll see this through together. Whichever way it goes, we'll see it through.'

None of us dreamt for a moment what sort of commitment that

would be, and what it would entail. But it was a solemn promise that was never broken.

Jimmy and I left Christie's for home late one Friday morning, longing to see Paul and Martin and be a family once more, hoping that we would never be separated even for a short time again.

Christie's were expert at arranging details like transport, and we accepted their offer of hospital transport, which provided a free lift home by car in place of a lengthy journey in a bumpy ambulance.

The car driver was very elderly and deaf and drove his new Japanese car up the M6 at over 80 m.p.h., weaving erratically from lane to lane. He flicked his cigar ash over his shoulder in our faces, and got lost for two hours dropping somebody else off in Morecambe. We decided that we'd rather hitch than trust a hospital car again.

Back home we wanted, and needed, a good holiday away from the nightmares of the summer. There was only one place that would be perfect, so we booked a fortnight in a holiday house on St Mary's, in the Isles of Scilly.

Only two months previously, such a journey would have posed no more than the usual logistics of reaching the islands in one day from home. The journey by train from one end of England to the other, including three changes of train, followed by a helicopter flight, all took precise to-the-minute planning. One late train, one connection lost, and the last helicopter flight of the day would be gone without us.

Travelling four hundred miles away from home to a collection of small islands twenty-five miles out to sea accompanied by an immuno-suppressed child with leukaemia made it slightly more problematic.

How well equipped was the small island hospital to deal with infection requiring intravenous antibiotics? If Jimmy suddenly became ill, how near was the nearest path lab to identify the type of illness and could it do a white cell count?

If the small hospital on St Mary's couldn't help, would that mean a helicopter dash to Truro, Exeter or even Bristol, and how much would it cost us?

It showed how much we longed for a break that we disregarded all these contingencies and relied on Jimmy's sense of wellbeing and enjoyment to protect him from illness while he was in a place that he loved so much.

The ploy worked. He left home weak and tired, with a white cell count so low that he shouldn't have been travelling on a train at all or been in contact with anyone in a public place. He was well every moment of the holiday.

The journey was exciting and picturesque. Jimmy snapped away with the family camera as we passed over the Tamar Bridge at Saltash, and he hung out of the little local train as it stopped at every station from Plymouth to Penzance, anxious to get his first sniff of the sea.

The helicopter flight held no fears this time. Twenty minutes hovering over the sea was nothing at all to worry about compared with facing death daily on the cancer ward. Living with leukaemia helps put life's smaller problems into perspective.

When we arrived at the house, the groceries we ordered hadn't arrived, and it was a Saturday night at eight o'clock. Shops in the Scillies always shut on Sundays, and there is nowhere open to buy food. Jimmy's continual hunger, caused by reactions to his drug treatment, remained unabated. We had to buy food. Within half an hour, we had explained our problems, and the cash and carry had been opened specially for us. Just the sight of Jimmy's bald head opened doors everywhere.

It was only ten weeks since Jimmy's treatment had started, but he had in this short time changed in appearance quite dramatically. After the first fortnight, his fine fair hair started to drop out, leaving bald patches, and within a month it was coming out in handfuls. The radiation treatment dealt a swift blow to all remaining little tufts, and Jimmy was now smooth-headed and hairless.

It was surprising how quickly we came to regard his baldness as normal. It somehow accentuated the beauty of his fine little features, although by September his face had become rather round and gross, and his whole body fatter and heavier, due to the steroids.

When he was at his most desperate for food, his loud and greedy demands made him look like a bald, overweight bovver boy; at first we tried to moderate his demands to fit in with life around him, but his need was too urgent.

It was just one example of the way the family had to learn to live with his bouts of unreasonable and uncharacteristic behaviour. Our only comfort was to keep reminding ourselves that this selfish, strident child was not the real kind and gentle Jimmy, but somebody temporarily under an unpleasant influence.

Jimmy's food obsessions varied. One week it would be tuna fish sandwiches, another it was cheese, then there were baked potatoes, hollowed out and mashed up with mayonnaise, salt and pepper; one fortnight it was sausage and bacon, another it was Quarter Pounder beefburgers. The fads never included anything sweet.

It was easy enough to keep a short-order kitchen running at home turning out bacon and sausage every twenty minutes, but difficult to explain if we were out with friends or in a public place. People witnessing his aggression over food must have thought we were indulging a spoilt brat. Poor Jimmy, it was very unfair. There were times when we found it hard to understand him, but even more when he himself couldn't understand what was happening inside him.

Our last family holiday together was also the last time Jimmy behaved physically like an energetic six-year-old. Long days spent out of doors in the clean, sea air soon banished memories of transfusions, drips and endless sickness, and Jimmy was strong, energetic, and only slightly irritable.

He wore a cap on his head to guard against sunburn after the radiation treatment, and the sight of our two little boys soon became familiar to the St Mary's boatmen, who nicknamed them Bird (Jimmy) and Scooby Doo (Martin).

Most people today are familiar enough with cancer to know that a completely bald head, especially in a child, is often the result of chemotherapy treatment; nearly everybody now knows of a relative or acquaintance who has suffered from some form of the disease.

We didn't want, or need, to explain anything to anyone. People seeing us soon summed up the situation for themselves; once I found half a dozen free boat tickets in my pocket to visit the other islands, and nobody in sight to thank. People are so moved by the sight of a child suffering from cancer that they often feel they have to do something, however small, to say how sorry they feel. Once, while out shopping back at home, I left Jimmy sitting in the street in his special wheelchair buggy. Feeling bored, he idly took his hat off and when I came out of the shop, I found people had been putting money in the hat as they passed quickly by, much to his amazement and delight.

Most days of the holiday were spent exploring and revisiting our favourite haunts on the off islands. It is difficult to think of anywhere left in Europe more beautiful and less spoilt by greed and mass tourism. The sea is clear and unpolluted and Jimmy loved to photograph the vivid blues and greens of the water, or the roughness of the Atlantic off notorious Hell Bay, or the friendly seals basking on rocks in the Eastern Isles.

He was ready for any adventure, the rougher and more risky the better. One of his favourite treats was to travel seven miles further out through the Atlantic swell to Bishop Rock Lighthouse. It was a two-hour trip, very cold and windy, tossed about on the high seas in an open launch, and he loved every minute of it.

Most evenings we would walk round the old garrison wall on St Mary's to see the lighthouses start to flash as it got darker. One clear night, by the light of a full moon, we walked across the headland a mile or more out to the unmanned Penninis Lighthouse where we stood on a rock in the path of the revolving beam, and listened in the dark to the eerie clanking of the old machinery.

On the way home, I tried to explain to Jimmy how our solar system is only one of many, and how tiny our planet is in relation to the universe and other galaxies. We talked about the insignificance of earth and man, and gazed up at the stars and thought how many thousands of light years away they are. Gazing up at the universe and reflecting on the smallness of man is an emotional experience; and as we stumbled over the stony track in the dark, hand in hand, I loved him with all my being.

Now that Jimmy is dead, the notion of Heaven being somewhere in that vast universe is depressing. It seems so far away, it is worrying to think that Jimmy's spirit is wandering the sky somewhere very distant from me. As mothers, it is instinctive at all times to want to know and account for each child in our care. We hold children's hands as we cross the road, we look round to make sure no child has wandered away. I still search for Jimmy as if he were a lost child who slipped away out of reach.

Walking the cliff paths for hours at a time, I saw Jimmy's illness in visual terms. I pictured it as though Jimmy and I had been walking along a cliffside path together, and I had been holding on to his hand as I always did, when he slipped from my grasp and started to slide down the steep cliff towards the sea far below. But I had managed to reach him and drag him back on the path. But although he had returned within my grasp, the path was so narrow that he was still in great danger of slipping again.

Every day seemed to be sunny and beautiful. We revisited our favourite white sandy beaches on St Martin's, and once again Paul built a car with front seats and back out of sand for the children to play in. If I were a little boy, I would love a creative Daddy like Paul. He designs, invents and builds anything from a Lego model with a motor, to a cathedral made out of wooden bricks which the children can then demolish.

Building a model car out of sand involved searching the beach for accessories, with old bottles as headlights and polystyrene for a steering wheel. Paul never sits anywhere for more than two minutes doing nothing, and his restless creativity is ideal for amusing small boys.

One hot afternoon, as we passed the tiny Old Town church with its quiet churchyard full of the graves of drowned sailors and servicemen, I left the boys and walked inside for a quiet moment. In spite of the happiness of the holiday, I couldn't stop my feelings of anxiety from re-emerging occasionally, and Jimmy's cancer was too heavy a burden to carry any further that day.

So I left the weight of my worries in that church, on the steps of the altar, and told God, if He was listening and always providing there was one, that I couldn't carry them any longer.

The two boys were excellent companions and playmates together, and romped round the islands, played hide-and-seek in the garden, or shared a glass of 'Dead Man's Blood' together at the pub where we often went to eat at night. Jimmy was less irritable than he had been, as long as we satisfied his hunger, and Martin was delighted to be back in favour again with his unpredictable brother.

On the last day of the holiday, Martin took all his clothes off on the beach as usual and burrowed down in the sand to play. Next morning we noticed a peculiar rash on his buttocks. By the following week, back home by now, the rash had become infected and looked similar to Jimmy's pre-leukaemic thrush.

Without so much as a day's wait, we were asked to attend hospital in Lancaster for blood tests, to rule out any possibility of another cancer in the family. The paediatrician and the dermatologist were worried and puzzled; it certainly had the look of thrush. Was it possible for leukaemia to strike twice in one family?

But Martin's blood tests were normal, and it eventually transpired that he was allergic to the sandhoppers that must have bitten his bottom when he burrowed in the sand.

Coming home was very sad. We all cried on the helicopter, looking down at the islands below, but little knowing Jimmy would never see his beloved Scillies again.

Within a couple of days, it was back to hospital for a clinic visit. Normally the children on their two-year course of maintenance chemotherapy go to clinic once a month, and for a bone marrow test under anaesthetic every three months. If the white cell count is very low, or infection a likelihood, the children go to clinic more often.

Clinic day routine was always the same. We would leave home about eight o'clock, having dropped Martin off at a friend's before school. The journey took about an hour and a half, and as soon as we reached Pendlebury, I would take Jimmy to the Path Lab for a thumb-prick blood test while Paul raced off to the clinic at the far end of the hospital to sign Jimmy in to avoid long waits later.

The Path Lab was down a narrow flight of concrete steps, through a shabby old swing door and along corridors of peeling paint. Paul was once allowed access to this behind-the scenes power house when taking photographs for the hospital. He found staff working in cramped, dirty labs, with their work benches stuck together with Sellotape where the surface had split with age. One corner of the lab was unusable because the ceiling was falling in. Fortunately the public were protected from sights such as these. The general dereliction of the 170-year-old hospital makes nonsense out of rebuilding it. The only answer must be a completely new building on the same site. To witness the dedication and cheerfulness of all staff made the working conditions they endured nothing short of a political scandal in the Thatcher boom years.

No chemotherapy can be prescribed without that first thumb-prick test which determines both red and white counts, and any abnormal cells present. After the test, we would head into the main building, along the main corridor past Gnasher the piranha and down to the clinic.

The clinic, next door to the oncology ward, consists of several very small consulting rooms, a theatre for bone marrow tests and a recovery room. Space is so cramped that most people wait in the passage; the nurses said that one doctor actually used a broom cupboard for years to see her patients.

An old bench seating three is thoughtfully placed on a slope where it acts as a see-saw. The passage runs downhill, making an excellent race track for the trundle toys and a set of double doors halfway down the slope acts as a crash pad.

Whenever we were there, most parents waited, standing around or squatting on the floor. There was a playroom not far away which was open most Wednesday and Thursday mornings, but when nurses were short-staffed the play lady had to lock up and go and help out, and the playroom was often unavailable. There were few chairs for parents, so we squatted in there, too.

The waiting time was often as long as two hours from arrival to seeing the doctor. The children became noisy and tired, and school holidays meant that brothers and sisters often came too, making things even noisier and more crowded.

On bone marrow day the children were tense and hungry as they waited for their anaesthetic. There were tears and tantrums, which couldn't be made better with a drink or a packet of sweets or crisps. The children had to be starved from the night before, and the last possible time for a snack was five o'clock in the morning. Jimmy liked to be woken with some toast or even sausage and bacon, then he would drop off to sleep again. Sometimes, when I was very tired, I would wake him at midnight with his snack so I could get an uninterrupted night's sleep; luckily Jimmy never checked the time.

Each child was given a quick checkup in the clinic before the doctor gave the Vincristin injection. Most children hate this painful injection, and there would be howls and screams periodically from the consulting rooms.

Sometimes Vincristin caused a burning sensation in Jimmy's hand or up his arm which could continue for a day or more; often his hand looked red and sore, and became stiff and painful for up to a week afterwards, so that it was difficult to write or draw if the injection had been in his right hand.

But he also suffered bad stomach cramps and backache which would strike him during the evening after his injection. During the following two weeks, he often had cramp in his legs, neck and jaws and he would frequently come home from school during the day when he couldn't tolerate the cramp any more without lying down. In the evening, he would wake up late and lie with me on the sofa until he felt more comfortable.

The bulk of the month's chemotherapy medicines were given over the first five days or week, although there was something to swallow every day. Those first few days after Vincristin and during the five-day course of steroids were the most difficult for us all. On the day after the clinic visit, Jimmy usually had twenty tablets to take.

It was a struggle to remember to keep taking tablets all day, especially when all Jimmy really wanted was to forget them and be an ordinary child again. He steadfastly refused to take any at school, and one day I cheated and laced his lunchtime flask of juice with soluble steroids. He was furious and felt I had been so dishonest that it was a long time before he trusted me again.

I apologized and truly regretted the deceit. There was no choice at all whether he took them or not; the least I could do was allow him to choose within reason when and how they were taken.

But my feelings were ambiguous as I doled out the medicines every day. It was very hard to insist that he took tablets which would make him feel more tired and grotty than he did already.

For several weeks after we returned home from holiday, Jimmy's cell count was still thought to be too low for him to be able to take any maintenance chemotherapy, so he went without any treatment at all for six weeks.

At first this didn't worry us because we were reassured by the clinic doctor that a little with Jimmy obviously went a long way, and with such a low white count, he wasn't in any danger anyway. Yet most other children had no difficulty tolerating the maximum amount of chemotherapy. We gradually became aware that Jimmy was not fitting into any of the predicted patterns, but our fears were met with bland reassurance that all was perfectly well.

That autumn Jimmy's acquaintance from playgroup days, who had suffered from leukaemia for four years, died at home in a nearby village. Jimmy had to be told. It took over a week before I could control my own sadness enough to tell him.

His questions were very much what we had expected. Why had this lively and bright little boy died of leukaemia? Had his treatment been any different from Jimmy's own? Was there a reason why he hadn't been cured? What was it like to die? Did he die in the night and was it like going to sleep and not waking up? Gradually Jimmy persuaded himself that there was some important difference in their treatment, and this was why his playgroup friend had died. But could he die too, he asked.

I had once asked Jimmy to tell me what leukaemia meant to him. 'Well, some people are all right and some people aren't,' he said.

So I reminded him then of his own words. Doubtless Jimmy always put himself in the 'all right' category and never thought about the possibility of his own death.

To hear of any death affected all the parents deeply. We not only grieved for the lost child and the family we knew, but such news also caused ripples of worry and insecurity, and we all felt less confident. Nobody wanted to imagine the pain and suffering that we might all face with our children one day, and we all felt great sympathy for each other.

Our confidence took a further severe battering just a month later. Another child from home, a two-year-old girl, was diagnosed with an identical leukaemia to Jimmy's. Amy was the third child cancer case since June in our small town, which has a child population of less than a thousand. Did this constitute a cluster, or was it mere coincidence?

In fact, the numbers over the past five years were even higher. Lee, a local child at the time he was diagnosed, was into his fourth year of survival since his leukaemia was first treated, and Jimmy's young playgroup friend brought the number to five. The true total of child cancers was five in four years.

Most people agreed that this was a matter for public concern, but to tell the press about it would sensationalize matters and might cause us all a gross intrusion of our privacy. Yet the health authorities should investigate this outbreak.

The first step was to write to the local MP, Mr Michael Jopling, who immediately informed the Minister for Health, Kenneth Clarke. There was an exchange of letters, and great care was taken by the Department in finding an expert to answer our requests for some sort of inquiry. Statistically, our cases did not constitute a cluster. We had too small a population and too few cases to be statistically accountable.

This was very frustrating news. There was an overwhelming urge to tell the world what had happened in our town, that three children had contracted blood cancers in three months. On one occasion, after hearing an item about cancer, I rang a BBC Radio Four programme to try and tell someone, but was amazed to find that I couldn't speak through the disabling grief that came suddenly and without warning.

Jimmy was unwell throughout the autumn, largely due to the after effects of the radiation treatment at Christie's. This reaction commonly occurs six weeks later and patients like Jimmy often suffer nausea, tiredness and extreme lethargy. His white cell count was permanently low, and his neutrophil protection cells against infection were too low for him to have his normal dose of chemotherapy drugs. Quite why so much notice was taken of the neutrophils was baffling. They were supposed to guard against bacterial infections like boils, and although Jimmy was low on neutrophils, he rarely had any problems with such infections. He seldom caught any viruses, and would often be the only person not to have a cold or sore throat in the family.

Perhaps he should have been treated at a higher level of chemotherapy. Often he went weeks without any, and then he was never given more than a maximum of 60 per cent of the optimum dose. We made an appointment to see the consultant to discuss our fears. Was Jimmy truly protected against his cancer returning, with such low doses of treatment? Logically, we felt, he couldn't be safe. A dose of 60 per cent of what he should have been given only eradicated 60 per cent of residual cancer cells. But the consultant, who was very approachable, articulate and willing to answer questions, was unworried about Jimmy's treatment. He told us they considered it safe and that it might even be to Jimmy's advantage, because he might suffer fewer long-term side effects from having less chemotherapy.

We also discussed our request for an investigation into our three local cases that summer, but the doctors at the hospital seemed less interested in searching for a cause. Their most urgent, immediate task was to halt the cancer and eradicate it.

However, they had decided in the circumstances to act on a request from Newcastle to submit our three children to body scans to detect selenium levels. This, we understood, had some connection with checking radiation levels. An appointment at Withington would be made.

But the appointment never came. Another family was asked to attend, and arrived to find nobody there to do the scan. Two months later, we enquired again. We were told it was all taking time, but we would be given an appointment. Nothing ever happened, and after six months we gave up. A valuable research opportunity was missed. If the scan had revealed nothing untoward, at least radiation as a cause could have been eliminated, although it was so many weeks since the children had been diagnosed, that some radioactive substances might have been undetectable by then.

Borchardt Ward was always full, usually to bursting, making it hard to find emergency beds for children with infections. Extra beds were often shunted in, some routine chemotherapy had to be postponed, and often cancer patients needing blood transfusions or urgent treatment for infections were admitted to other wards.

Jimmy suffered only two infections requiring a hospital stay, and during the first, when his cell count and resistance to infection were very low, he lay in the cystic fibrosis ward next to children with serious chest infections.

A cancer ward roughly twice the size of the present one would only just be big enough to deal with the increasing numbers of children needing chemotherapy. This is not because the incidence of childhood cancers is on the increase, but rather because cases are being diagnosed in time for treatment to begin, and children who would othewise have died within two or three weeks, if left at home, are now reaching hospital before it is too late.

There was often discontent at the overcrowded conditions, and the children themselves, accustomed to Borchardt, hated being put on other, unfamiliar wards. Plenty of people found fault with the system, but never with the kind and dedicated people who tried to operate it with the minimum of resources in cramped and shabby conditions.

During these months before Jimmy could return to school, I taught him each morning at home, trying to follow the school curriculum. But he needed to return to school, to be with his friends, and failing that, a home tutor would give him new ideas. Jimmy and I had been together almost all of every day for six months.

The Education Authority's Special Needs staff sent a home teacher for an hour and a half every day which gave us a short break from one another.

One of the commonest instincts that parents have towards their sick children is to protect and guard them from life itself, and it is all too easy to overprotect a child with leukaemia. But in doing so, parents rob each child of fulfilling whatever potential he has, even one that has been limited by illness. Although the next year or two may, indeed, be the last in that child's life, it is still absolutely necessary for a parent to let go of a child sufficiently for him to be what he will.

When Jimmy went away from us for the first time since his illness started, it felt like letting go to see him packing an overnight bag, and taking his tablets with him, with a note full of unnecessary instructions to cover every eventuality.

Both boys had stayed often enough with Becky and Jonathan Gorrigan, but leaving us for the weekend now took on a new significance. I had to learn to trust somebody else to look after Jimmy; and I had to release him from my care so that he could be himself, have lots of fun and live his life to its new limits.

With our children away, Paul and I watched videos, climbed Helvellyn, and wandered round our empty rooms feeling strange. It was not a relaxing time for either of us; instead, it was the sort of time when concentration wanders, risks are taken and accidents are more likely to happen, as we later discovered.

The boys, by contrast, had a wonderful time with Karen and John and their children, as they always did.

Just before the end of the Christmas term, Jim was finally fit enough to return to school. His sensitive and supportive teacher had spent time preparing the other chilren for Jimmy's return, answering their frank questions about cancer and persuading the group to be protective towards their classmate instead of teasing him about his baldness.

He arrived in the playground one afternoon for his first experience of school in seven months. He was mobbed by all the children, who set up a chant of 'Jimmy! Jimmy! Jimmy!' but he soon managed to merge back into school life and disliked any extra attention. He was very upset when a child in the playground labelled him as an egg head, with no hair, and he refused to believe that egg head could be a compliment and meant he was very clever at his work.

Christmas that year hardly happened. Emotions at Christmas run high, and my thoughts were constantly back on Borchardt, picturing a row of lethargic, wispy-haired children attached to their drips, too sick and weary to enjoy anything. The sight of two or three hundred healthy children at our Christingle service celebrating the children's festival was too moving to contemplate. How many more Christmases would Jimmy enjoy?

Nobody enjoyed this particular one because we all got flu, with the exception of Jimmy. We didn't even need an excuse to miss Christingle because we were in bed, and the only reason for getting up at all on Christmas Eve was to make the mince pies to leave out for Father Christmas, with his glass of sherry. Christmas Day was just as miserable except for Jimmy and Martin, who were too busy playing with their new toys to notice how ill the grown-ups were feeling.

My birthday came and went, along with New Year. One of the most unpleasant aspects of this particular flu had been the sickness which accompanied it; slowly the flu went, but my sickness stubbornly persisted, day after day.

Despite this constant nausea, it was strange how no skirt in my wardrobe would button up round my waist any more. Fancy putting on weight and feeling so ill . . .

A pregnancy test revealed all. The baby was due in mid-August and initial feelings of shock and horror were soon replaced by delight. It was an accident of fortune and the best mistake we had ever made.

# FOUR

## Crisis

Jimmy had been given so many wonderful toys in the six months he had been ill that when his seventh birthday approached, we tried to find a tiny fragment of real life to give him, rather than an object. The cost was of no importance, but it had to be something which would add a new dimension to his life.

It was just as well that cost was not a factor in the choice; his birthday present came absolutely 'free to a good home'. It was a male kitten, aged eight weeks, predominantly black but with splashes of white colouring, and he was one of a litter of about six kittens born to a farm cat.

Tinker fascinated Jimmy from the start; he was the kitten who fell down the back of the heater, and loved to have his tummy tickled. His brothers and sisters climbed the curtains and tumbled from the potted plants as we tried to choose the right pet for Jimmy.

Jimmy enjoyed the new responsibility of helping to look after the kitten, though he could be very stern when Tinker was badly behaved. But he turned out to be an intelligent cat, able to use a cat flap within a week or two and to leap up on the big crossbeams in our old barn of a living room, watching life from a safe distance when the house was too busy for comfort.

We all loved Jimmy's kitten and he grew into a handsome, graceful and affectionate cat with more than a strong hint of Egyptian aristocracy in his beautiful narrow face and superb deportment. He soon became a well-established member of the family and gave Jimmy much enjoyment.

After our quiet Christmas, Jimmy returned to school on a permanent basis, although this often meant attending only in the morning or the afternoon if a whole day was too tiring for him. The sight of our two little boys setting off for school in the morning gave us the happy illusion of being an ordinary family again.

Jimmy's taste in food became increasingly adult and very sensible. He leaned quite naturally towards food that was good for him; he loved brown bread and raw fruit and vegetables, and he refused to eat white bread at all. He preferred juice to squash, though he liked nothing better than a good cup of coffee at breakfast time with his porridge. He ate well, in spite of the weird aberrations his monthly steroids caused, and he experimented all the time with new foods. He loved cheese, egg or tuna fish sandwiches, raw carrot sticks, fruit of any sort, nuts, and the coleslaw I often made for us.

In spite of the constant stress of living with Jimmy's uncertain future, the months from Christmas to Easter were not unhappy. My pregnancy was running normally, an amniocentesis test had reassured us that the growing baby was normal, in spite of my age, and things seemed to be progressing as well as they could.

Walking to school each morning with my three children, one still inside and the other two by my side, I felt we had reached the ultimate family goal – watching our two alert, loving and sensitive children enjoying a safe childhood in the midst of a community that cared about them. The sun shone most mornings and the world around us looked soft and beautiful.

In reality, we were experiencing a period of normality in the middle of Jimmy's life-threatening illness, and our precarious happiness and contentment might be shattered at any time. But the future was a long way off, too far ahead to contemplate. The next eighteen months, while Jimmy remained on chemotherapy treatment, were taken care of with certainty. No need to think about relapse until the end of that time, and bone marrow transplantation would be that much more successful by then. We had no worries about our unborn baby. There was no reason to think that its birth and babyhood would be anything other than completely ordinary.

Looking at Jimmy now, it was hard to tell he was anything other than a normal, healthy seven-year-old. His hair, although still very short, had grown back quite thickly, and he had lost his surplus steroid weight and looked his normal self again. An appeal had been launched by the town's Rotary Club to raise money for the childrens' cancer ward, largely inspired by Jimmy's cheerful bravery as he faced his treatment. The news that there were now three children under eight years in the town all suffering from acute forms of child cancer spurred the whole community into action and the year-long appeal, launched in January, began a flurry of fund-raising activities organized by every club in the district.

The appeal was publicized on Border Television with a news item which included an interview with Jimmy. It was suggested that he should ride his new bike on film to illustrate his fight and fitness, which appealed to him very much, and he recorded his interview with only a trace of shyness. He was very proud to see himself on television, and played the video recording to his friends whenever he got the chance.

In February, Martin failed a routine sight test at school and an appointment was made for him to see an eye specialist. Although Martin frequently collided with furniture and often bumped into big obstacles without seeing them, we assumed that this was because he was left-handed, naturally clumsy, and not so well co-ordinated as Jimmy, who was always agile and dextrous.

But the specialist confirmed that Martin's sight was very poor, and he also had a squint. He would always need to wear glasses and, in addition, the better of the two eyes was to be blacked out for some months, in order to make the other eye work harder and improve its sight.

If we hadn't already faced the constant anxiety of Jim's cancer, the news of Martin's sight would have been quite a blow. Most children with patched eyes find school work difficult and life in the playground doubly so. Although we worried about this, it was little in comparison with Jimmy and his hospital friends buying a lease of life with their toxic chemotherapy. Dealing as we had to with problems of life and death, it would always be difficult to relate to lesser ones in the real world where children were healthy. A patch, when seen in comparison with a drip, seemed an easy option and we expected Martin to manage his handicap as best he could.

This was by no means easy for him. The plaster patches with which we'd been supplied almost tore the skin off his face when removed, so instead we used padding and a pirate's patch. But that didn't feel comfortable, and eventually we blacked out one lens of his glasses. He stumbled on through life at school, his writing even more hesitant than it had been. He frequently tripped over things in the classroom and his knees were always bumped and scarred from falls in the playground. The frames of his glasses were easily broken during rough play; pairs went missing, or got bent. One pair was run over by the wheels of a car, another swept away when he fell in a flooded stream. Life with a patch was very hard for Martin.

Jimmy couldn't have been more feeling or sympathetic. He knew exactly what it was like to be handicapped by an imperfect body, and, seeing Martin's daily struggle, he thought having leukaemia was a better deal than wearing glasses and a patch. He was comforting and compassionate to Martin, and so very proud of him when his efforts finally paid off, and we were told six months later that it wouldn't be necessary to patch Martin's eye again for the time being.

Every month we travelled the 180-mile round trip to clinic at the hospital, and it was always the same story I had to report; Jimmy had been quite well, but suffered from cramps and pains and tiredness and had only managed half-days at school. The doctor we saw each month reassured us constantly that things were satisfactory. Jimmy liked him more than he liked most of the doctors he'd encountered during his illness. To him it seemed that the doctors were to blame for all the needles, drips, injections, transfusions and anaesthetics he had to put up with, but this particular doctor was skilled at doing Jimmy's Vincristin injection and rarely left him with a sore hand and stiff arm.

Because the doctors felt satisfied with Jimmy's low white counts and small amounts of treatment, they were confident enough to cancel his regular three-monthly bone marrow test. This was rather surprising because we hadn't requested a complete cancellation, only a post-ponement so it wouldn't clash with half-term. But Jimmy was considered such a low risk that the doctors decided not to bother with his test for another three months, and he completed six months without a bone marrow test.

On May Day holiday, we walked through woods near home just as the new leaves of the beech trees were at their most delicate green and acres of bluebells carpeted the ground. The boys skipped on ahead of us, playing hide-and-seek, darting round trees and jumping out from bushes. It was like a sudden glimpse into the future, when Jimmy would be cured and all his normal energy and zest for life return. We stood and watched with enormous hope and confidence. We had never felt so solidly optimistic before that Jimmy's tough little body was winning its fight against malignancy.

Not only was Jimmy well that month, but the next one too. He radiated strength and stamina, riding his bike every evening with Paul just as he used to. It was during this time that he made his strange, prophetic statement to me one night as I kissed him goodnight.

'Mummy, while you're there, my light will never go out,' he said.

Since Jimmy had become ill, I always kissed the boys goodnight

twice, once when they were awake and again before I went to bed late
in the evening. It was a reminder of how precious they were, and a
celebration that Jimmy was still alive and well.

The children's lives had become very precious to us, and Jimmy's
illness taught us to appreciate them, and how very fortunate we were
to have them. The sight of children in the street being bullied, slapped,
kicked and smacked by parents for small misdemeanours was sickening,
and the verbal abuse handed out to them was almost as bad as beating
them physically. Perhaps it is only the threat of losing a little child
which reminds some parents how valuable children are.

Both relatives and friends came to stay with us throughout spring
and early summer. Nobody had thought it right to visit just after
Jimmy's initial treatment, so a steady stream of nieces and nephews,
cousins, aunts and uncles came now for weekends, which we all enjoyed
very much.

The weather continued to be fine and sunny during May and June
and Jimmy's eyes became sensitive to sunlight; so we bought him a
pair of 'real cool shades' and he was allowed to wear them at school
in the playground.

As a family, there were some fine and memorable days spent visiting
places of interest in the early summer. They are especially memorable
because, although we obviously did not know it at the time, they were
the last days we were able to spend together out of doors. One glorious
Sunday we took Granny Anna back to her old convent boarding school
in Skipton, where she had been sent in 1917. It was over sixty years
since she had last seen the school corridors, classrooms and refectory,
and the same day we also visited Bolton Abbey, where she told Martin
and Jimmy about the school picnics she remembered when she was
little.

The cool woods by The Strid provided an ideal picnic place and
Anna fascinated Jimmy with tales of the legendary depths of The Strid,
where the body of anybody who fell in and drowned might take two
or three days to come to the surface of the deep and dangerous river.
The dungeons at Skipton Castle were equally interesting to the boys,
but Skipton lacked a good toy shop open on Sunday for them to spend
their pocket money. They finally settled for two luridly coloured teddy
bears, one orange and one purple, which they often played with. Only
ten months later, Martin chose the purple bear as one of the treasures
he placed in Jimmy's coffin.

During half term, we were visited by the boys' cousins, Matthew and Jonathan. The big boys took their little cousins out every day, looked after them, bought them treats, bathed them and played football with them. Nothing was too much trouble for them; our boys had fun all day, and we had a rest.

One day we all walked round Buttermere and 14-year-old artist Jonathan handed out paper and pencils so that we could all try our hand at sketching the spectacular view across the water to the fells beyond.

Jimmy was greatly influenced by Jonathan, and it was largely due to his cousin that Jimmy enjoyed drawing birds so much. The two boys loved each other loyally.

But Jonathan was anxious about Jimmy's illness and no amount of reassurance could convince him that Jimmy would be all right. The cousins' visit was a high spot of the summer, and their departure left our children flat and sad.

Most Sundays we took a picnic with us, and walked all day on the fells. But the weather was so hot one Sunday in June that we took the boys caving, where it would be cooler underground.

The limestone caves of North Yorkshire provided plenty of visual excitement, although the humid weather made the day at ground level weary and irritable for Jimmy. The cave exploration involved walking several miles, and Jimmy needed a piggyback frequently. He used his camera enthusiastically to photograph the weird shapes made by the limestone, and the stalactites and stalagmites, and he bought himself a souvenir lump of haematite. Considering that he had leukaemia and his thirty-nine-year-old mother was thirty-four weeks' pregnant, cave exploration was quite an achievement.

After such a challenging day, it was sad that an accident killed the pet hamster that evening. It was having a run over the breakfast bar while its cage was being cleaned, when Martin scooped it up in his hand, turned to show us, slipped off the tall varnished stool and fell on top of Harriet Hamster, who died instantly. Martin was very guilty and distressed, but Jimmy was inclined to giggle after the initial shock had passed.

It was just five weeks before the baby was due that staff at the maternity hospital first noticed that it was small for dates, and my weight gain had become a loss. But the weather was so uncomfortably hot, the heat alone might have accounted for this.

One Wednesday afternoon at the end of June, Paul complained of a pain in his stomach. The pain became worse by the hour, and by midnight, the doctor had diagnosed acute appendicitis. Next morning he was taken away by ambulance to Lancaster to have an emergency operation.

Jimmy was very worried by the insecurity of his Daddy being ill and in hospital, and both children were too upset to go to school that day. Paul had his appendix removed late in the evening, and settled down to enjoy a five-day rest, recovering in hospital, cocooned from reality.

As the days went by, and he realized what a relief it was to be away from home and from the constant worry of Jimmy's illness, even our visits disturbed his new-found peace. He didn't want to be reminded of reality, and was even more reluctant to return home.

His absence made life harder physically than anything I had ever experienced before in life. The extra effort involved in keeping the business running and being solely responsible for both boys, in temperatures up in the high eighties with a thirty-six-week bulk to drag round, was exhausting. The baby inside was jittery and restless and plagued with long bouts of hiccups.

Jimmy and Martin invented a new game; naughtily they would strip off their clothes, jump in the stream which runs by the park and position themselves, one at the top of the waterfall and one at the base. Taking Martin's pants, Jimmy would sail them down over the rocks and rapids to Martin, who had to catch them before they shot past downstream, heading for the River Rothay. They never played a game which made them giggle more, especially at the prospect of Martin having to return home minus his pants, should he fail to catch them.

The day of Jimmy's school trip fell while Paul was still in hospital. The trip was a day-long walk, and he couldn't go without an adult to help him in case he became tired and had to return sooner than the others.

The only person who could possibly go was Paul's kind and willing assistant, Viv. It was another very hot day, but Jimmy completed the walk the same as everybody else did, and it was Viv who returned exhausted while Jimmy skipped all the way home. To see Jimmy with such energy fed our optimism constantly, and we looked forward to the future with increasing confidence.

During Paul's absence, the boys were taken out for a boat ride which suddenly turned into an exciting adventure.

Jimmy's godfather and godmother were David and Jean, whom we had known for many years before Jimmy's birth. Their four children, although much older, were all very special friends to our boys, and their big house and garden provided plenty of scope for games of monster and hide-and-seek both in summer and in winter. Our two families always met to spend a day together over Christmas, and the boys loved anything which involved being with the Earnshaws because it always felt very special to them.

Every visit to their home at Scandale Brow was a treat for our boys, but this hot, sunny Saturday David and Jean had persuaded the Lake Warden on Windermere to treat Jimmy and Martin to a ride in the police-style launch. But the routine run down the Lake had changed into an emergency dash when smoke was seen at the far end, and after a high-speed rush along the Lake with sirens blaring, the Patrol found a speedboat alight, and its occupant swimming to safety. The fire destroyed the boat before the fire brigade could arrive, but the real-life emergency thrilled the boys and made an exciting tale to tell Paul.

Paul spent only four days convalescing when he returned home from hospital before getting back to work. There was only a month to go before the baby was due, and I had planned it carefully so that I could be with Jimmy at Pendlebury for his bone marrow test, which was expected to take place two weeks before the baby's birth. The following week, if all went well, I would still be at home to help Jimmy through the worst week of his chemotherapy treatment.

The concern about the small size of the baby was mounting; but the obstetrician knew how important it was for me to be with Jimmy on bone marrow day, so he decided to delay doing anything until the day after the test.

The bone marrow test was clear, and all was well. Paul was still very tired after his operation, so I drove part of the way, something I rarely did. The baby kicked in an agitated manner against the steering wheel, then all went unusually quiet, and it was completely still for hours.

The scan next morning showed why the baby had been agitated; there was very little amniotic fluid left for it to float and move about in, a sign of serious foetal distress. Labour would be induced at the beginning of the following week, the consultant decided; but just before I left for home, a sudden afterthought struck him: to run a foetal heart monitor on the baby, as a precaution.

The printout from the monitor showed erratic jumps which staff called phase two dips, though at first they doubted the accuracy of the monitor. But the machine was working perfectly. The baby was in deep distress.

There was just time to leave a message for Paul, who had no idea where I was, before the ambulance arrived to take us to Lancaster, where the Maternity Unit had a full-time theatre and a Special Care Baby Unit.

The heart monitor there showed the same erratic dips and our baby was clearly fighting for its life.

A Greek doctor sat on the bed. 'You need a delivery,' he said.

'When?' I said. 'Tomorrow, or Saturday?'

'Oh, no hurry,' he laughed. 'No hurry. Twenty minutes from now, no hurry.'

There was just time to jot down on a paper towel the chemotherapy dosages Jimmy was due that day; they had all been changed the day before, and nobody except me ever handled Jimmy's medicines. Within five minutes I was undressed, attached to a drip, catheterized and breathing oxygen through a mask before being put to sleep. There was no time for fear.

I woke up at about six o'clock to find we had another son, weighing four and a half pounds. He was slightly premature but alert and beautiful, and he went straight to the breast as the other two babies had done and enjoyed his first feed as his Daddy arrived to meet him. Then followed that precious time of mutual observation and closeness as we stared at Christopher Patrick, and he stared back at us with a calm serenity.

The baby spent the night in the nursery of the ward, and although he was feeding well, his glucose levels were very low. So he was transferred two floors below to the Special Care Baby Unit where, seven years before, Jimmy had spent his first ten days. I visited him that afternoon and saw him warm and happy in his incubator.

The boys came to visit that evening, but the disappointment of not seeing their new brother was modified by their excitement at going camping for the weekend with Paul. The tent was pitched by Windermere, and they couldn't wait to get back, and ride their bikes round the campsite before bedtime. Seeing Christy could wait until next day, but camping couldn't.

Next morning, the baby was sleepy and reluctant to feed. His skin looked sallow, as though he already had neo-natal jaundice as both his brothers had done before him. By midday, he was restless and unhappy, and when the children arrived in the early afternoon, Christy was refusing to feed. The doctor on duty was uneasy about his condition, and by the time the baby started vomiting, he had already done various tests and decided to start antibiotics without waiting for the results.

His suspicions were well founded. By early evening it was almost certain the baby had something called necrotizing enterocolitis, or NEC for short. This is an illness caused by some sort of unidentified bug which attacks the bowel, and occasionally perforates it, leading to gangrene in the colon, and serious infection throughout the body. Christy was vomiting, and passing sticky black stools. The consultant had arrived, and we discussed how I could tell Paul the news that night. It would be difficult to locate one small tent on a crowded site, and there was no telephone he could reach.

Christy's condition worsened. The diagnosis was confirmed, and he was in an intensive care incubator, wired up to monitors and looking tiny, remote and very vulnerable. Antibiotics are used at once to treat the illness and these had already been started, thanks to the perceptive and quick-acting doctor to whom Christy certainly owed his life at this point.

There was little time to reflect on the extraordinary string of tragedies that seemed to hit us, one after another, and not one of our own making. Life, which at times seemed like a bad dream, was rapidly developing into a full-blown nightmare.

The baby was to be transferred to Manchester next morning. The immediate problem was whether to leave Jimmy and stay with Christy at St Mary's in Manchester, or whether to follow the baby a couple of days later when I felt stronger. To add to our problems, the wound from my Caesarean operation had become infected, and it would be an extra risk for Christy if I were to be handling him.

A patient, avuncular consultant with shiny brogue shoes and a slow, deliberate way of explaining things listened while I juggled with family priorities. There was nothing more I could do to help Christy; he wouldn't miss me at all, but Jimmy would. Separation from the new baby was bad enough, but parting from Jimmy was worse. There was a small measure of self-protection in letting Christy go alone to Manchester; our lives were in such turmoil and trouble already, and I hardly dared to love this little baby we hardly yet knew, who might very well die. To know him would be to love him, and the agony of watching him die was too much to contemplate. Christopher would go alone, and I would join him as soon as I could, probably mid-week.

An X-ray next morning confirmed the worst. Christy's bowel had perforated. By midday, he was critically ill, but still stable. An ambulance with a ventilator on board could not be located, but it was so urgent to get him to the waiting surgeon at Manchester that staff had no choice but to transport him without one. He was placed in a special travelling incubator, and I kissed him goodbye and cuddled him for just a moment as he was lifted between incubators. A Sister from the Special Care Baby Unit travelled down the motorway with him, and I watched the ambulance pull slowly away carrying our poor little baby with a feeling of utter desolation and disbelief. The only useful thing I could do for Christy was provide him with expressed breast milk. Most of it was poured down the drain, but I intended to try and keep the milk flowing by using the breast pump three-hourly in anticipation of a time when he might feed again.

His journey was slow and careful, to maintain his stability, and he reached Manchester in excellent shape in view of his condition. Preparations were under way to operate immediately, and by seven in the evening, we heard that the operation had been a success, and although the entire transverse section of his large bowel had to be removed, there were two healthy ends to join back together again, without leaving any of his bowel outside his body. More often than not, surgeons have to leave part of the bowel outside temporarily, and the baby is left with a stoma bag until the bowel can be replaced.

The news throughout Monday continued to be hopeful. Christopher's condition was stable, and he could perhaps be off his ventilator that night.

Visitors came and went; Roger and Maureen appeared, with Forton, a blue rabbit they had bought on the M6 services just south of Lancaster. There was hardly space in the room for all the beautiful flowers. The pain of separation from Christy alternated with feelings of profound relief that he would be all right. Thoughts of Jimmy's vulnerability brought frequent tears, and the trips to the breast pump to feed a baby that couldn't be seen or held prompted some depressing thoughts.

Even if Christopher recovered well, he would need very special care during his first few weeks. How could my care and attention be divided between a sick baby and a sick child? The practical problems of looking after both Christopher and Jimmy in the months ahead made our lives seem dreary and hopeless with defeat and exhaustion. There seemed no end to our misfortunes. Of all the babies that could have contracted NEC, it was our poor little underweight scrap that was fighting for his life. Fate had chosen our family yet again. Life seemed to be on a runaway downhill course veering dangerously out of our control.

On Monday evening, doctors at Manchester decided to try and let Christy breathe for himself. But it was too soon, and his condition deteriorated suddenly. Replacing the ventilator into his lungs caused bleeding; his jaundice levels were very high, and his heart not as stable as it had been.

But he faced each crisis with strength that amazed the staff. By Tuesday evening, he was so poorly that we decided to go to him next day, however bad my own infection was. Early on Wednesday morning, at about one o'clock, staff were told to inform us that he might not live through the next couple of hours. The anguish of waiting was too extreme, and sleep brought wonderful oblivion for an hour. At four o'clock, I woke expecting to hear that Christopher had died. Instead he had rallied, and regained a weak hold on life.

After waiting three hours to find a doctor willing to take responsibility for discharging me with an infected wound with an open hole in it, Paul and I drove down to Manchester to see Christopher.

This reunion aroused ambiguous, mixed feelings. It was the most longed-for visit, at the same time as being frightening and risky. To love and touch a baby that was still very likely to die would make losing him even more painful. Yet to hold back would be cowardly, especially if Christy knew subconsciously that we were with him, and the slight touch of our fingers on his tiny arm might help him to fight on with greater strength.

The Neo-Natal Surgical Unit was overcrowded, very hot and extremely intense and noisy. Each small nursery had six or seven intensive care incubators, each one bleeping or whistling for attention. Nobody had time to stop work long enough to talk about Christopher. Instead, nurses pointed us in the direction of the right cot.

But no directions were needed, because something rather primitive and strange happened as we walked through the door. Paul searched the room for the right cot, but I knew instantly which one was Christopher's because I could recognize his strong smell. It was the smell of a new-born baby, sweet yet a little musty, and its familiarity took me straight to Christy to breathe in his own special smell that came through the portholes of his perspex greenhouse.

From that first moment of recognition, there was no choice about whether to risk loving and losing. He desperately needed love and protection as he lay so isolated, wired up to a dozen different machines, the ventilator pushing his chest in and out so roughly. I held his tiny fingers, and he knew I was there. Even his erratic heart beat slowed down to a more even rate on the monitor screen.

It was harder for Paul without the strong maternal biological urge to bond with the baby. He said afterwards how useless he had felt, perched on a stool near the incubator getting in the way of the doctors and nurses who were round Christy's little box almost continually. It was hard to see the baby at all. The ventilator hid his face, and his body was covered with a forest of tubes and leads connecting him to the machines which controlled his existence.

We had to leave Christopher, and return home, wondering if we would see him alive again. His life was still very much in the balance as each small problem quickly became a major crisis. My presence on the unit would cause anxiety; nobody at Manchester wanted the risk of contact with a wound infection from another hospital which could spread to both other babies and post-natal mothers. Jimmy and Martin needed us both at home, where we would help them to face the baby's precarious future and the possibility that he might not live.

Jimmy was sad, but entirely practical. He thought it was pointless leaving packs of disposable nappies lying around in the nursery to remind us of Christy. 'Put them away, he might die, and then we wouldn't need them,' he said. Often, at night, he couldn't sleep. He would creep upstairs for a cuddle and as we lay together on the sofa, we talked about life and death and Heaven. Christy's illness gave him the chance to ask directly about his own. 'Could I die too?' he asked.

'It's as you said,' I reminded him. 'Some people make it and some don't.'

In a superstitious way Christopher's terrible bad luck made Jimmy's future safer. Ill fate had struck us so often, it was beyond belief it would strike again.

Instructions had been left that Chrisopher should be baptized as a Catholic, in the family tradition, rather than die unchristened. The Catholic chaplain at Lancaster had refused to do this when Christy first showed signs of illness, because he considered the baby was not poorly enough. But a priest was found at St Mary's without delay, and nurses reassured us that baptized babies often put up a better fight.

Christopher was still so critically ill that his condition changed frequently, and an improvement at six o'clock in the morning could revert to a serious deterioration by midday. We were asked to phone the unit every four to six hours, because things changed for better or worse so rapidly. We imagined that such a critical period could only last for a few days until we knew one way or the other whether Christopher would live, but he hovered, undecided, far longer, and it was three weeks before the staff expressed any real confidence in a future for him.

But nobody could hazard a guess as to what sort of future that would be. We had longed for him to live; but were the doctors being too clever by half, and might his life be blighted by handicap or brain damage?

Feeding started at the rate of one millilitre of breast milk per hour, given by drip; his bowel was healing and holding together well, but the surgical staff were anxious that the medical staff might overload his gut with too much food, while the medical staff were seriously worried that Christopher was being starved and might suffer brain damage as a result. Christy's life still hung by a thread until a successful compromise was found.

Our visits to St Mary's continued every three days in a familiar pattern of optimism on the way there, replaced by profound pessimism after we had seen the baby and been reminded how very ill he continued to be. His colouring looked both yellow and grey from jaundice, his eyes were sunk in their sockets and his skin had lost its moisture and elasticity, leaving it stretched and wrinkly. He looked like an Ethiopian famine victim.

In the second week of August, Paul and the boys joined a coach and travelled to London with a party of children suffering from leukaemia from all over Cumbria.

Some weeks before, Greenpeace had invited the children and their families to see the first London visit of the new *Rainbow Warrior* campaign ship. The guests were to be accommodated in a student hostel for two nights, and entertained with parties and trips.

Greenpeace provided a rousing welcome and endless free hospitality, to give everybody a memorable time. There were rides in the ship's inflatable dinghies, a reception and disco when the crew danced with the children, and a visit to the Tower of London. Paul included Hamleys and the Planetarium on his itinerary, and the Cumbrian party were all very impressed with the generosity of their thoughtful hosts.

The London visit provided an opportunity for me to stay with Christopher for three days in Manchester. His ventilator had been removed two days previously, and I expected to see an almost normal baby who might even breast-feed.

But he was so frail and poorly, there was nothing to do except sit patiently by his incubator watching him sleep. It was strange to hear him cry; the ventilator had prevented him making any noise, but now he cried when he was hungry or uncomfortable, and it was distressing to witness his pain and fear now that his face could be seen. It was far from a pleasure to sit and watch him without being able to comfort him.

It was not until the third day that he was allowed a brief cuddle in my arms while his incubator was being cleaned. He was still connected to several monitors, and his wires trailed in all directions. The moment arrived and I sat very still ready to receive my baby into my arms. Various machines had to be reset or unplugged. Suddenly his body went quite still and his eyes rolled back in their sockets until only the whites were showing. His nurse had noticed even before the alarms sounded on his monitors. She flicked his feet roughly to remind him to breathe again, and he did so immediately. The incident, although brief, was very frightening, but it never recurred.

Nevertheless, the neurologist was sent for and found no obvious brain damage. Reflexes and responses were good, he said, but it would be some time before Christopher stopped constantly rolling his eyes and started to behave normally.

Jimmy and Martin were impatient to visit Christopher but we thought it unwise for them to see him before there was any certainty that he might live. After three weeks, when he seemed to be improving very slowly, we took the other two boys to spend some time with him.

The traffic that day was very heavy. We waited two hours at Pendlebury for Jimmy to be seen at the clinic for his regular monthly check, and arrived much later than planned on the other side of the city at St Mary's.

We were cheerful and optimistic, and the boys were very excited at seeing Christopher after so long.

What they actually saw was a tiny yellow scrap of a human being, terrified and pathetically thin. He weighed only three and a half pounds, and his huge eyes rolled about in his tiny head.

We tried to explain to Jimmy and Martin why Christopher was such a forlorn little being. He had suffered separation from his mother soon after birth, missing all love and cuddles and human touch. He had almost died from his illness, he must have felt the pain of his operation and scar, and every half hour or so, he'd been terrified when yet another needle was put in his foot or hand or arm for the constant testing that is necessitated by the use of high technology machinery.

Christopher hadn't been able to see, we told them, and a mask had covered his eyes to protect them during his light treatment for jaundice; and he had been prevented from moving at all for over three weeks, having been artificially paralysed to keep him still while on his ventilator.

But at least he was alive, though not sufficiently strong yet for us to relax or celebrate.

It was a sad afternoon as we stood round his open cot. Both boys tried to cuddle the baby, and Jimmy took photographs. There was even a family portrait of us all, Paul looking profoundly sad and Christy wild-eyed and fearful in his arms. We left, depressed and tired as usual and we knew Christy still had a long way to go on the road towards home. A traffic warden had even given us a parking ticket as a parting gift.

These visits were never happy; there was little the boys could do except hang over Christopher's cot, and the novelty of that soon wore off. Jimmy was pale and tired from the journeys and Martin bored and frustrated.

Then, just when nothing good seemed to have happened for several days, we found when we visited that there were fewer nurses looking after Christopher and his cot was in a quieter corner of the room. The next time, a few of his machines had been unplugged and taken away and within a week, he had been promoted to the nursery next door. The staff had been unwilling to release him back to Lancaster, but changed their minds suddenly. With only two hours' notice, he was on his way by ambulance back to the Special Care Baby Unit which he had left five weeks before.

The caring staff were shocked by Christy's appearance. They could hardly recognize the little wreck that arrived back in place of the calm, round-faced baby they had sent. Christy was more confused than ever by his move and rolled his eyes all the time, unable to focus on anything. If something frightened him suddenly, his eyes disappeared altogether in his head, and only the whites were left showing.

It was impossible to say then whether he was brain-damaged; but the first basic step was to try and turn him back into a human being from the terrified little animal he had become. His cot was put on its own in dim light; all the nurses were asked to love and cuddle him constantly as part of his nursing care, and his feeding was altered daily to promote a steady weight gain. He breast-fed by instinct, with a strong, demanding suck, which was at least one good sign that he would be a survivor. Even as he began to gain weight and relax a little, nobody expected him home for at least a month, or longer.

Important things were happening at home for Jimmy. The new school term had begun, and he was now a junior school pupil, with a smart new uniform of white shirt, blue tie and jumper, with grey shorts and long grey socks.

Even more exciting were the first pair of football boots, and the Liverpool kit, passed on by his cousin Jonathan.

One of our most stalwart and wisest supporters was the Vicar of our Parish Church, the Reverend Lewis Higdon, and throughout Christy's illness Lewis had visited, cared deeply and prayed earnestly, although we were not Anglicans and did not attend church. One wet afternoon he called on us, just as I was sewing nametapes on Jimmy's new uniform. Considering that just a year ago, we had no idea whether Jimmy would ever live long enough to be a junior, marking his new uniform was like making a gesture of confidence in his ability to survive cancer; every nametape was a celebration of his living and a strong hope in his future. Lewis prayed in thanksgiving, both for Christopher and for Jimmy.

Christy was improving so quickly after just a week's tender, loving nursing that the consultant decided home would be the best place for him as soon as possible. There was very little anyone could do for him except feed and love him, which was better done at home than in hospital. If nursing staff were confident that I could feed him adequately, he could go home.

The Mother and Baby Units provide a halfway house for mothers to take over the care of their babies before going home. But however kind the nurses, most mothers feel rather uncomfortable, being discreetly assessed by the staff over the course of a weekend. Being caught by Sister changing a nappy on the bed felt like being caught by the teachers smoking behind the bike sheds at school.

It had put the family under considerable strain to visit Christopher daily, and Jimmy was looking tired after his first week as a junior. He was irritable in the evening, and found the heat of the Special Care Baby Unit altogether too much to tolerate.

It was a great relief to bring Christy home, not least because the daily journey of seventy-five miles to visit him was very time-consuming and expensive and Jimmy was beginning to need extra care and support at home through this new and tiring phase.

Jimmy had made a 'Welcome Home' banner, and a sign for the nursery door saying 'Chris's Room'. It was quite nerve-racking, after six weeks of waiting, to be entirely responsible for our tiny, weak baby. For the first two days, we jumped every time he sneezed or coughed; after so many clever people had spent so much time and expertise saving Christy's life, it would have been tragically ironic if he had come to any harm at home through inexperience or carelessness.

We were just starting to relax sufficiently to savour the sheer novelty and joy of life with our beautiful new baby, when a phone call shattered all our delight, replacing it with something new and unexpected to worry about. The Sister on the Special Care Baby Unit who had taken such loving care of Christy had developed shingles on her face. She had been in close contact both with the baby and with Jimmy. Realizing the full significance of this very serious situation, staff at Lancaster had contacted Manchester urgently, and it was Pendlebury who broke the news to us. Not only was it a threat to weak little Christy; but poor Christy himself might pose an equally serious threat to Jimmy, should the infection spread. The chickenpox virus can be fatal to children with leukaemia.

Pendlebury decided that Christy must have two injections of gamma globulin, and for Jimmy the only answer was a heavy dose of an antiviral drug. There can't be many injections more painful than the gamma globulin, something which poor Jimmy knew only too well after being subjected to a double one the Christmas before. It had been given into his buttocks, leaving him sobbing with pain, and humiliated by the indignity of it. We knew what to expect before the doctor arrived at home to give the injections to Christy.

Prepared though I was, and accustomed to seeing all Christy's suffering in hospital, the reality was infinitely worse than the nervous apprehension. Christy, who weighed less than four pounds, had no fat or muscle on his buttocks, and no bottom in which to put the injections. Terrified of being pricked with a needle, he still cried piteously every time we undressed him or changed his nappy, but there were small signs of improvement as he gradually learned to trust us. Fifteen minutes of struggling to inject him with the gamma globulin, and he reverted to the eye-rolling terror of earlier weeks as he felt the stinging pain. All of us with him shared his ordeal. It was pain heaped on pain, caused by freakish bad luck.

Jimmy found the antiviral drug equally hard going. Within two days, he was too tired and lifeless to struggle through more than half a day at school. The pills were awkward to swallow, and robbed him of all appetite.

In spite of all this, we recovered our good spirits sufficiently by the weekend to act like a normal family. We went shopping, like everyone does, and wheeled our baby in a pram through the streets. We played at being an ordinary mother and father, with three beautiful boys – but only for one week. Within seven days, our lives were catapulted into new, uncharted depths of anguish and anxiety.

# FIVE

# Relapse

Jimmy was due to attend clinic for his routine monthly check just ten days after Christopher came home and took his place as the new baby in the family. The staff at Pendlebury knew about Christopher's misfortunes, and Christy's surgeon worked both at St Mary's and the Royal Manchester Children's Hospital, so news had travelled between the two hospitals throughout the summer.

Staff at Pendlebury had always emphasized that their care of children with cancer extended to the whole family; any event of importance within the family was their concern, largely because of the impact it might have on the psychological wellbeing of their patient. We felt they had shared our pain and anguish that summer as we waited to see whether Christopher would survive.

So we looked forward with pride to the day that we could show our beautiful little miracle off to everybody at Pendlebury. It was a Thursday in late September, and instead of regarding clinic day as a tense, yet tedious obligation, the joy of taking Christopher made it into a happy and relaxed sort of outing.

Paul carried the baby in from the car park, but stopped just far enough away to let Jimmy take over and be the one to present his new baby brother to all his friends who worked at the clinic. There was much excitement, and no shortage of admirers to hold the baby; Christy tolerated the cuddles and handling with his usual calm stoicism.

Jimmy went to the path lab for the usual thumb-prick test and we waited the customary hour and a half to see the Scottish GP who took a clinic once a week, and who always saw Jimmy.

Jimmy took second place to the baby as we related the misadventures of the past few weeks to the doctor, and it was some time before we got round to talking about Jimmy. Everything was quite routine, even our mention of Jimmy's tiredness and lack of appetite. That was nothing unusual and of no urgent concern, and the doctor started to fill in Jimmy's prescription folder, which we would then take to the pharmacy for another half-hour wait before we were ready to go home with all the drugs he needed.

He mentioned, as he wrote, that he was still waiting for just one more set of figures from the blood test results, but that these shouldn't make any difference to the amounts of chemotherapy he was writing up for Jimmy. But then the phone on his desk rang, and staff in the adjoining office requested him to go through to take a call. Paul realized at the time that this was extremely unusual; any normal call would have routinely been put through to the doctor in the consulting room. But I was quite oblivious of anything untoward, looking after Christopher and thinking about when he would need his next feed.

The doctor came back into the room and sat down at the desk before he started to speak. Without any hesitation, with his eyes on our faces, he said, 'The lab has found some suspicious-looking cells in Jimmy's blood, and I'm afraid that this does, in fact, change everything that I said before.'

He waited a few moments for the significance of his words to sink in.

'I think you understand what this means. There is a very small chance, and I stress it is very small, that these cells may not be what we think they are. But in the meantime, we will have to stop Jimmy's maintenance chemotherapy, and you will have to come back next Wednesday for a bone marrow test to see what exactly is happening.'

I asked him if the antiviral drug Jimmy had been taking against shingles might have caused some strange reaction which would produce odd cells on the slide under the microscope. He thought it was possible, but unlikely. The likeliest explanation for the immature blast-type cells that had been spotted was that Jimmy's cancer had returned, and he was suffering a relapse. But there was always room for doubt, and nothing could be confirmed for another six days until after the bone marrow test.

Paul felt there was nothing left to say, and he left the room with Jimmy and the baby. He knew there were other questions I wanted to ask, and his first thoughts were to protect Jimmy. I remained seated while the whole world seemed to rock and tilt around me.

'I know you understand what I am trying to tell you.' The doctor struggled to find words to express how bad things were.

'It couldn't be worse, could it?' I asked, but I didn't need an answer.

The Liaison Sister, Alison, had educated us so well that I knew without being told again that only about 5 per cent of children relapse while still being treated with chemotherapy drugs. The percentage is so minor, and their chances of a cure after this so small, that we had considered this too improbable to worry about. Children who relapse later, after their chemotherapy treatment is complete, have a much better chance of long-term survival.

Jimmy was playing outside, but for once I couldn't control the tears; he looked up and saw them with some surprise, but I couldn't stop to speak to him in case it made matters worse. We were taken to a quiet corner for a cup of coffee, while one of the nurses led Jimmy away to help her change Christy's nappy.

Alison arrived; we asked her if she thought there was any hope that the suspicious cells were aberrations caused by the antiviral drug. With her customary blunt realism, she said no, and told us not to build up any hopes in the next few days. She was certain beyond doubt that Jimmy had suffered a relapse.

The giver of bad news such as this has a miserable job; it would have been so much easier to give us hope and say the things that we most needed to hear. Instead, Pendlebury always tell their parents the exact and honest truth, which is harder to bear at the time, but easier to come to terms with in the long run. We always appreciated their directness, although, at crucial times, such unadorned truth-telling seemed to lack compassion. I am sure this was not the case; and, to be fair, no words of sympathy and understanding at that dreadful moment would have been adequate.

There were only ten minutes to have a drink, resume control and greet Jimmy with calm faces and casual confidence. He was already suspicious at my earlier behaviour and confused by the turn of events. Nothing mattered any more but getting away from the hospital and back to the safety of home, as far away from the relapse as possible. Our warm and sunny day of pride had been so cruelly transformed into a day of sheer horror.

It seemed quite surreal, on the journey home, to sit in Jimmy's favourite Little Chef café and see nondescript people living ordinary lives, and know that our shattering news had not stopped the trivia of everyday life. The café was housed in a narrow sort of cabin, and outside the windows, the sun dared to shine on a field of waving grass. With a sense almost of outrage, I realized that the beauty of that scene remained unaltered by Jimmy's relapse. All around us there were sales reps relating tales of triumph and failure, and an elderly couple smiled to see our little family, and the tiny baby asleep in my arms.

Over the next few days, Jimmy was quite unaware of the significance of his relapse, but we swung from heavy pessimism to ridiculous hope several times each day, if not each hour.

We told very few people, and those who knew almost refused to believe and encouraged us to try and find obscure explanations to account for something that was only too easily explicable. It was unnecessary to worry Granny Anna about the relapse before the bone marrow test confirmed it, so we said nothing. But she was with me in the house next day when Karen rang. Although nothing at all was said on the phone, Karen immediately picked up the low note of worry and tension.

'Has Jimmy relapsed?' she asked at once.

I warned Jimmy's new teacher that we were expecting bad news, although Jimmy continued to go to school for half-days. On Friday, it was his first football game and he wore his kit and new boots and came home with his eyes shining. On Saturday afternoon, the sense of foreboding and despair were so great that I wheeled the baby round the village to escape the feelings of dread and fear at home.

During their stay in London, the children had been given a Greenpeace album of songs which they played and danced to. One of the songs was Dire Straits' 'Why Worry?'. The words seemed so appropriate that I played the song over and over again. Why worry, the song asked. Jimmy's relapse was so dire in itself, it was almost too bad to worry about. One could worry about something so dreadful in anticipation of it happening, but there was no point in worrying now that it had happened.

But the song was only partially accurate: 'There should be sunshine after rain,' it says, by way of comfort; but there's very little sunshine after a catastrophic relapse like Jimmy's. Only a month before, his bone marrow had been declared clear of cancer cells, and then, in the space of a few days, the leukaemia cells that must have been left lurking in the marrow had suddenly multiplied so swiftly and aggressively that vast numbers of them had spilled out into his bloodstream and were now being carried to every corner of his body. Most relapses are detected in the earliest stages while still in the bone marrow; it is extremely unusual for a relapse to have progressed so rapidly as to be detected in a routine blood test only four weeks after a clear bone marrow test.

One of the things that we did to celebrate the first and only week of family life with the three boys before the disastrous clinic visit had been to buy a new television and video. Throughout our week of waiting for confirmation of Jimmy's appalling news, the children continued to enjoy the novelty of having the video, and they were completely oblivious of our anxiety and fear.

I felt as if I moved through those days like two different beings sharing the same body; one person performed the social functions of talking, laughing, greeting and smiling, while the other being inside felt the constant horror of the situation we would face with Jimmy the following Wednesday morning.

At last Wednesday came, and we explained to Jimmy that he would have to have a special bone marrow test to check whether his bad cells had come back. We waited for the results of the test in the clinic passage for an hour and a half but this time it wasn't necessary to make an appointment to see the consultant. He came to us. Jimmy was taken away to play somewhere so that we could talk in private. He was very upset about this and went unwillingly and suspiciously. We very rarely talked about him to his doctors unless he was present. Christopher was clutched firmly in my arms, and nobody could have separated us, but for once I needed him far more than he needed me.

'You can tell by my face what I have to say to you,' the consultant began. The facts were given without comment in a very matter-of-fact, clinical way. Jimmy had relapsed very seriously, and the leukaemia cells had flooded from the bone marrow into his blood.

The first option open to us was to go home and do nothing about it. Without further treatment, Jimmy would be dead within eight to ten weeks.

The second option was to start all over again with intensive induction chemotherapy, and follow a relapse protocol. The chances of his going into remission were only fifty-fifty. If he did, the remission wouldn't hold without a bone marrow transplant, and we would need a perfect match from one of us, preferably a brother. Even if we had a match, and it was only a one in four chance that we would, then he still only had a small chance of a cure, perhaps 20 per cent.

Because the 'go home and do nothing' option had been put first, I thought it was the one favoured by the consultant in view of the hopelessness of curing Jimmy. It was, I thought, a deliberate attempt to dissuade us from putting Jimmy through further treatment, perhaps because it might cause him even more pain and suffering, and more anguish for his family. The worst possible news was given to us so bluntly that I longed for someone to say, 'This must be terrible for you – we're so very, very sorry, because we love Jimmy too, and we share your feelings.'

Perhaps no oncologist the world over could say those few words when facing the parents of a dying child; to feel each individual loss in a business which deals with complete failures frequently might involve staff too deeply and render them emotionally unfit to face each tragedy. Perhaps they were afraid that to show any emotion might cause us to break down and lose control.

Paul and I discussed it as the tears ran down our faces. There wasn't much time and already I could hear Jimmy's voice in an adjoining room. The relapse had, in effect, delivered a death sentence on our precious son, and the consultant had to act as a hanging judge in announcing it.

The easiest option that day would have been to creep away from this bad place and never, never return. No more treatment, no more blighted little lives and no more crying, dying children. But would we ever be able to live with ourselves if we hadn't at least tried to give Jimmy every possible chance of survival? Even if only 10 per cent of children in his predicament survived, we couldn't deny him the chance of being one of the lucky few.

The only thing to do was choose the second option and decide what to do next if and when Jimmy went into remission. The consultant showed a glimmer of optimism. He thought Jimmy's chances of a second remission were slightly over the odds because his first remission had been achieved so swiftly. It was, he said, the option he would take. Every avenue would then be explored, and if all failed, at least we would have the small satisfaction of knowing that everything possible had been tried to save our son.

But Jimmy, at seven years old, surely had the right to choose for himself. We could explain what the options were, and help him to decide.

The consultant agreed to talk to Jimmy, but got nowhere with him. Just like any shy boy of his age, Jimmy didn't respond easily to adults in authority he hardly knew. He looked at the wall, nodding with agreement at everything being said, and probably understood nothing.

We were given just a few days to go away and decide what we were going to do. If we opted for starting more treatment, the sooner the better; the relapse protocol would begin the following Monday when Jimmy would be admitted back on to the cancer ward for at least a couple of weeks or possibly longer. The consultant said he would talk to us at any time as soon as we had made up our minds; whatever our decision, he would support it. If we chose to stay at home and do nothing further, nobody would persuade us to do otherwise. If Jimmy had a better chance of survival, it might have been different. Children whose parents do not wish to start a relapse treatment programme have actually been made wards of court by doctors who thought their chances of success were good; but Jimmy's chances of success were not good.

We arrived home, fetched Martin back from Granny Anna's, having broken the news to her, and put Christy to bed, so that we could all talk the problem over together and offer Jimmy the chance of choosing whichever option he preferred.

We all cuddled up together on our big bed, and explained to Jimmy that his leukaemia had come back. He could either do nothing, or fight on. If he chose treatment, it would mean having lots of needles and drips and lumbar punctures again. He would feel ill and be sick, lose all his hair again, and have to stay in hospital.

Without any hesitation, he chose to keep fighting on.

'I'll fight all the way,' he said. We all held each other and cried together.

Martin was very hungry, and while I went out to fetch him some fish and chips for supper, Jimmy asked Paul what would happen if his treatment failed. Paul told him he would die and go to Heaven. It was the first time that we had to tell him, directly, that he might die soon. Paul was very upset.

Later that sad day, we played Jimmy's favourite game, Trivial Pursuit, and after the boys had gone to bed, one of our Health Centre doctors who had been told the bad news by Pendlebury offered to come and sit with us to answer any questions we might have, and to help us if he could. We accepted gratefully.

We talked to Alan until half-past three the next morning. During that time we were able to ask him questions we hoped we would never need to ask any doctor; we needed to know how Jimmy might die, so that we could build up the courage to help our son through anything and everything. Agonizingly sad though it was, he described the usual sort of illness and death that children with leukaemia often suffer, and his honesty and courage provided us with a likely picture of things to come, which we then put to the back of our minds, hoping we would never need to refer to it again.

Being realistic about the possibility of death did not in any way banish any optimism we had left. We still held on to our hopes that a remission might be achieved, and we phoned the consultant and announced Jimmy's own decision.

Intensive chemotherapy was to start the following Monday, and we devoted the next few days to doing all the things that Jimmy especially wanted to do. School was forgotten; Jimmy didn't want to have to tell his friends about what lay ahead, and he knew it might be many weeks before he could return. He looked paler by the day, but he approached all activities with a frantic sort of energy and stamina as if he knew that time was limited, and he might never visit these places again.

The knowledge that these small adventures might be Jimmy's last chance at living was almost too hard to bear. We cried often, but quietly and secretly; it was the very beginning of a grieving process which still continues, day by day, and includes many facets of grief, of which the writing of this book is just one.

Jimmy adored funfairs, so we took him to Frontierland at More-cambe. He was absolutely fearless as he attempted every possible ride and amusement that he could pack into four hours. Some he repeated over a dozen times; to reach the top of the slope for the helter-skelter mat ride involved running up many steps, and he did this again and again, his hair flying in the wind, his eyes wild with excitement as he attacked each run down with manic determination. The cable car was unstable and wobbly, but Jimmy felt no fear, only the thrill of danger. He bought himself a captain's cap to wear in hospital the following week, and his strength never flagged for a second.

We had already arranged that Christopher's emergency Manchester christening should be supplemented the next weekend in the Anglican church at home. There was to be a special blessing in thanksgiving for our baby's recovery and in acknowledgement of the sincere and powerful support the Vicar and his congregation had given us during Christy's fight for life. In truly ecumenical fashion, Lewis decided that a Catholic baptism could be completed in the Church of England, and he had planned to perform this blessing as part of Harvest Festival on Sunday morning.

This had been planned the week before we found out about Jimmy's relapse during our brief respite from worry and sadness; but now we were quite certain that it had to be a strictly private affair, away from the public gaze. The following week marked the start of a difficult journey for Jimmy and all those who loved him, and we went to church quietly and privately on Saturday afternoon not only to bless our baby, but to seek strength and blessing on this frightening voyage through uncharted waters, much as knights must have sought a blessing before setting off on the Crusades, from which many knew they might never return.

It was a hot, sunny autumn day, and we dressed smartly for the occasion. There were the five of us, with Granny Anna. Godparents had yet to be approached and asked, so Jimmy and Martin stood in as proxies.

Martin was not in the holiest of moods, and as we left home to walk to church, I noticed something clutched in the palm of his hand. It was the novelty he had bought for 30p recently – a most unpleasant-looking pile of trick plastic dog dirt. His Dennis-the-Menace plan was to plant this nasty mess on the baptismal font as a joke, but it was confiscated just in time.

The service of blessing was short, but thankfully rather solemn and formal, to avoid emotion. Christopher was well-behaved, Martin restless, but Jimmy was almost indifferent as he turned away from the proceedings.

Talking about it later, he admitted that he felt awkward during the service because God had let him down by allowing his cancer to come back. He viewed God in much the same light as the consultant. Both had been figures of authority that he no longer trusted.

The last day before he was due to return to hospital, he chose the theme park of Camelot as the place where we should all spend the day. It was his second or third visit, and once again, he was quite fearless on all the rides. By this time, his face was so pale that passers-by noticed, and turned to look at him; but he saved all his strength for climbing up the rope walks or bouncing with his wiry agility on all the clever equipment in the gymnasium fun-house.

There seemed to be no limits to his strength and stamina. His face

beamed with happiness; no adult anticipating prolonged cancer treatment starting the next day could possibly have been so fun-loving and
carefree.

Paul and I paused to watch him clambering effortlessly overhead
across a rope bridge; if anyone deserved to succeed, Jimmy did. And
surely, we said, with such gritty courage and strength and sheer love
of life, he must be in with the best possible fighting chance.

Throughout the day, the Tannoy system in the theme park relayed
on loud speakers everywhere a most beautiful selection of classical
music, from Bach and Byrd and Thomas Tallis to Vaughan Williams.
It was all based on a theme of courtliness and elegance befitting
Camelot. It brought the most unexpected joy to this saddest of days,
and I wanted to find whoever was responsible and thank him or her
personally.

We left at five o'clock to go to David and Jean's house for supper.
Jimmy had chosen his favourite meal of roast turkey, and such an
occasion would normally have been a very special treat for our children.

We arrived home to complete our packing, and on the doorstep was
a box of groceries, everything that a parent would be very glad of
during a stay on Borchardt Ward. The person who so kindly assembled
it from her new grocery shop was Lucy, Amy's mother, who knew only
too well what sort of food would be most useful. The news of Amy's
diagnosis of leukaemia had been broken to Lucy as she nursed the
family's new baby daughter, born just a few hours before. The whole
family, including the new-born baby and Lucy's husband, Brian, had
lived on the ward for a month the autumn before.

Monday morning dawned, a perfect autumn day. We packed up the
car with Jimmy's bag and all the things the baby would need for a
fortnight, and arrived at midday. Two hours later, we were still sitting
waiting in the clinic passage for someone to tell us what we
should do. No matter what time of day, somebody always seems to be
sitting, waiting in that uninspiring place; and whenever anyone
questioned any delay, the answer was always the same – 'The doctors
are at a meeting . . .'

Jimmy had become very hungry and tired waiting. But when he was
finally admitted and saw we had a cubicle to ourselves, to allow a little
privacy for breast-feeding the baby, his spirits rose and he suddenly
remembered all the presents and treats people had given him before.

Sitting on his bed, wearing his captain's hat from Morecambe, it seemed very cruel to remind him why he had returned. As soon as he unpacked, he demanded that I resume my former role of hospital slave, waiting to pander to his every whim. At a wave of his hand I would rush off to the kitchen and make tuna fish sandwiches or locate a pork pie or bacon butty at midnight.

But this time we had Christopher to look after as well; the baby made more noise than Jimmy, so his needs often took precedence. The mildly tyrannical rule Jimmy had formerly exercised from his hospital bed became a thing of the past.

Only the parents of a sick child are allowed to stay on the ward. Brothers and sisters are not permitted under any circumstances except one – that of being breast-fed. The Family Care ladies responsible for allotting accommodation made certain we knew the rules; and however much I sometimes wanted to replace breast with bottle, it was necessary to continue breast-feeding just to allow Christopher to stay with me. After his illness and separation, we were only now beginning to become familiar with each other and nothing could be allowed to interfere with this late bonding process.

Having the baby also opened other doors. A convenient and roomy Mother and Baby Unit just down the corridor from Borchardt was allocated to us, instead of a bunk in the parents' house across the grounds.

Being amongst many other children fighting for their lives helped to lessen the horror of Jimmy's relapse. At home, he was a rarity and in hospital he was one of perhaps six or seven children having a very last chance at staying alive.

Visitors from home came every day and they all helped to keep Jimmy's spirits up, despite his sickness. Many of the most toxic drugs he had had before were repeated, with the same results as before. He would start to vomit within minutes of the medicine entering his body through a drip in his hand or arm.

One of the new experiments was to give high doses of steroids every day through his drip instead of in tablet form. The drug made his arm and hand ache and sting so much the first time that he cried throughout that hour. Next day it was given slower and more diluted, with no pain.

A photograph of Jimmy's painted clown face, with its wide grin and mischievous eyes, looks at me now from the back of the kitchen door. Gillian, one of Jimmy's friends at the *Westmorland Gazette*, had spent the morning making him into a laughing clown, despite frequent delays to empty the vomit bowls. Nobody looking at the picture could ever guess what a bad day it had been. Jimmy was never miserable; he was often impatient, sometimes cheerful, sometimes irritable but never miserable.

It was a busy and unsettled week on the ward, and we were so grateful for the degree of quiet that our little cubicle gave us. We could at least shut the door against the constant noise outside. Opposite, a little boy with an inoperable tumour on his liver screamed throughout the night after his mother went home; further down the ward, a toddler with a tumour of the bowel sobbed hysterically for his mother.

There were such serious staff shortages due to lack of cash that the ward was staffed at night with only one experienced oncology nurse and three agency nurses, but rarely the same ones twice. They arrived on the ward at the start of the shift with little knowledge of oncology and chemotherapy, and both parents and children were distressed at the number of unfamiliar faces on the ward each night.

Resident parents became very worried at the inexperience of these nurses, and one night a deputation gathered to go and see the Director of Nursing to protest. Jimmy was too sick for me to leave him, but we were very concerned that the agency nurse looking after him and other children that night revealed that she had spent the day nursing an old lady with shingles. She was quite unaware of the danger that our children faced from contact with chickenpox and shingles.

The outcome of all this was a letter to the Area Health Authority, which we wrote with the deputation next day, and some excellent publicity in the *Observer* soon afterwards. When the Prime Minister's Office read the article and heard that bone marrow transplants and chemotherapy were being dangerously delayed by staff shortages, they rang the hospital direct and within two weeks, Borchardt had an extra senior nurse, experienced and trained in oncology.

But the new Bone Marrow Transplant Unit, built with charity money, could only use four out of its total of eight beds because the Health Authority were unable to fund and staff more than four. Much of the important work in the labs was done by a research scientist whose role was vital in determining the treatment of the children. But the government provides no funds for medical research and his salary was paid by the Leukaemia Research Fund and by fund-raising parents at home.

We made friends that week with Geraldine and Nick, whose nine-year-old son, Jordan, had relapsed at the end of his maintenance treatment. Jordan had Non-Hodgkin's Lymphoma and was further forward with his relapse protocol than Jimmy. He struggled on for weeks before gaining a remission, which only lasted three or four weeks before more strange cells appeared. But a glimmer of hope and more treatment took Jordan eventually to the Bone Marrow Transplant Unit, where his sister was found to be a perfect match and donated marrow for him.

Everyone hoped that his transplant would be successful. But at that time, with infections and cell count so low that he only managed the occasional visit home, he looked so weak that Jimmy positively bounced with health in comparison. The unpredictability of cancer led to Jimmy's death first, but sadly, poor Jordan died exactly six months after Jimmy.

Geraldine looked after Christy whenever Jimmy's need of me was greater than the baby's. She would walk up and down the ward talking quietly to him, and her calm and gentle face made him relax and beam up at her.

The presence of a healthy baby on the ward had an uplifting effect on morale. The nurses loved to cuddle and hold him, and he often brought a smile to the faces of even the weariest, most depressed little children.

A fifteen-year-old girl, the youngest of her family, lay isolated and expressionless, day after day, as cancer gradually engulfed her whole body. She was very thin, unable to walk alone, and sometimes I was sure her adolescent dignity suffered when one of the male nurses led her very gently and slowly down to the toilets. She was extremely depressed, her head hanging down, missing her friends and even her birthday at home. A chronic chest infection caused her to cough continually, tiring her out even more.

But when one of the nurses visited her with Christy, she smiled and put out her hands to touch him. The risk to Christy, frail and vulnerable himself, from catching the chest infection was outweighed by the joy he brought her, as she played with his tiny little hands. With fingers crossed, we took him to see her every day and he never failed to produce a smile and even a chuckle. She knew what a fight for life Christopher himself had faced.

'If Christy can do it, I'll keep trying too,' she once said to me. She died just a few weeks later.

Martin and Paul looked after each other at home. Martin took my place and behaved like a grown-up in my absence, but his short visits to hospital were as difficult as ever they were before. There was so much I wanted to say to him, but as soon as he arrived, he desperately needed me to do trivial things for him, like buy him a drink or crisps.

Whenever we saw one another, it was vital for him to show me how much he missed me and resented my absence by being cross with me. But after he had punished me for leaving him, life would revert smoothly back to normal. We relied on him to be versatile and rock steady, and he never let us down. He accepted sudden changes and unplanned events in his sturdy, robust way, and we often had to remind ourselves that he was only five years old at the time. His behaviour became very mature.

Maureen arrived nearly every day on the ward as before, relieving the pressures on me by staying with Jimmy while I had a hurried meal in the canteen or half an hour's sleep. Staying with Jimmy until the early hours, then getting up twice during the night to feed Christopher, left very little time for sleep. The Mother and Baby Unit was adjacent to a ward, and it was impossible to let Christopher make any noise in the night. If he refused to settle back to sleep after a feed, I cuddled him or walked the floor to prevent him keeping the children close by awake. There were at least half a dozen doses a day of extra iron, vitamins and minerals to give the baby, but Maureen's expert technique ensured that most of it went down his throat and not his bib.

The doctors and consultant observed things quietly, but not much was said. One of the most important prerequisites of repeating Jimmy's treatment was that he himself actually wanted to. The staff made it quite clear they would be unwilling to treat him if it caused him too much distress. We had agreed that if the moment came when Jimmy told us that enough was enough, we would stop all treatment by mutual consent. With such a small chance of success, the quality of his remaining life was very important. We all agreed that to carry on treating if it became obvious that the treatment had failed might rob Jimmy of all enjoyment of life left to him. There are some parents who never give up, and request staff to continue chemotherapy right to the very end. This was not the course we chose.

It would have been impossible to comfort Jimmy through his sickness and discomfort without continuing to hope. But only one person during those weeks gave us any reason whatsoever to hope.

1. Jimmy was dearer to us
than we could ever have
imagined possible.

2. A small bright little boy
wearing red wellingtons.

3. As our two babies became little boys, it was hard to believe that life could be so happy.

4. Martin wanted nothing more than to be good friends with his older brother.

5. Jimmy, Doggy and Dawn.

6. A month before Jimmy was diagnosed he looked as fit and well as any six-year-old, as he and the others roly-polyed back down the steep slopes of Skiddaw.

7. The picture Jimmy asked his dad to take. His eyes looked weary and resigned as if he couldn't fight the fatigue any more.

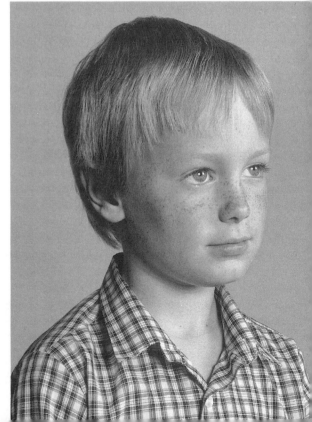

8. June 1988. Jimmy has leukaemia. Our last night at home.

9. Learning to live with a drip.

10. He always had a smile...

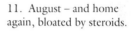

11. August – and home again, bloated by steroids.

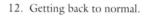

12. Getting back to normal.

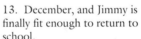

13. December, and Jimmy is finally fit enough to return to school.

14. Rushbearing in July 1989, with Christy on the way – feeling tired together.

15. Cuddling Christy at last.

16. Jimmy's first day at Junior School, September 1989.

17. Hopeless and helpless: Paul and Christy.

18. Good buddies on our holiday in Scarborough, one of many examples of people's support and generosity.

19. Jimmy's last birthday, December 1989.

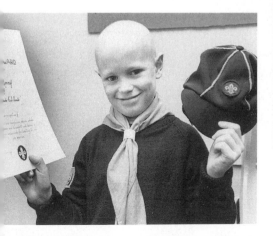

20. Measuring up to *Bluebird*.

21. Jimmy receives the Baden Powell Award for Fortitude.
(© *The Westmorland Gazette*)

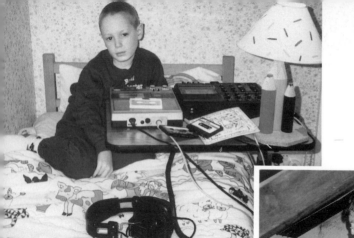

22. Jimmy begins to understand.

23. Paul building Jimmy's railway: a race against time.

24. The first and last portrait of us all together – February 1990.

The Registrar, in one short meeting, put a whole new light on things.

She came to explain the relapse protocol in detail, including how long Jimmy would need to stay in hospital and how often he would attend clinic for outpatient treatment.

She was, she said, very optimistic that Jimmy would go into remission, on the grounds that his first remission had been achieved so easily. Two of the drugs in the relapse protocol were completely new to him, and might therefore be very effective.

The A protocol had not included these drugs. Piling on large doses of new drugs, she thought, made his chances very good.

Next came the problem of a bone marrow match. She thought that if Martin proved unsuitable, the baby might provide a match for his eldest brother. Although babies are normally eighteen months old before their bone marrow is taken for transplant purposes for a brother or sister, it might be possible to extract small amounts from Christopher over a period of time, and these could be stored until Jimmy was ready to use them.

Her casual words of hope planted new seeds of optimism in our minds. It was impossible to think of anything else over the next few days; it was what we most wanted and needed to hear. With another ten days to wait until the next bone marrow test, we enjoyed this measure of hope, knowing that it wouldn't be interrupted by bad news until then.

Jimmy was able to go home earlier than we had expected and his last few injections were given there. His fine, blonde hair was quickly reduced to a few wisps again. He pulled it out in handfuls because the constantly falling hair tickled his face and made him cross. He hid clumps of pulled-out hair on the carpet to make me laugh, and I used to rub a damp cloth over his pillow several times each night to rid him of the tickly hairs.

That week at home he still had plenty of energy. He would watch a three-hour video recording of *The Lion, the Witch and the Wardrobe* nearly every morning, hardly faltering for a moment in his concentration. He loved the clear-cut fable of good versus evil, with good triumphing at the end. He recognized the analogy of Aslan with God, and the White Witch with Satan, though he was apt to get confused and sometimes the White Witch became Mrs Thatcher, whose manner from television interviews he had seen annoyed him intensely.

He was still experiencing pangs of hunger throughout the day after the steroid doses, so he wrote out his orders and menus as a joke. He ate beefburgers, toasted cheese sandwiches, bacon and egg sandwiches, and baked potatoes with their cooked middles mashed up with cheese and salad cream. He wolfed his food down and often woke up for a midnight feast as well.

At the end of this third week of treatment, his injections had been completed, and Paul took him for a ride in a motor boat on Ullswater. Paul's assignment was to photograph a marina on the shore.

It was a very windy day, but despite the squally weather, Jimmy drove the boat and smiled at the camera, with his blue hood hiding his bald head, and his cheeks pink from the sharp wind. Both his top front teeth were missing, and his gappy grin expressed all the fun and excitement he was having at the wheel of the boat.

But when he came home, he was tired and shivery and went to sleep in our bed. Before long he started to vomit, and by ten o'clock his temperature was too high. Wearily we rang the ward. We knew it was an infection that would need hospital treatment and intravenous antibiotics, but dare we postpone the journey and upheaval until morning?

Although we had become accustomed to packing up at a moment's notice, the separation never became any less painful. Just at a time when we all needed to be together, we were forced, time and again, to part.

This time we decided to risk it and wait till morning, though we would check the temperature at half-past two. The alarm clock was set and duly went off; Jimmy's temperature was 103.5 degrees despite the paracetamol we had given him. A move had to be made without further delay.

The idea of waking Christopher, packing nappies and food, pram and chair for an indefinite period was too much to contemplate at that hour. So, for the very first time, we swapped places and roles. Paul took Jimmy alone to Manchester, and I stayed at home with Martin and the baby. The business had to remain open for Saturday morning, and then I would look after both children at home for the weekend, until early Monday morning when we would change places.

One of the couples whose help we called on frequently throughout Christopher and Jimmy's various crises were Sam and Marion. Although both retired as doctors, their lives in retirement couldn't be busier; on many occasions they abandoned plans and arrangements to help us out, and once again it was Sam I turned to on Monday to give Christopher and myself a lift to Pendlebury.

Travelling to Pendlebury for Sam was a familiar journey; his long career in paediatrics had included a period spent working there, and his associations with the hospital remained.

When Sam and Marion, both very familiar with childhood malignancy in the North-West area, realized that Jimmy was unlikely to live long, rather than keep their distance and avoid the pain of watching him die, they set out to become two of his very special friends, who enlivened and enriched his dwindling life in its very last stages. They had known Jimmy since birth, but needed to become better acquainted with him so that they could discover the sort of things he liked doing best. He felt comfortable and at ease with them always, and they gave him their friendship without ever considering the loss they would soon experience, as did all those special friends who loved him until the end without ever counting the personal cost. The memories Jimmy had of Sam and Marion's Christmas parties, to which they invited all the little children they knew, included chocolate finger biscuits arranged in a tiny silver cup, and eating so much with such greed and excitement that we thought he would be sick.

So it was Sam who often provided urgent transport, as he did early that October morning. Paul and I spent five minutes together before he returned home to work. Jimmy's fever was still uncontrolled. The powerful combination of two different antibiotics had so far failed to work, but there were several combinations left to try.

Jimmy was suffering such a severe infection, which proved so obstinate to treat and so unwilling to respond to strong treatment, that by Wednesday even the doctors were concerned. Infections in immuno-suppressed children are commonplace, everyday eventualities on a cancer ward, and they are looked on as expected hazards, although occasionally they can prove fatal.

Jimmy's white cell count was so low that the bone marrow test had been postponed for that week. So we had another week's grace before finding out what impact his chemotherapy was having on the leukaemia. In the meantime, his temperature rose steadily as soon as each dose of paracetamol tailed off, and he was particularly ill during the night.

The ward was very cramped, and Christy perched in his little seat at the end of Jim's bed, or tried to sleep in his carrycot, which was pushed in a corner wherever we could find enough space. Christy's nights were disturbed because of the noise around him, and the bright lights shining overhead made his normal daytime rests into mere catnaps. He woke frequently with a startled jump; children cried and shouted all around, whatever the time, and there was constant background noise from all the televisions during the day. Within hours of arriving on the ward, Christopher would become tense and jumpy and irritable. We had all worked so hard at home trying to make him a more relaxed and settled baby after his horrifying start in life that it was highly frustrating to watch him rapidly lose ground when he had to live on the ward, away from everything familiar, quiet and peaceful.

On Monday night, about eleven o'clock, we noticed that the bandage that secured Jimmy's drip in the vein in his hand was soaking wet, indicating that the drip was leaking out. Somehow the drip had become displaced and the antibiotic had leaked into the tissues of his hand. He shouted with pain as his hand swelled, but the staff were so busy with an emergency admission that it was some time before they could investigate. Removing the drip needle would mean waiting half the night for a duty doctor to come and resite it. At last they unwrapped the bandage, and found his poor hand distended, and the skin puffy.

Jimmy couldn't take much more; he waited with terror for the gentle Chinese doctor to arrive about two hours later. Normally he controlled his fears, and looked away while needles were put in his veins, but this particular night, he had let go of his built-in control, and showed us all the fear he usually hid. He had to be carried into the treatment room, and there, despite her light, expert touch, he shouted in protest and screamed in the hope that he would be left alone.

Sitting there with Jimmy struggling on my knee, it felt very uncomfortable to be on the wrong side as usual. My natural inclination was to take his side and protect him from those whose job it was to hurt him. Instead I had to side against him and help the doctors do unpleasant things to him. Only six weeks before, I had watched Christopher repeatedly roll his eyes in terror as needles were stuck in him and I frequently helped to hold him down to make the job easier for the staff. It was a strange, unnatural sort of motherhood to assist people in hurting my children, even for the best possible reasons.

Two days later, on Wednesday, the doctors hit on the winning combination of antibiotics necessary to kill Jimmy's bug, and his temperature slid down and stayed down. On Friday morning, with two emergency admissions in the night and a newly diagnosed child just arriving, Jimmy's bed was occupied by somebody else before nine o'clock. The ward had never been more crowded, and although the doctor had suggested keeping Jimmy in just another day, there was no bed left for him and no choice except to discharge him. We sat on our bags with Christopher on the ward floor waiting for a lift home. There were five more waiting days until bone marrow day.

We returned on Wednesday, afraid to hope. We sat longer than ever in the passage, probably nearly three hours, as we waited; but there was a delay that afternoon in getting the results, and we had to leave for home before they were available.

Later in the afternoon, we talked by phone to one of the clinic staff who told us that while there was some improvement in Jimmy's marrow, with fewer immature blast cells and even some normal white cells, he was still not in remission. We might have to be prepared for an intensification of the treatment, but no doctor would be available to speak to until next morning. She revealed that the doctors had hoped for better results, but that things could be worse, and second remissions did take longer than first ones.

But the doctor next morning was clearly not satisfied with the rate of improvement. It wasn't as good as they had hoped for or expected. But there was to be no speeding up of the treatment to hit the leukaemia harder. The relapse protocol had to be followed as planned, because Jimmy was still part of the UKALL relapse trials; this meant that there would be no further treatment during the next week.

Logically, it would be unlikely that the next bone marrow test would show any further improvement unless there was more treatment given in the interim period, and the protocol did not allow for this. Jimmy's only real hope lay in a delayed reaction to the treatment he had already been given. This was unusual but not completely unheard of.

We were called in to see the consultant after the following week's bone marrow test. The grim expression on his face made words unnecessary. Every time he gave us yet more bad news, we thought there couldn't be anything worse to hear, but we were always wrong.

We could hear Jimmy running about outside, chasing the nurses and teasing them; we talked briefly and the consultant agreed to press on with treatment for another fortnight. The next stage of the relapse protocol gave Jimmy two very powerful drugs he had never had before. If these failed to bring about a remission, nothing more could be done; and there could be no bone marrow transplant without remission. Testing for a bone marrow match now seemed quite futile.

We left Jimmy on the ward, about to start an eight-hour blood transfusion, and took Christopher to see his consultant at St Mary's, on the south side of Manchester. John Gorrigan was sitting reading a Roald Dahl story to Jimmy when we returned; he had driven down to Pendlebury on his half-day off from the practice where he is a GP to stay with Jimmy while we were absent. Geraldine and Nick were on the ward with Jordan, so there were plenty of people to talk to as the hours crawled by. The transfusion finished at ten o'clock, but despite the lateness of the hour, Jimmy wanted to get home as soon as possible rather than stay overnight. He had started to hate hospital, and dreaded the idea of staying in.

The next stage of the relapse protocol involved four days of drug treatment as a day patient. Without Karen's powerful support as she drove us down, looked after Christopher and helped to nurse Jimmy through hours of violent sickness, these distressing, bad days might have been even worse.

The first day we arrived as requested by half-past nine, which meant leaving home at eight o'clock. It was nearly midday before treatment started. In spite of all his brave efforts to ignore the sickness and keep active and cheerful, within half an hour Jimmy started to vomit.

It was the same every time. We would start to play Monopoly, but we never managed to finish a game. The vomiting was almost nonstop for the first hour. We had to support Jimmy sitting up, so that he wouldn't choke as he retched. Then he would drop back, exhausted, sleep for ten minutes, and wake up vomiting again.

Not even the strongest antisickness medicine made any difference until after four or five hours, and then the nausea would subside and Jimmy would sleep for an hour. It was strange that he might complain about small inconveniences in life, like running out of pocket money, or not having any sweets, but he never complained about the big things he had to suffer.

Each day's treatment would end with half an hour's recovery, and despite several hours of vomiting, Jimmy would then slip off the bed, having got rid of his drip, and make off up and down the ward on the nearest trundle toy he could find. He very rarely thought about himself as ill. The moment he walked through the ward door, and out of the hospital, he acted as a normal, healthy child again. Being ill was reserved for hospital in his mind. If his body had been as healthy as his bright little mind, he would have lived the long and active life he so richly deserved.

We returned to hospital every few days for another treatment session, and despite his sickness Jimmy never expressed any strong reluctance about having to go for more chemotherapy. It wasn't until weeks later, when he came to dread visits to hospital almost more than death itself, that we glimpsed the real fear and horror he suffered during these ordeals.

One journey was particularly memorable. Jimmy developed painful stomach cramps, probably in anticipation of his treatment, and Christopher joined in with loud screams. Having stopped to deal with the chaos, the only solution was to reach Pendlebury as quickly as possible. Karen inadvertently drove through a contraflow section of the M61 at over 70 m.p.h., both children still screaming, and was picked up by a speed check. Fortunately the police accepted our plea of mitigating circumstances when the summons arrived a fortnight later, which saved us at least £100, possibly more.

Paul took Jimmy alone for the last day of treatment, driving back at midnight through floods to reach home, where Jimmy demanded a bacon and egg sandwich despite the usual day of continual sickness. His stoicism was heroic and his cheerful stamina truly remarkable for a seven-year-old with little fun left in life.

But his efforts were in vain. The chemotherapy was having no impact whatsoever and the leukaemia cells were multiplying even after such hard treatment. It became inevitable that the relapse protocol would have to be stopped. But should we tell Jimmy it had failed, or could we expect him to guess before too long?

It was the beginning of November, and the consultant predicted Jimmy would probably have about six to eight weeks left to live. It would be doubtful whether he would see Christmas.

The idea of Jimmy dying at Christmas was absolutely horrifying. We wanted him so very much to enjoy one last family Christmas. It meant so much to us that we were offered just a little further treatment in the form of daily tablets that might temporarily halt the progress of the disease. The last thing we wanted Jimmy's life to be was a replica of Narnia under the reign of the White Witch – always winter, but never Christmas. Our wishes were granted and Jimmy was permitted his ninth, and last, Christmas.

✳

# SIX

# A Season for Living

The relapse protocol was abandoned in November and Jimmy was now deemed terminally ill. He remained, in himself, quite a strong little boy still capable of enjoying all sorts of experiences.

We had very little time to consider how best to spend his remaining few weeks, or, at the most, months. There were no family conferences, or grand plans; instead we adopted the ideas that we had already half formed in our minds. As he was still able to enjoy experiences, we would give him as many, and as varied a programme, as his health and our limited resources could stand.

To do this, we needed the co-operation of other people around us, so we let it be known quietly that Jimmy's treatment had failed, but that his family were not going to sit and do nothing in the precious time left to him.

On hearing news like that, one's first shocked reaction might be to dash out and buy Jimmy an expensive toy while he could still play with it. But rather than overcrowd him with material things, how much better, we suggested, if that same money were used to buy him an adventure or unusual experience.

Contemplating the weeks ahead, and Jimmy's eventual deterioration, the strongest natural inclination of any parent, myself included, would be to withdraw the dying child from life altogether, and wrap him tightly in a protective cocoon of love. Without the intrusions of other people, we could then savour every last moment of his life just for ourselves.

But we had always shared his life with those who loved him. From the moment that he was born and his existence became independent of mine, I respected the highly individual little person Jimmy soon became, who had rights and preferences of his own.

Our code of parenthood was in perfect harmony with that of Kahlil Gibran, who summed it all up in *The Prophet*: 'Your children are not your children; they are the sons and daughters of life's longing for itself. They come through you but not from you, and though they are with you, yet they belong not to you . . .'

Jimmy had matured into a most sociable child, who loved his friends.
It was important that he should share his last weeks with all the people
who loved him, not just us. We had no right to choose how he should
spend his limited time, and he would have resented it deeply if we had
sought to keep the rest of his life exclusively for ourselves.

He not only made friends easily with children of his own age; he
was equally at home with adults and it was these adult relationships
that now became important in his life, partly because he found it
increasingly difficult, as he became weaker, to tolerate the rough and
tumble of playing with children. He hadn't lost touch with school
altogether, thanks to the dedication with which the staff organized a
steady flow of letters from every child, so that every fortnight, Jimmy
received bundles of letters, drawings, word puzzles, jokes and games
carefully put together by each class in turn. But this was very different
from actually meeting his old friends themselves.

We had invited a couple of his classmates round after school on
several occasions, but without great success. Life had continued at
junior school without Jimmy, and it was hard for his old schoolmates
to relate to him in person after so many months.

His friends would arrive, straight from school, shy and ill at ease.
Jimmy looked odd with his bald head and pale skin, and there was
very little left in common between them. Eventually, his friends would
be tempted by the model railway track Paul had built in the attic, and
they would climb up the ladder to the attic and run his engines, under
Jimmy's instruction.

But he tired easily, and when the others wanted a change of activity,
it was Martin who gleefully led the way and played with them, while
Jimmy would collapse onto the sofa to watch television. Then he would
find the room too noisy and realize that he couldn't keep pace with
his companions any more and the afternoon always ended in resentment that it was Martin now that Jimmy's friends preferred to play
with.

So it was inevitable that he should spend most of his time with
adults. They made allowances for his tiredness and didn't expect
anything of him, and they geared their activities to allow for the fact
that Jimmy was not just very ill, but slowly dying. Death still seemed
a long way off whenever Jimmy enjoyed a short, sharp burst of energy,
pounding modelling clay or drilling and sawing up in the attic.

The model railway took up more and more space and time; and although Jimmy spent all and every day with me, his evenings were with Paul engaged in a joint project to convert the big old attic into a complex electric railway system. Work on the railway had started the year before, when Paul spent most of the winter crawling about under the eaves, flooring the attic and building the track. Jimmy had spent some of his own savings on Hornby engines, and Paul bought a trunk full of old Hornby models and transformed them all back into working order.

But the track was too small and they demolished it to make way for a bigger one. The news of Jimmy's relapse had brought all railway work to a complete halt and everything lay in bits. There was little point in Paul carrying on alone; but after we accepted that Jimmy was terminally ill, and his time was limited, Paul put everything he had into rebuilding their railway so that Jimmy could run his trains on the bigger and better track before he became too ill.

It was a race against time; every evening, whether we were at home or in hospital, Paul disappeared up the narrow ladder and worked until the early hours of the morning, building the low surface over which the track would run, introducing tunnels and loops and links, stations and sidings. Much of the work involved the electrification of the system, and Jimmy's light touch and dexterity contributed greatly to the project.

Jimmy used his railway until he no longer had the strength to sit up and operate his trains from the control panel. As his anaemia made him sleepier, he took his pillow and duvet upstairs, and made himself a bed to sleep on in the middle of the floor so that he could run trains and rest at the same time. When we tried to explain that Heaven would be the very nicest thing he could imagine, he chose to think of it as a vast model railway layout.

When Jimmy's treatment stopped, it left us free from frequent hospital visits. One of the trickiest problems we envisaged was explaining to Jimmy that he wouldn't be going to Pendlebury any more. He knew it was essential to his very existence and we thought he might be very frightened if we suddenly stopped going. Things turned out differently; he continued to be checked at clinic once a fortnight until two months before he died, by which time he felt so ill, it was a relief for him not to endure the journey any more.

The abandoning of the relapse protocol brought a new freedom, that of being able to travel out of reach of home or Pendlebury, and the first move was to take a few days' holiday together, our first for fourteen months. Jimmy had been feeling very low that second week in November with a bad cold, but we planned to leave, if at all possible, on Friday afternoon. Sonja and her husband, Martin, had been inviting us to their home in York for years; Jimmy was very keen to go, and it was now or never as far as he was concerned.

But on the Wednesday before, the day of his last bone marrow test, it looked unlikely we would be going anywhere, even home. Jimmy's chemotherapy, coupled with a bad cold, had left him very depleted. His platelets were low, he needed a transfusion both of platelets and red cells, and he had an ear infection requiring antibiotics.

He came round from his anaesthetic very slowly, and we waited in the recovery room for nurses to find a hospital bed so that the transfusion could start. It was midday and as each hour passed it became less and less likely we would return home that evening.

Jimmy lay, sick and listless, on two chairs. There was no bed available anywhere in the hospital so staff tried to make him more comfortable with blankets and pillows.

We waited four hours and then started to pack up to go home; there was nothing else for it but to return next morning. But as we left, the doctor arrived and urged us not to go. Jimmy's platelet count was so low, he might start to bleed at any time, and it was dangerous to take him home.

At last a bed was found on an unfamiliar ward. Paul left us to go home and look after Martin, and Christopher, Jimmy and I tried to settle down next to an angry little boy who pelted us with toy cars from his cot.

The twelve-hour transfusion began that evening; whenever transfusions continued through the night, it meant a restless, uncomfortable and disturbed night's rest for Jimmy because nurses have to check blood pressure and temperature so frequently. Jimmy liked to have company on these occasions, and we often talked quietly through the early hours of the next morning.

It was a very special night, when we said a lot of special things to each other. For once, Jimmy was angry about having leukaemia.

'Why is it always me that gets all the bad luck?' he grumbled. 'First I get leukaemia, and then it comes back and now I end up having to stay in hospital. It's always me that gets all the bad luck.'

I asked him why he was increasingly unpleasant and mean to Martin. 'Because he hasn't got leukaemia, and he can go to school and be with his friends,' he replied.

Then the conversation, for some reason, turned to Heaven, and how it was the best place anyone could go to. I asked Jimmy what he most wanted at that time.

'To be in your tummy again, like Christy was, where it's all warm and safe and I would like to be born as a baby again, but this time with a body that works properly,' he said.

I liked the idea of reabsorbing him back into my own body. But Jimmy, ever logical and practical, didn't think it was really possible to re-enter the womb and emerge the same, only better.

'We don't know everything in this world that there is to know,' I told him. 'What's to say that we can't do that?' Jimmy recognized the words of the Professor in *The Lion, the Witch and the Wardrobe*, who told the children the same thing when they came with tales of a land beyond the fur coats in the famous wardrobe.

I consciously worked to expand Jimmy's concept of reality and the possible, so that he would accept the notion of Heaven without too much logical disputation when the time came to explain that he was dying.

'I want to be Jimmy again, but better next time,' he said, and finally fell asleep.

The trip to York took place as planned. We also wanted to visit the Yorkshire coast, and had already booked a family room in a very grand hotel in Scarborough, fully expecting that we would never reach there because Jimmy would be too weak. At least we had taken out an insurance policy to cover us if we had to abandon the visit.

We stopped at Gargrave on the evening journey to York, for a meal at The Anchor, where only six months before we had been a happy family rounding off a perfect day out with Granny. The children had played in the pub garden with the teddy bears they had just bought in Skipton. The evening sun was casting long shadows across the Leeds and Liverpool Canal which ran alongside the garden, and we had been reluctant to leave for home after a good meal in a pleasant setting.

This time it was winter, cold and quiet. Jimmy lay across the bench seat impatient for his food to arrive, but he couldn't eat it when it did. He looked so ill, it seemed the height of folly to be attempting to go on holiday. The easiest thing would have been to admit defeat, turn round and go straight back home. Instead, we opted to drive on and return the next day if things hadn't improved.

Sonja and Martin Davis's Victorian house in York was on three floors, linked by steep flights of stairs. The children loved its unexpected treasures; the large bathroom was more like a glasshouse at Kew Gardens, trailing with ferns and verdant exotica; while the music room with stripped pine floorboards was an oasis of peace and elegance.

The boys slept at the very top of the tall house in a room next to ours. We were warmly welcomed, although the effort of hiding the awful sadness Sonja and Martin felt at seeing Jimmy for what they knew would be the last time must have been a considerable strain for them.

We spent Saturday morning visiting the famous Yorvik exhibition where we all enjoyed the gimmickry of travelling through the ages in time cars, and sniffing the smells of Viking York. Jimmy needed his wheelchair buggy at all times because he was too weak to walk, and the Saturday crowds of shoppers outside bumped and jostled us. After the customary visit to a toy shop and half an hour in a café for Jimmy to have a chocolate milk shake, we left the city centre for Sonja and Martin's house.

We would have been forced to give up sightseeing with Jimmy in the afternoon if Martin hadn't come to the rescue by providing a taxi service from place to place. The weather was freezing, the coldest week of the winter, but York Minster proved a good warm place for winter tourism.

The organist was warming up for Evensong, and we bumped Jimmy's buggy over the ancient uneven paving stones while little Martin skipped round tombs and behind grilles. Jimmy saw the candles left burning by people who had requests for prayers.

'Is it the Bishop's birthday?' he asked, but only half innocently.

It was the Rose Window with the setting sun shining through its coloured glass that captivated us all, but especially Jimmy. We squinted up at it, high above, then we looked down into a mirror, reflecting from below all its magnificent detail.

No doubt it was the story of the lightning strike that started the fire in York Minster in 1984 and the subsequent rebuilding of the roof and window that made it so fascinating to the children.

The next place of interest commanding at least two hours of time was the National Railway Museum; *Mallard* itself, the fastest steam engine in the world, was there to see and touch. A video film with footage of *Mallard*'s recent steam runs ran constantly nearby. Interest was flagging a little when big Martin arrived, bringing Christopher to me for a feed. He took the other two children and disappeared for an hour and a half, during which time they met an old railwayman, who took them behind the scenes to places that visitors don't usually see.

The weather was still below freezing and next morning, early, Paul and I left the three children and walked the city walls along paths slippery with frost and ice. When we returned, Martin and Sonja were giving the children their first violin lesson, which they enjoyed enormously.

We left York with great sadness and reluctance and headed for Scarborough and the Royal Hotel. The local Lions Club at home had offered to help pay for the family to have a short break together and it was thanks to their generosity that we could afford such luxury.

The hotel is Regency period, with an imposing hall, sweeping semicircular staircases and mirrored galleries along each of the landings. Our room was dark, with no view at all, but the luxury inside more than compensated for looking out on a brick wall. There was a double bed and a double sofa bed and ample room for everyone including Christopher in his carrycot.

We had chosen the hotel solely for its indoor swimming pool and Jacuzzi, which proved the holiday's chief attractions. Jimmy was in the pool within half an hour of arriving, and swam twice each day. It was designed to resemble an oasis in the desert, and the lighting was so effective that one could almost escape into the realms of fantasy and forget that we were on the east coast of England, three doors down from Marks and Spencer in a seaside resort in November with a dying child.

Jimmy looked a little better but continued to be extremely irritable all that week, directing his ill temper and resentment at poor Martin, whose only fault was in being Martin, and not having the illness that Jimmy had to put up with every day. We tried to be understanding and sympathetic to Jimmy's angry mood, but we had to protect Martin, too, and prevent him from retaliating. Jimmy's furious reactions were uncharacteristic, and we watched with great sorrow as illness transformed his personality into one that was unfamiliar to us.

Jimmy refused to eat anything except tuna fish and mayonnaise sandwiches; it was a Sunday and not even room service could oblige, so we bargained at Reception; they clearly thought we were trying to humour a spoilt brat. Without meaning to put a special case, the truth slipped out. The sandwiches arrived in half an hour, presented on a silver tray and served with fresh orange juice. The bill we were given when we left made no charge for anything the children had, meals and room service included, but when we pointed it out, the management insisted the bill was correct.

Monday was a fine, sunny day. We explored the beach, and Paul and the boys dug a big sandcastle and waited for the North Sea to come in and wash it away. They were not disappointed as the tide raced in with a brisk east wind behind it.

I stood and watched while Christy slept in his pram and suddenly I couldn't stand the pain any more, knowing that Jimmy would never build a sandcastle again. It was something he loved to do, something he rarely had the opportunity of doing.

He ran up and down the beach, carrying water, mending broken defences and dancing with excitement as his castle crumbled. Turning my back on him, I crumbled, too, crying those deep despairing sobs which are such a tiring feature of grief at its rawest. The future just then seemed impossible – to help our precious little boy, who loved life so much, to leave it all behind.

We were very rarely allowed the luxury of feeling our emotions with any depth or for long; life's trivia would intrude, and tears had to be hidden or brushed quickly away because a shoelace needed tying or a nose blowing. Within seconds of profound grief, one could be laughing again at something funny one of the children had said. We were well practised in quick recoveries and the lightning mood changes necessary to accommodate the children's needs.

That cold November afternoon we wheeled Jimmy round Scarborough Castle with the icy wind whipping off the sea. The mellow stone was golden in the late sunshine and we raced up and down little hills and round the perimeter of the cliff-top grounds, shouting and laughing.

Next day, the sun had gone and the blue skies were replaced with a depressing iron grey. We drove to Whitby, with great expectations, but the little port looked pinched and shabby as we shivered in the wind, with greasy chip papers flapping round our feet, and litter left overflowing from unemptied bins.

Whitby Abbey was more stimulating and I wheeled Jimmy round, telling him about the life of a medieval monk who had to get up in the night to pray. 'Sounds very like having Christy!' he commented; with Christy sharing our family room at the hotel, the boys suddenly became aware of his twice-nightly shouts for milk.

Whitby Parish Church was even more fascinating, with its high wooden pews, and large ear trumpet hanging by the pulpit for the benefit of the Vicar's deaf wife in Victorian days. The Ten Commandments were engraved in wood on the wall, and Jimmy read each one through, thought about it, then imagined a few examples of ways in which people might break them.

I never wanted to miss any opportunity to teach Jimmy as much general knowledge as I could. A small voice inside me argued that it was pointless if he was going to die so soon. But I ignored such defeatism, arguing back that the world was such an infinitely fascinating place, he should know as much about it as possible in the short time left. Now the Ten Commandments joined all the other snippets of knowledge he was so hungry to learn, and even if he couldn't recite his nine times table, he could speak authoritatively about global warming, the changes being enacted in Eastern Europe and where Africa was on his globe.

We were cold and miserable as we made our way back to the escapist oasis pool at the hotel via Robin Hood's Bay and McDonald's. It had been a most enjoyable few days away, a risk we had taken which had paid off. Everybody felt better for it except Tinker, who came home with a cat virus and mites from his brief stay in a cattery.


A new sort of routine evolved at home for Jimmy and much of it involved adults giving him their time each week. Sam and Marion both set about getting to know him better and invited him to spend a morning each week with them, helping with the weekly bread-baking, and playing cards and bagatelle.

In a very short time, the three of them had fallen into a familiar routine for Jimmy's visits; the bread was baked by midday, and Jimmy helped to make little individual loaves with our initials carefully picked out in oatflakes.

The bread-making fulfilled Pendlebury's label of 'quality time' if anything did. Even when he felt too tired to do anything much at home, Jimmy would still go bread-baking. He always asked me to explain to Sam if he felt especially weary; he was too embarrassed to mention it himself, but he said it was all right to tell Sam.

'He knows about cancer, and he knows about children too,' he told me. 'And they both understand when I feel tired.' He was absolutely at home and comfortable with them, even when he felt poorly.

On Saturday mornings, he would spent several hours with his teacher, Janet Benson, in whose class he had been for the last few months at the infants school. Together they would play Monopoly, or watch a video, and there were always little bits of news from school that she had saved up to tell him, special things she knew he would enjoy. If she hadn't managed to see him any week, there would always be a letter written in big print that he could read himself, and she never forgot to tell him the latest exploits of their cat, Cloughie. Jimmy's passion for Monopoly was nurtured at the Bensons', where they taught him to play.

She always made the very best tuna fish sandwiches in the world, he said. The secret was to put the fish and mayonnaise in the blender and make a fish pâté. These Saturday mornings were as precious to him as the bread-baking days, and he looked forward to them both each week. They were brave people, who let themselves be close to Jimmy and accepted the sadness his loss would inevitably bring.

One day our reporter friend, Gillian, took Jimmy on a mystery tour, accompanied by her boyfriend, Michael. He amused both boys with his imitation of Orville, the ventriloquist Keith Harris's duck that was popular on television. Michael was soon nicknamed Orville. He and Gillian took Jimmy to Coniston to see a mock-up of Bluebird, Donald Campbell's boat in which he broke all records and died in the last attempt as the boat broke in two on Coniston in 1967.

Jimmy had been intensely interested in a television play about Campbell and his speed attempts called *Across the Lake*, and when he borrowed a video film of it, he would replay the actual film shot at the time of the tragic accident.

Since Jimmy had been ill, he had developed a morbid sort of fascination with other people's disasters. Perhaps it was because he knew that something bad was happening to himself, and it was reassuring to know that bad things happened to other people too. He would ask all sorts of detailed questions about how accidents happened, and the sinking of the *Titanic* was another event about which he wanted to know more and more. He borrowed a book about it and the part he always turned to was the chapter describing how the great ship sank, drowning men, women and children too. The notion that children drowned was particularly significant to him.

Gillian and Orville also took the boys to Blackpool to swim at the Sandcastle. Orville had a car phone and Jimmy's little voice gave us a running commentary as they headed south along the motorway. He rang from Blackpool outside the Tower, and his confidence hurtling down the water chute floored even Orville. We met the boys back at Milnthorpe, where we were visiting friends.

'Don't worry about getting lost in Blackpool, or finding somewhere to park, because I was born here and I know it like the back of my hand', Orville had boasted to the children.

As they drove into Milnthorpe, Martin commented tartly: 'I can tell you which way to go, because I know this place like the back of my hand, though I suppose the next thing you'll tell us is that you were born here as well!'

After many telephone calls and whispered asides, we were requested to take the boys to Cark, on the Furness Peninsula, to await a surprise. We knew that Gillian had arranged with a company director she had met to bring a plane up to Cark Airfield and take the boys for a ride over the Lake District, flying over Ambleside if possible.

Cark Airfield looked more like a farmer's field than an airport, so even as we arrived, neither Jimmy nor Martin could guess what they were about to do. Cows grazed by the runway and the piggeries seemed rather better appointed than the control tower. An aviation club were assembled for a day's parachuting, but there was no radio link with the control centre and we could only guess when the pilot was arriving by the distant sound of his small, single-engined plane.

His arrival did nothing to calm the nerves of reluctant passengers. As he came in to land, a waiting plane loaded with parachutists suddenly and without warning chose that moment to taxi onto the runway in the path of the landing plane. He aborted his landing in a steep climb and leap-frogged safely over the offending plane. He seemed quite unshaken by the manoeuvre and insisted they practised it frequently while training.

The plane could only seat about four passengers, so Christy, Orville, Gillian and I waited on the ground while Paul, Jimmy and Martin joined the pilot and his five-year-old daughter for their flight. The only people who knew about the trip were David and Jean; the plane flew up Lake Windermere, over Ambleside and up towards Rydal, and suddenly the pilot spotted a message picked out in white sheets hundreds of feet below in the garden of Scandale Brow. He circled and dropped height to inspect the message. It said 'Hi Jim!' and came from David and Jean.

Back at Cark, as we waited huddled up in the cold, sunny morning near the wartime Nissen huts, we felt that if we blinked momentarily, we might open our eyes to see the ghosts of eager young airmen dressed in their leather flying jackets, sitting outside their huts in Lloyd Loom armchairs, playing cards and waiting for the order to scramble.

The flight was a great thrill for Jimmy and Martin, and a good photo opportunity for Paul. We drove back and rushed straight round to Scandale Brow to thank Jean and David for their thoughtful message and all the excitement it had caused.

The news that Jimmy was terminally ill spread very quietly and discreetly all over the district, and his plight fired young people to think of anything at all that they could do to make the rest of his life challenging and stimulating.

Young staff at a local outdoor centre temporarily transferred their support of the BBC Children in Need appeal in November to a Jimmy Appeal, to raise £400 to buy him a games computer.

But their generosity almost backfired when their youthful enthusiasm galloped ahead of common sense, and they printed leaflets headed: 'TIME IS RUNNING OUT FOR JIMMY . . .' The notice, with a photograph of Jimmy, was an information leaflet solely for the benefit of staff and students, and pupils at a nearby comprehensive, who were joining with the centre to raise funds for the computer. Unfortunately, the printed notices were pinned up in various places round the town, and friends who saw it said nothing because they assumed we knew.

The notices had been up for five days before we discovered them. Jimmy was still strong enough most days to skip round the shops if there was something he wanted to buy and we really didn't know whether he might have seen them, with a picture of himself, and said nothing about it.

Jimmy didn't actually know that he was going to die. To have told him that would have meant explaining his treatment had been a failure. He had worked so hard and uncomplainingly to beat his leukaemia that it was something neither of us could tell him outright. We had hoped that it was a truth he would gradually see for himself as he became more ill. A gradual acceptance and recognition of death would be kinder than a stark, dramatic announcement from us.

Fortunately, he wasted little time reading notices, and never read that Time was Running Out for him. Instead, a games computer was delivered to him in December, with software bought for him by his friends at Greenpeace.

One Wednesday evening, there was a programme on television about an organization which sent children like Jimmy on holidays of a lifetime. The next afternoon, Jimmy's headmaster rang to say that he had managed to contact the organizer and had told her about Jimmy. She had a flight leaving on Saturday morning for Norway and Sweden, where the children would visit the real Father Christmas at a theme park called Santaland in the middle of Sweden. The all-expenses-paid trip lasted four days and hotel accommodation was provided. If Paul could reach Heathrow by eight on Saturday morning, there would be places on the flight for the three of them, including Martin. They simply had to answer yes or no.

The answer was an immediate 'yes'. Fortunately both the boys still believed in Father Christmas, otherwise the entire trip would have been based on a falsehood. Jimmy had asked me, when he was about four years old, if Father Christmas really did exist. Unwilling to shatter his illusions at such an early age, but equally unwilling to tell him a lie, I put the ball back in his court.

'What do you think?' I asked him. 'Do you think there really is a Santa Claus?'

Jimmy wasn't very sure. He shrugged and shook his head.

'Well, Father Christmas is there for you if you believe in him,' I told him, but I saw quite clearly that he didn't. So long as he kept the truth to himself . . .

I expected him, the next Christmas, to be wise and superior to Martin, who was still a firm fan of Santa's. Oddly enough, though, Jimmy's faith in Santa's existence was absolute, and he had blotted out all doubts from his mind.

We had just fifteen hours to arrange visitors' passports, pack warm clothes, locate hats and gloves from last winter and make sure that Jimmy had everything he needed for four days. My place on the trip was never disputed. I didn't have one. Christopher couldn't go and somebody had to stay to look after him.

It was the only time I felt angry and resentful, not because I wanted to go to Sweden for four days, but because I wanted to see Jimmy's face as he saw Santa and all the other delights laid on for the trip. To be apart from him for four days meant those precious days were lost to me forever from a supply which was already severely limited. They were four days we could never replace or catch up on.

The party of about forty children, brothers and sisters and parents, flew to Oslo and then travelled into Sweden by coach. Having settled in a pleasant hotel in the Swedish lakes area, then visited Tonteland, which looked authentically like Santa's real home. Each child sat on his knee in his traditional wooden house while the real-life reindeer grazed outside, and trolls peeped out from little houses scattered round the grounds. Many of the children, like Jimmy, were very poorly, with little hope of living much longer, and Santa's gentleness and affectionate patience provided everyone with a touching experience. Even the adults said they could believe in a Father Christmas like the one they had met and the children were never in any doubt – except Martin. Paul overheard this conversation that night:

Martin: 'Do you think that really was Father Christmas, Jimmy?'

Jimmy: 'Well, they'd hardly bring us all this way if it wasn't.'

Martin: 'Yes they would, if the grown-ups were trying to do something to please us.'

The hotel and courier looked after the children very well, and there was a tour doctor and nurse travelling with the party.

Included in the excursions was a visit to a factory making traditional Swedish wooden horses, and an afternoon spent sledging in the snow on a nearby slope. Geraldine, Nick and Jordan were on the trip with Jordan's elder sister, and Jordan enjoyed sledging so much, he took a Swedish sledge home to Preston, where he waited all winter for snow, without success.

An hour-long video shot by a parent recorded Jimmy on several occasions; he and Martin found a fisherman fishing through a hole he had drilled in the ice on a frozen lake, and were filmed drilling their own hole.

There was also film of Jimmy leaving Tonteland on the coach, when Father Christmas boarded their bus and approached Jimmy for a quiet chat. Later in the trip the video camera caught Jimmy, quite unaware of being filmed, quietly picking up Paul's camera and surreptitiously taking a picture with it, just like Daddy.

The video even manages to record an impish Jimmy being mischievous to the courier as she handed out stockings full of little presents for the children on the last day of the visit. Each stocking was handed over in return for a kiss, but Jimmy plotted a way to avoid kissing this very large and ample lady by grabbing the stocking and dashing for his place on the floor.

It was a helpful and very enjoyable break for all three at a time of unimaginable stress and sorrow. The sorrow, if anything, was heightened by such a happy visit. Watching Jimmy having such fun, unaware that life was running out and that his time was so limited that each day had to be special, was very difficult for Paul to witness without feeling depressed. What made matters infinitely sadder was Jimmy's own zest for life and the way in which he accepted challenges and grabbed life with both hands.

My time passed in a mist back at home, longing to see Jimmy again, but not wishing his visit to flash by too fast. The loose covers on one sofa needed washing and mending, which took care of Sunday. At five that evening, the phone rang, and Jimmy's voice said 'Hi Mum!' from Sweden. It took the boys nearly twenty minutes to tell me what they were doing, and the call was the very best £20 we could have spent on anything.

On Monday evening I had been invited to go to a Greenpeace function with a friend, Janine, whose eldest son is now cured after contracting leukaemia four years before when they lived in Ambleside.

The parents of children with leukaemia in Cumbria had been asked to a hotel to meet the Greenpeace antinuclear campaigners from all over the world, who were having an international conference near Keswick.

That day they had visited Sellafield, but having been unwelcome guests inside the complex, they had instead toured the perimeter fence with a Geiger counter, registering unacceptably high levels of radiation.

The campaigners came from Europe, Australia, America and the Far East; the evening began with a speech and reception at which we all had to introduce ourselves, one by one, and state our reason for being there. I was there because of Jimmy, but even just thinking about his leukaemia made me feel very emotional. I waited my turn nervously as the Greenpeace experts each gave bold and articulate summaries of their work. At last the eyes of the sixty or seventy people there rested on me.

'I'm here because my seven-year-old son is dying of leukaemia,' I said. There was total silence throughout the large room. Nobody breathed. I looked down with tears blurring my vision, and felt very guilty. The information that I had told a room full of strangers was the very thing that I had never said outright to Jimmy himself. What would his reaction have been if he had heard me?

It was an interesting evening, talking to so many committed people from round the world. But the longest conversation I had was with a mother who had lost a five-year-old girl four years before. Her husband had worked at Sellafield and her little daughter had developed leukaemia. Treatment had been progressing well. Suddenly she caught chickenpox and was dead within two days. The grief of losing her daughter had not lessened with time, despite having two more children since her death. It made our future as a family seem even more hopeless.

It was more precious than ever before to take Jimmy and Martin in my arms in a huge hug when they arrived home at midnight from Sweden. Jimmy was first through the door; he burst in and ran straight to me. I had looked forward to his return with great longing because I knew that this time he would come back. Sooner or later, he would never come home, run through the door, and bring his love and vitality into our home.

Jimmy's meeting with the real Father Christmas was announced at school and in the Anglican church, at Christmas plays and carol services. It inspired people to look for the positive in a situation that was almost too negative to believe.

The next big day on the horizon was Jimmy's eighth and last birthday. He longed for the usual birthday treats, but we dreaded the arrival of yet more material presents. We had no room to put anything else with the sheer volume of toys and books. And the burden of always being the recipient instead of the donor was a humiliating one sometimes.

But our feelings were irrelevant and Jimmy's were the only ones that mattered. We wanted to give Jimmy the best birthday he had ever had. We invited all the friends that always came to his birthday parties, and a local hotel very kindly lent us their private pool for a splashing time of water games and competitions.

Everybody understood the sadness of this last birthday; Jimmy was so vivacious and excited, while we helped him to celebrate this special day knowing it would be his last. People flocked to our home throughout the day, from breakfast time to after midnight. We were never alone and we shared that extraordinary combination of happiness and sadness with all those who shared our love for Jimmy. Memories of that day in the beginning of December conjure up images of a sea of loving faces, and the sight of Jimmy, splashing about in the pool with his friends like any eight-year-old.

Among Jimmy's most treasured presents were a Paul Daniels box of magic tricks, a Lego Technic crane for him to make, and his own set of Monopoly; he also coveted a series of microscopes for children called PolyOptics, and in addition to these, there were games, toys and books and a tape of music by Smetana which he liked so much, he used it constantly on journeys to Pendlebury.

Just a few days after his birthday, he insisted on going out to spend some of his birthday money on yet more toys. There was hardly enough space to store his existing new toys and this obsession with spending money as if there was no tomorrow (which for him, of course, there wasn't), seemed greedy and selfish. Just because Jimmy was ill didn't exempt him from the occasional good telling-off.

'Do you realize just what trouble lots of people went to in order to make your birthday a happy one?' I asked him impatiently. 'These things don't just grow on trees, people had to spend their own money buying them for you. Doesn't that mean anything to you? Why do you want to go on and on, spending and buying? Where's it all going to end?'

How can anyone be cross with a child who is about to lose his happiness, his childhood, his potential, his world and his life? Yet this sort of disciplining probably made him feel safer than if we had suddenly stopped correcting him altogether. It was very important to behave absolutely normally with him and he would have felt very uneasy and anxious if nobody ever told him just how far he could go, and when he had pushed his luck too far.

One of the very best things about Jimmy was that he only ever needed things explained once before he had a perfect grasp of the facts or the situation. As soon as we had finished this conversation about material greed, he disappeared, only to return half an hour later with a sheepish grin on his face, and the information that there was a letter for us in our mail box downstairs. It was from Jimmy himself, and he had written a thank-you letter:

'Dear Mummy and Daddy, Thank you very very very much for my Lego Tecnic it was my best present. Thank you for the party and the swim you arranged, lots of love, Jimmy, XOXOXO'

A couple of weeks later, Jimmy swallowed his pacifist tendencies and joined the army for the day.

After careful planning between the commanding officer, and his godfather and godmother, David and Jean took Jimmy to the army's firing range at Warcop, near Appleby, and he became a Tank Commander for the day. The army let him fire a shell and even gave him the reusable brass casing and the small parachute marker as souvenirs. They dressed him for the occasion in an army beret, and he rode in a tank and was even offered the opportunity to drive the tank, but declined.

But life wasn't all sweetness and love. Jim's relationship with five-year-old Martin was getting more difficult. All his tiredness and bad temper were directed at Martin, and family relations were often quite strained as we faced Jimmy's death approaching closer by the day, but were forced to intervene on Martin's behalf to save him from Jimmy's anger.

We longed for a reconciliation between the two, and, in the absence of any definitive medical explanation for his illness, we even began to wonder if the depths of Jimmy's anger weren't partly to blame for his leukaemia returning. Could it really be true that an unhappy mind caused a sick body? Had Jimmy been unhappy all his life?

These thoughts haunted Paul, who was finding it increasingly hard to be the object of Jimmy's adoring hero worship, especially when this was at the expense of Martin, who would be pushed to one side. Jimmy never let Paul alone for a second when he was at home with us, and he had geared his own life and its interests and activities to make him more and more like his father.

Something had to be done to change Jimmy's fundamental outlook and convince him that it wasn't his brother's fault that Martin was as healthy and robust as Jimmy was weak and poorly. We wondered how efficient hypnotherapy might be and whether it could reactivate Jimmy's body to fight his cancer again.

Pendlebury regarded such therapy as alternative medicine and while they had no objections to it, they were yet to be convinced that it did any good, something they themselves had no time or resources to investigate. Most parents, they said, resort to alternative therapy at some stage of their child's illness but most of them are reluctant to mention it to the practitioners of conventional medicine in case it should be disapproved of. Nobody wants to annoy the busy people in whose hands the lives of their children rest.

We told the hospital that Jimmy would be having hypnotherapy and they wished us good luck. It was only a small step, but while we called it 'treatment' we could continue to believe that we hadn't given up hope, and that treatment was continuing. Jimmy was taking just one chemotherapy drug, to keep the cancer in check for as long as possible, including Christmas; this drug had never achieved a remission, but might there not be a first time, and might it not be Jimmy? At least it gave us a flickering hope to cling on to.

For just a couple of days, we put so much importance on hypnotherapy that we began to believe that making Jimmy's mind more peaceful might cure his body. Unrealistic though this was, it gave us a short break from despair and life seemed altogether better temporarily.

Bernadette, a doctor, hypnotherapist and mother of four, who is married to Ian, Jimmy's local GP, had known Jimmy all his life, and kindly offered to try to help him defuse his inner anger and find peace. Jimmy was sometimes uncomfortable and reluctant at the start of the session, but Bernadette's gentle storytelling lulled him into a happier mood, and he was always smiling with contentment after she had gone.

Jimmy would curl up on the bed; this is where we envisaged he would be when he could no longer get up any more, so it would be a good place in which to learn how to escape from his physical pain into mental calm. Bernadette was thinking ahead to the time when Jimmy's illness might become very painful and she tried to suggest ways in which he himself could control his pain.

Although his power to control his pain turned out to be limited, because once bad pain had taken hold he was too upset to think logically and calmly, the sessions were nevertheless very valuable. They made him feel happy and he loved Bernadette with her gentle voice, lively eyes and beautiful face who made his mind feel unworried with her inventive stories about the magic unicorn who had the power to take away suffering.

Pendlebury's original prediction that Jimmy might not live to see New Year was off target. The chemotherapy drug had banished the blast cells from his blood, confining them to his bone marrow, and though they could break through and multiply at any time, the drug had borrowed a little quality time for Jimmy, just ready for Christmas.

# ✳

# SEVEN

# Time Running Out

A fortnight before Christmas, we went down to Pendlebury for a clinic visit, dreading the day, which couldn't be long, when the doctors would send us home for good, unable to treat Jimmy any more.

Our links with the rambling old hospital, staffed with so many kind, down-to-earth familiar faces, had become very close; in months past their role had been active, but now it was passive. At first they had been able to throw Jimmy a lifebelt as he threatened to drown, and he had clutched at it and kept his head above water. But the tide had turned suddenly and dangerously, sweeping him beyond reach, and the lifebelt was no longer enough to keep him afloat. They united with us as helpless watchers on the shore, unable to prevent this tragedy as it rolled towards its inevitable denouement.

Despite our acceptance that Jimmy's life had only a short future, the success with which the doctors treated him during this month brought us renewed hope and more uncertainty. It was not unusual that the chemotherapy drug had contained the leukaemia back in his bone marrow; it wasn't even significant enough to justify another bone marrow test to check there had been no last-minute remission. But we couldn't help hoping that Christmas might bring a miracle. If Jimmy's body had behaved so unpredictably at every stage of his treatment, was it not possible that it might do so again, but this time in his favour?

The clinic visit was cheerful, with Jimmy displaying his new Paul Daniels magic tricks to the nurses. There were shrieks of laughter as he teased them, and, ironically, many of his tricks were based on illusion, much as the visits themselves were.

The reality was the consultant's expressionless face and his failure to comment in any way on Jimmy's strength and vitality, which were quite irrelevant to his actual condition. Jimmy's rosy cheeks, bright eyes and impish energy would normally have elicited the approval of the clinic staff, but nobody ever said: 'Doesn't he look well!' as they might have done before. A careless comment like that, said casually and with no intention of making a medical evaluation, might have given us cause to hope. But the staff were careful not to provide any grounds whatsoever on which new hope could be built.

No Christmas, however well prepared or lavish, could have been special enough to mark our two family milestones: Christy's first Christmas and Jimmy's last. So we chose to have an ordinary sort of Christmas. Jimmy and I went to the junior school play, held in the church where only a few weeks later his own funeral would take place. That night we walked together through the darkness, hurrying in our excitement, and sat close to one another so we could whisper about the production and all the people he knew taking part. It was both comical and sad, as we enjoyed the light-hearted play but missed Jimmy's participation in it. He had become a self-conscious observer of the life he should have been enjoying.

Although we lived each day as it came, naturally our thoughts tended to wander towards the horror of the future as we tried to brace ourselves to guide our young son gently through it, right to the very end.

The church, that evening of the play, was alive with the presence of young, bright, energetic and healthy children but the thought of death and funerals was never very far away. It was hard to banish the mental picture of the small coffin that would come to rest in front of the altar; but that night he was still at my side, his head touching my arm, his foot kicking mine to communicate some small detail I might have missed.

The only way to live cheerfully through these extraordinary weeks was to accept the inevitable and live life on a normal, mundane level to prevent the true horror breaking through and affecting our behaviour. We took our lead, as we so often did, from Jimmy. He faced each day as if he were a normal child, looking forward to Christmas, helping to post the cards, decorate the tree and wrap the presents. He had the feelings and reactions of an ordinary child and it was just his body which had become abnormal. With such sturdy good sense, the example Jimmy set us gave us no choice but to hide our true feelings and behave as he did.

As always on Christmas Eve, the children were allowed to choose our guests for a candlelit dinner after Christingle. They chose David and Jean and their entire family, which meant that with grannies included, there would be more than a dozen people sitting down to dinner with us on the most magical evening in the year.

Preparing food for so many gave me the chance to miss Christingle

in church. It was such a moving occasion to see hundreds of excited
children helping to light the world with their oranges and candles, it
would be extremely hard not to cry at the contrast between the youthful
congregation, just setting out on life, and Jimmy, equally young and
hopeful, just setting out on his downhill journey towards death.

The evening was noisy and very jolly, just as we had planned, to
help us live entirely in the present rather than dwell on the sadness
that lay ahead. The presence of a baby in the family at Christmas always
helps to bring the Christmas message to life and we rejoiced in Christy's
survival and celebrated his strength and tenacity, without which he
would not have been with us. It was very significant to Jimmy that
this particular Christmas was Christy's first; he showed his baby brother
the manger he had helped to make, and the lights on the Christmas
tree, and moved his little chair to just the right spot for Christy to see
the sparkling tinsel catch the light. But despite the mood of conviviality
throughout Christmas, it was impossible not to feel a sombreness in
us all just behind the jovial exterior.

Jimmy hated to admit how frightened he was at the notion of Father
Christmas breaking into his house; he was always afraid of burglars or
intruders and there was little to separate Santa's unorthodox arrival
through the skylight from anybody else who might choose to enter
our house, undetected, in the night. It mattered little that he now
knew Father Christmas, and that he was the very same gentle,
sympathetic man on whose knee Jimmy had perched. He remained
nervous and unwilling to sleep on Christmas Eve night.

The skylight was left open to prevent Father Christmas from coming
to harm trying to descend one of our blocked-up chimneys, and the
children wrote their names on the empty stockings, hung them up and
tried to sleep.

It was well past midnight when Paul crept in to make his first attempt
at retrieving the stockings, but Jimmy was too restless for him to be
able to risk anything. So we went to bed and set the alarm for three
o'clock. About two, Christy woke for a feed and seizing the
opportunity to grab the empty stockings, I crept into the boys' room.
Just as I unhooked them from the bedpost, there was a flash of
lightning and heavy rolls of thunder as a sudden freak storm broke
almost overhead. By some small miracle, Jimmy remained asleep and
the magic of Christmas unbroken; and for one little boy, Father
Christmas lives on forever, his reputation intact, the thrill of his visits

never diminished by Jimmy having to grow up and discover the truth.

We were joined on Christmas Day by Granny Anna and Miss Thompson. Mary Thompson has been a friend to children all her life as a teacher, headmistress, and special companion to any child privileged enough to spend time playing chess with her at home, or throwing sticks for Settle, her dog.

Both Jimmy and Martin were fortunate to be among Miss Thompson's many friends and spent entire afternoons enjoying Kipling or Pooh Bear with her, or learning chess moves or solitaire, or chasing round the garden with Settle. When Jimmy became ill, Mary provided Martin with an anchor of security, and together with Granny Anna, the two elderly ladies brought order and routine to his chaotic life, taking and fetching him from school, and always being there for him when Paul and I were not.

It was Jimmy's idea to invite Mary. We thought she might refuse if we asked her, but we knew that Jimmy's request would never be rejected. She very kindly agreed to share what she too knew was Jimmy's last Christmas.

It was a perfect day. There were surprises, great excitement and pleasure, love and laughter; the children were never too noisy, the adults never irritated. The morning was devoted to opening stockings and presents, and with Christmas dinner timed to fit in with Christy's feed and the Queen's speech, the hour before lunch was set aside for indoor fireworks. This surprise for the boys came from their Great Aunt Fra, an auntie to Paul and an expert at treats and surprises. Jimmy and Martin each received a special card chosen by Fra, every month by post, with a little extra pocket money inside. But instead of buying toys for Christmas, Fra followed our line of creating an experience instead and her indoor fireworks provided an exciting diversion, with small explosions, occasional minor volcanos and plenty of acrid smoke.

The fireworks were just one of several outstanding things about Christmas which made Jimmy think it was the best one he had ever had. A month later, Paul made a tape recording with Jimmy during which they talked about the past year. What had he thought about Christmas, Paul asked.

'The best one ever,' he replied emphatically. 'It was the best one because Granny and Miss Thompson were there, too.'

My fortieth birthday, three days after Christmas, coincided neatly with an important day for Jimmy.

Jimmy had to be eight years old before he could join the Cubs, but by the time his birthday came in December, he was already too tired and weak to go to the Cub hut every week, so his enrolment had never taken place.

In spite of this, the Scout Association, who knew about Jimmy and how hard he had fought for life, wanted to reward his efforts while he was still able to appreciate the importance of such an award.

The award the Scouts suggested was the Baden Powell Award for Fortitude; work had been going on in the background to authenticate it and letters had been exchanged between local Scouts and head-quarters. Jimmy knew nothing of this until the week before; and no award could be made until he had been officially enrolled.

The date chosen happened to be my fortieth birthday, a day which progressed from forty to fortitude.

The uniform we had inherited in a bag of jumble the year before was made for an altogether bigger Cub. The green jumper reached Jimmy's knees, but the cap was big enough to cover his baldness perfectly. He was feeling very tired and irritable after his enrolment in the morning and fortunately he failed to appreciate the honour being paid him by the presence of such important Scouting leaders at the cere-mony in the afternoon, otherwise he might have felt too shy to appear.

It was ironic that although Jimmy accepted the Fortitude award with shyness and modesty, the only thing he really wanted in life was to be an ordinary Cub, lacking all qualities of fortitude but well qualified in mischief-making. But all his family were extremely proud that the Scouts should recognize his personal bravery and courage and give it public recognition and praise while he was still well enough to understand.

It wasn't the sort of birthday present most mothers would want to receive; but it was my best birthday ever, and the Cubs who attended the ceremony in our studio came prepared to make a whole birthday cake disappear in just five minutes.

Observers watching us that evening, drinking champagne in a restaurant, laughing and eating with friends, might have thought us quite unfeeling to be celebrating a birthday while our son was left at home, with only weeks to live. But it was just these terrible circum-stances which made it more important than ever to celebrate something frivolous for just an hour or two before turning again to the frightening reality of Jimmy's short future.

Christmas week was a traditional happy mix of visiting and being visited. New Year brought a new decade, and as everybody around us invested hope in the future, we tried not to look forward to grief and emptiness, but stay in the present while Jimmy was still with us, or look back to a better past when he was younger and healthy. It was with great reluctance we left the eighties, when Jimmy had been with us almost throughout. We didn't want to travel into the nineties without him.

It had been two weeks since Jimmy was last checked at Pendlebury. His blood test before Christmas had given us a small bonus because no leukaemia cells had been detected in his blood. The cancer was still contained in his bone marrow and this had given us the tiniest of flickering hopes that the only drug which Jimmy was still taking might achieve its very first miracle and produce an unexpected remission.

We kept this small hope quietly hidden so as not to raise the hopes of those around us; but in the end it was without foundation. The thumb-prick test in the New Year detected the blast cells circulating in his bloodstream again. The drug was becoming less and less effective in the path of the advancing cancer.

We approached hospital visits in these weeks without fear; we thought there could be no more bad news to give us that we didn't already know. The news that the cancer was winning again hit us unexpectedly hard, proving the resilience of the human capacity to hope. Thinking that Jimmy still had a little quality time remaining, the doctor prescribed the same delaying drug for another week.

However, it was becoming noticeable that Jimmy needed a blood transfusion. He was increasingly anaemic, breathless, pale, listless and tired. Whenever he ran anywhere, he would get sudden painful headaches; and it was no good advising him to walk, not run. Children of that age run everywhere to fetch the things they want. But he was adamant that he didn't want a transfusion, even if it could be done on an outpatient basis. He said it was too uncomfortable.

It was as if he suddenly knew that a transfusion was no longer helping him to stay alive; it had lost its life-giving properties and wouldn't be able to make him feel better any more, so why waste what time he had left doing something boring and uncomfortable?

Perhaps we should have recognized his greater wisdom. He grudgingly agreed to have a transfusion, which, it transpired, may well have been responsible for prolonging his life beyond quality and into pain during the next few weeks.

Despite increasing tiredness and decreasing stamina, Jimmy filled each day with frenzied activity. Whatever he chose to do could never be put off until he felt better. He drew and painted, photographed, catalogued his collection of slides, ran his trains and made inventive Lego models. Each weekend, the children played with Becky and Jonathan, and we sat back and marvelled at Jimmy's energy, even wondered if some mistake had been made and it was some other child who had relapsed and was now slowly dying.

To love a dying child requires great courage, and Karen and John and their children fulfilled their commitment not only to Jimmy, but to us all as they shared those anxious weeks with us. Each Sunday the children played, we expected it to be the very last for Jimmy, and each week he struggled on. One Sunday he danced a wild sort of jig with John to the ragtime music he loved so much, and another Sunday he raced round the adventure playground in the park swinging from the ropes and hiding in the wooden fort before collapsing exhausted back in his buggy to be wheeled home. He knew just how to make the most of his limited strength, and chose only his favourite activities on which to expend it.

One of the things the four children liked doing best of all together was arranging a sort of ghost train which the grown-ups had to submit to one by one. It was an ingenious idea and involved the children in dressing up, daubing face paints on each other and creating a sort of play making full use of loaded water pistols, noisy toy-gun caps and fake spiders as props. Our narrow passage was plunged into darkness, and the adult victim had to walk past the four doors from behind which the children would leap out with various unpleasant or frightening surprises. The grown-ups always got wet, usually screamed and sometimes ran for cover and the children never tired of this entertainment.

The highlight of Jimmy's last active month was reached when he drove a fully loaded British Rail express passenger train at 110 miles an hour from Oxenholme to Lancaster one wet Saturday afternoon.

Janine, who had already fixed it for Jimmy to go to London with Greenpeace and have his own games computer, rang British Rail and told them that Jimmy loved trains and that he had very little time left to enjoy them. Within two days, it was arranged for him to spend an afternoon on the railways and ride in the cab of an express, and we were all invited to accompany him.

It wasn't just any train that BR laid on for Jimmy to drive. When we arrived at Oxenholme Station as directed, it was the fastest, newest locomotive which had been moved up to Glasgow the day before specially so it could be on its return journey at precisely the right moment for Jimmy to climb aboard the cab and get behind the controls.

It must have taken quite a lot of fixing for British Rail to allow Jimmy to take the crowded train up to 110 miles an hour between Oxenholme and Lancaster. As the train speed increased to its maximum, we could imagine the bewildered passengers and the slopped coffee behind us; then it was Martin's turn at the controls, after which the driver brought the train and its passengers safely to a halt at Lancaster, where we disembarked.

All afternoon we were looked after most courteously by senior management, who took us next on a Pacer from Lancaster to Barrow, travelling across the Kent Estuary by Morecambe Bay. Then Jimmy's energy started to flag. He was weak and very tired, and had to be carried between trains.

At Barrow the station buffet produced hot chips and Coca-Cola while British Rail held up the train's departure. Jimmy revived sufficiently to take over the controls of another powerful locomotive from Lancaster back to Oxenholme at 100 miles an hour. Martin was never excluded and his face beamed at the importance of applying the brakes for the next stop.

All four drivers that we met had been told about Jimmy in advance. They responded with kindness and compassion and it was the most exciting afternoon any young railway enthusiast could wish for. It was also Jimmy's last big adventure and took place not a moment too soon. Only a week later, he would have been too weak to enjoy it; as it was, the excitement was almost too much for him and he arrived home completely exhausted.

Jimmy rarely made special requests or demands on us to do any particular thing. But if he did, we tried very hard at this stage of his life to answer his wishes. Although his musical tastes were varied, he loved the jollity of traditional ragtime jazz, and often played tapes and records of two local performers, the banjo player Chris Sands and pianist Patrick Sykes who performed ragtime under the professional name of The Edwardian Duo.

Jimmy wanted to hear them playing live, but their concert bookings were too far away for him to travel. So we decided as Jimmy couldn't go to them, we would ask the Duo to come to us and play a programme of their music specially for Jimmy at home in our living room.

Jimmy had often seen the Duo and knew them well, because Paul took the publicity shots for their record covers and leaflets. No concert at home could be complete without photographs and Jimmy set everything up to record and shoot the event in full, just like a smaller version of his father at work.

The Duo came expecting to play just two or three numbers, but they were kept hard at it for nearly an hour playing requests and encores. They had assumed Jimmy would be almost bedridden, and that he would sit quietly and listen. Instead, he leapt frenetically from tape machine to camera, checking the recording levels and setting up his next shot throughout the performance. He was using Paul's big camera which is not automatic; and we both felt just a little embarrassed at this young poseur strutting about, stepping over wires to get himself the best shot while the music was being played.

The Duo came specifically to answer a request from a dying child and were surprised at how well Jimmy looked. He was dying, but not beaten yet. Our uneasiness at the way he had copied Paul changed to admiration when we saw the superb pictures he had taken. Far from being an exhibitionist, he had simply been working very hard with a camera that needed brains to make it function. The results were excellent. He already had the makings of the good, competent photographer we had hoped would eventually succeed his father. We were filled with a sense of futility at the waste of his bright little life and quick brain.

Friends continued to visit; they came apprehensively to say a quiet 'goodbye' and were astonished at their visits becoming occasions for happy sociability round the dinner table in our big living room.

For Jimmy, it was normal life continuing; for us, it was joy and sadness combined. One Friday evening, by secret prearrangement, the doorbell rang and Jimmy answered it to find his much-loved cousins, Matthew and Jonathan, on the doorstep, just arrived three hundred miles from Poole with Cate and their father, Gunnar. The joke backfired a little – it was very dark and wet and Jimmy couldn't see clearly who was there, so he didn't recognize them.

Jonathan and Jimmy drew birds together. Matthew, who had

recently passed his driving test, took Jimmy out in the car or wheeled him down to the park in his buggy. There were games of Trivial Pursuit, shopping expeditions and time for them to admire and cuddle Christy for the first time.

Thanks to Jimmy, we have a precious souvenir from this happy weekend when the four cousins were together for the very last time; using the family camera, Jimmy photographed us all through the two days. The only person missing from the pictures is Jimmy who was too busy to think of including himself.

Cate and I had never really faced Jimmy's illness and death together. The initial shock had left her very shaken and frightened, and it was a subject neither of us knew how to begin to discuss on the phone, or in the rare and brief moments we were alone together without any of the children. It had been impossible to travel to Poole for our usual happy visits since Jimmy's diagnosis, and we had never shared our grief together except once when we were out shopping and I suddenly started to cry in the street.

This was yet another family occasion with no chance for Cate and me to be alone for long enough to talk about Jimmy's death. The things that we both wanted to say so much were left unsaid but the familiar closeness I needed on many occasions was there. Perhaps we would both have been too upset to be much support to each other, and if our emotional controls broke down we neither of us would have been any use supporting our respective families. To Jimmy himself, Cate was the zaniest, most inventive, most original of aunts, who hid Smarties in his wellingtons and saw how his mind was working almost before he did, and he loved her with the same intensity and devotion as I will always do. Never mind that we were unable to share depths of our grief together; instead, her adopted role was often as safety valve, comic relief and welcome normality. The weekend over, Jonathan and Matthew hugged Jimmy goodbye without showing him their tears.

The next visit to Pendlebury was the last and confirmed that Jimmy's leukaemia cells had multiplied so fast that treatment was not appropriate any more. The news came as no surprise and it was almost a relief to feel that we would be free of the hospital for ever.

Pendlebury had changed unavoidably in our minds from being the friendly place that saved Jimmy's life to being the noisy, chaotic, impersonal surroundings in which we received nothing but bad news.

Now that nobody there could help us make Jimmy better any longer, it was time to go home. We hoped to be able to make Jimmy's eventual death a family affair at home, though not without Pendlebury's constant support and expertise reaching out to us there. This never actually materialized and our distance from the hospital added to our feelings of isolation and certainly made immediate hospital support an impractical proposition for staff.

Jimmy himself was glad to be free of these visits. His experiences during the last few days of intensive chemotherapy in autumn had left lasting fear of being in hospital.

The last transfusion had brought little improvement in Jimmy's condition. He waited patiently for a couple of days to feel more lively, expecting his new blood to work at any time. But when nothing changed, he never questioned why; he seemed to accept the slow deterioration he had already begun to notice.

When he needed to rest more during each day, the time was right to make changes in the children's sleeping arrangements. We had anticipated the need to swap things round, but it was important to choose just the right moment, so that it would seem like an exciting, novel idea and not a retrogressive step towards the day when Jimmy would never get up again.

I suggested to him that if we moved Christy's little cot out of the nursery, Jimmy could have this room to himself, leaving Martin alone in their old room. Both boys welcomed the change with genuine excitement, but it was Jimmy's enthusiasm and pleasure that was so touching, it was almost too sad to watch.

We moved his bunk bed into the nursery and borrowed an adjustable table from Paul's studio to fit across the bed. Jimmy collected lots of treasures to store on the shelves I had cleared for him, and brought in a few of his favourite books.

Requesting that I should reread books I had read to the children a couple of years before was one of the little ways in which Jimmy had started to regress back towards a safer time in his life, when Mummy and Daddy had been able to take care of all the bad things that frightened him.

But although a little boy again in some respects, he was still fascinated by technology and among the essential items in his room were two tape recorders and a bank of recording equipment. His interest dated back to the time when we used to make audiovisual slide shows. He loved copying tapes, making his own recordings and checking the sound and recording levels, just like Daddy did.

When all his things were in place, he babbled on happily about having his very own room for the first time in three years.

'I can keep all my best things in here, and I can draw birds on my table and I can come in here and have a rest on my bed whenever I want a bit of peace and quiet and it's just what I need, though of course I'll have to give it back to Christy when I'm better, probably about the time I go back to school,' he said. But when he thought about going back to school, he fell very silent and the moment of happy excitement was gone. He had momentarily forgotten something that he had already silently guessed – that he wouldn't ever be going back to school.

Only a few minutes after this conversation, I tried to take photographs of both the boys sitting on Jimmy's bed, surrounded by his recorders and books. Jimmy always smiled for the camera, but not that day. The face that looks at us from his exciting new room is frowning and unhappy.

It was impossible to know the right thing to say about things like going back to school. One day he actually said he felt as though he was never going back, and I couldn't deny it, though I didn't confirm it either. He had been anxious about all the school work he was missing, and it was hard to tell him that it would never matter without telling him exactly why.

To say something like, 'Oh, you'll soon catch up,' would have been a lie, and might have given him hope that he would return to be with his friends one day. He hated any sort of dishonesty when dealing with his treatment.

We never made false promises, but sometimes it was necessary to answer questions in a very general or ambiguous sort of way. We never lied to Jimmy; but if we needed to hang on to even the faintest hope, so too did he, and to be told that he would never return to school lacked all hope.

But the excitement of having his own room had temporarily made him forget that his life at school was over. I felt unutterably sad. I don't know how we controlled the tears hour by hour, and day by day over the months. It must have been a combination of practice and control, so that tears were shed quietly, and out of sight. It was a great tension in our lives, never to allow our natural emotions to be fully expressed. When people frequently asked, 'How do you manage?' I always answered that it was Jimmy himself who led us, who dictated the pace of life; and if he felt calm and undramatic, then so did we.

We never knew at what stage he must have realized that his treatment had failed. He would never have forgotten the talk we had together in September and that he only had one chance, and that if it failed, he would be leaving this world to go to Heaven. My anxiety about how much I should tell Jimmy came to a climax one day, and I rang a children's hospice and even Great Ormond Street Hospital in my search for some counselling and guidance. Nobody could offer us any help.

We didn't want to tell him outright that he had failed, because he hadn't. It was the treatment which had failed. There were various conflicting pieces of advice which did nothing to solve the problem of whether we should tell him that he was going to die soon. His consultant warned that if we didn't tell him, he would ask directly. Children always did, he said. In fact Jimmy never did ask directly. Gradually the truth dawned on him and his question, when it came, was asking me to confirm what he already suspected.

In any case it was too soon to say anything about death at this stage. Jimmy was still wringing every living moment out of every day, wasting not a second as he flitted from one activity to another.

He would be drawing, or painting, or recording, or bread-baking. He didn't do things in a half-hearted way; he entered wholly and entirely into whatever was on offer. One day, he started to print with Elin's mother, Pam, using sponges and huge sheets of paper on the floor. This rapidly became a hand- and foot-print experience, and he flung his clothes off, soaked large areas of his body in bright poster paint and set about experimenting. Later he sat on the bathroom window sill wearing only his pants, washing his painted feet in the wash basin, grinning boldly for the camera. We were frightened that if we told him outright that he was soon going to die, we might deprive him of all the fun and love of life he still had in him. The idea sounded right in theory, but was quite wrong for Jimmy at this time.

One afternoon, he thumped, bashed and battered a lump of clay until he was panting, and then made coil pots and little flowers. Every day there were at least two games of Monopoly. The board was the only little space left in the world in which he could succeed, and winning became painfully important.

He had watched friends playing and learned clever, sharp ways of acquiring property and bankrupting others. His ploy was to buy up Mayfair and Park Lane, put hotels on them and wait until we fell in his trap. If another player happened to buy one of these first, Jimmy would angrily refuse to play on. Under normal circumstances, we would have lectured him on fair play and the pleasure being in playing, not winning, but it was obvious that his aggressive play was helping to express the anger he felt and nobody ever resented his need to be a Monopoly tycoon.

Jimmy's home tutoring continued whenever we both felt in the mood, and one morning we chose to think about music. We listened to Bach and Beethoven, but it was Mozart he enjoyed most of all. He had heard passages of Mozart in Paul's audiovisual shows, and he was a composer Jimmy could always recognize by the style, even if he didn't know the particular piece.

One piece he did know well was the middle movement of the Clarinet Concerto, and we listened to this slow, sad music so we could describe to each other the mental images it inspired. Jimmy fetched his globe and put it on the table. At the end, we agreed that it was probably the most perfect music ever written, and Jimmy described how it reminded him of the world, spinning slowly and infinitely in space.

The next time I heard the piece, it was being played at his funeral. On fine nights now, when we can see the stars, I search the sky as if his soul might be up there somewhere and I hope very hard that he isn't lost in the vastness of space.

Another morning, we talked very seriously about the ecological problems facing the world. We drew diagrams to illustrate the greenhouse effect and the damage being done to the ozone layer by CFC emissions.

Jimmy not only understood, but set about suggesting a few small ways in which we could help improve matters by changing the way we all live. He drew bad eco habits on one side of the paper, and put a big X through each example, and countered it with a drawing of the right action opposite. He chose to contrast a car carrying one passenger, with a train carrying five hundred on the other side; there was an electric light left burning wastefully countered opposite by somebody switching off lights and saving power. The work was neatly done, with much ingenuity and more care than usual.

Although Jimmy was still up early each morning, he was becoming more tired each day, and we could see that his body was not keeping pace with his mind any more. One day, amongst the post, was a card sending us a message of condolence on Jimmy's death. Fortunately it wasn't a day he went to fetch the post, so he didn't open it himself. It had been sent by a very kind old lady who had known Jimmy well as a little baby, and she had become confused by somebody else's death in the town, thinking it was Jimmy's.

The arrival of the card was bizarre while Jimmy was still up and running, but we laughed it off, and hid it from him. That day, he bought a light for his prized red BMX bicycle, and insisted that it had to be tested in the dark. His chosen cycle route passed the flat of the card sender, and we hoped she wouldn't choose that moment to look out and see a ghost pedalling by. Unfortunately his test run exhausted him, and he never wanted to ride his bike again.

There was nothing Jimmy liked better than spending money, but even a shopping spree was now too tiring for him.

Karen shared his enthusiasm for a good spend, and they departed with their purses one morning to a local gift shop that sold unusual novelties and toys.

It was the last time Jimmy went shopping, and he bought a little wooden pop gun with a tiny cork on a string, and a joke pair of false teeth which acted as pincers, and could grab or pick up small items. He spent the very last of his money buying individual bubblebaths for me and he chose strawberry- and lemon-shaped ones, and a little car like an old VW.

Although the effort of all this exhausted him so much that he collapsed on his bed with a headache for half an hour, he soon recovered, and teased us all with the false teeth. Christy was sitting in his little chair playing with a rattle, when Jimmy crept behind, grabbed the toy in his pincers, and dangled it in front of Christy's face. The baby made an unfamiliar noise, a bit like choking, and burst into giggles. Jimmy repeated the joke endlessly and always raised a laugh out of Christy. He was very pleased to be the first person to make his baby brother laugh.

One sunny, warm Friday in February, I decided to take advantage of the weather and have an outing to the park with all three boys. It was something we had done hundreds of times before, but never quite like this. I wheeled Jimmy in the big buggy, carried the baby on my back in the carrier and Martin cycled along on his bike.

We walked round the beautiful park, past all the favourite hiding places, past the big slab of rock that Jimmy could climb at only two, past the adventure playground and past the river where the two boys had played so happily during the hot weather the summer before.

We stopped by the thick bushes, where Jimmy and Martin used to stumble through the undergrowth, climbing trees and alarming the birds. I hoped he might be able to play for a little while. He climbed reluctantly out of the buggy, walked a few steps, but gave up immediately, too breathless to stand any more. The fine day was starting to turn sour on him, and he urgently needed to go home. We started out briskly but Martin tripped while wheeling his bike and grazed his chest and tummy. He was bleeding and wailing, which made Christopher cry too. The walk home was a pathetic sight, with me wheeling Jimmy in the buggy with one hand and the bike with the other, carrying the screaming baby in the backpack and dragging Martin who decided he couldn't and wouldn't walk. The illusion we had tried to foster, that life was normal despite everything, was shattered once and for all.

Although Jimmy's activities were becoming more limited every day, it was the onset of pain which finally changed his life from being active to inactive. It was not only the pain itself but the strong drugs needed to control it which robbed him of the desire to do anything except lie, half asleep, during the last few weeks of his life.

The last active weekend was livened up by a flying visit from Cate and Gunnar, who came this time without Matthew and Jonathan. The very last time Jimmy left the house, it was to drive to Kendal at over 80 miles an hour in Gunnar's car, on Sunday morning, to have a burger and French fries at McDonald's. No last outing could have been more fitting and appropriate.

Jimmy's pain started that evening. He tried to eat his dinner and couldn't, lying on the floor at my feet complaining that his tummy hurt.

Pendlebury explained that his pain would certainly be coming from his swollen spleen, and next day it became rapidly worse. We'd always had a joke about Mummy's healing hands being able to magic any hurt away, and he lay on the sofa begging me to rub the pain better. My hands felt rough, so I rubbed them with baby oil and massaged the place where it hurt.

It was at this point, when Jimmy's pain started, that Ian, his GP, started to call daily and entered his life in its final phase. We had decided weeks before that it was unnecessary to worry Jimmy with regular visits whilst he was still out and about and active; and although he hadn't seen much of Ian while Pendlebury supervised his treatment, we discussed every development most carefully with him and he was ready at any time to bring us the constant back-up and support that he knew he would need, caring for Jimmy at home. His visits were never hurried, and he always managed to sense the prevailing mood and respond to it sensitively, bringing comfort when we were despairing, and cheerfulness when we felt like smiling. His unhappy job wasn't made any easier by Jimmy's fear and distrust of doctors by this stage, but nobody could have given him more dedicated caring than Ian did.

Morphine was prescribed immediately, but at first it did very little to ease the pain. Whenever he felt the pain begin, Jimmy wouldn't let me take my hands off his tummy and I spent hours massaging him front and back with oil. The warmth and love comforted him, but it wasn't a very efficient method of pain control.

It was half term and we had planned to take the children with Jonathan and Becky to the cinema nearby to see a film called *Honey, I Shrunk the Kids!* Jimmy was excited at the prospect, and I wheeled him the short distance in his buggy and carried him up the stairs. Derek Hook, friend and cinema owner, had put comfortable chairs in a special little gallery over the main part of the cinema so that we could be private and special.

But as soon as the first short cartoon started, Jimmy began to wriggle on my knee and writhe with pain. I made light of it, hoping the film would take his mind off his discomfort, but within five minutes he was begging to be taken home so that he could stretch out and make the pain in his tummy better. It was always in the same place, on his left side just underneath his ribs.

I realized how serious he was and carried him down the steep stairs, put him in the buggy and ran wildly home through the rain, trying not to bounce him about too much. It was half an hour before he would let me take my hand away from the site of his pain.

'Why do I get all the bad luck?' he asked again.

On Friday morning, four days later, he was pain-free and confident enough to want to try for the cinema again, only to find that the film had been changed that day. 'Why, oh why do I always get all the bad luck?' he repeated.

I usually managed to stay outwardly calm through these periods of pain, because it was important to prevent fear and panic in him, which would have made the pain very much worse.

By staying calm, even casual, I wanted him to think that if Mummy was there, as usual, as I had been all his life, talking to him normally and reassuringly, accepting the pain as nothing particularly surprising, then he would accept it as well, and not become too distressed.

For a mother to accept pain in her child as normal seemed utterly contradictory. Mothers fight for their children, champion their cause, protect and make better; yet I was not fighting any longer for my son. Would he think I had changed sides? I knew my role was to guide him gently and as painlessly as possible down the road towards death, and yet I always felt how absurd and nonsensical this was for a mother to do.

My strongest feelings of guilt were that I could not fight for his life any more. 'Do not go gentle into that good night,' urged the poet Dylan Thomas, yet I was aiding and abetting a gentle death to take place. I couldn't even rage at the 'dying of the light', as the poem advocated. Jimmy's light was already almost out, his body spoiled and blighted. There was no future on earth for it after leukaemia had laid waste.

The recurring pain around his spleen continued throughout that first week. Within a few days, the spleen had become swollen, making his stomach look bloated on one side. But he did not want to lie in bed, and instead he occupied his favourite sofa so he could still manage to play the occasional game of Monopoly.

Jimmy's friend and pastor, Lewis, saw that the time had come for Jimmy to become used to his frequent presence and our conversations often led purposely to thoughts about Heaven. Jimmy listened, but didn't join in. Instead he drew his vision of the road to Heaven. It was a very geometrical diagram of straight lines meeting at one point of soft yellow light. The lines were leading to Heaven. Jimmy described his journey through life like walking down our passage towards his bedroom, where a soft yellow light shone in the warm room at the far end. Inside his room was a big armchair that was so comfortable, he would sit in it and never feel aches or tiredness again.

Playing Monopoly required stamina and concentration Jimmy no longer had. Instead he devoted all his passions to a new game called Pass the Pigs. The game consisted of two little pigs which had to be thrown up in the air, and the position they landed in determined the score.

Suddenly, one Friday afternoon during his umpteenth round of Pass the Pigs, a bad pain started that made him moan and cry. He was breathless and his heart was beating so rapidly, I was alarmed enough to fetch Paul. The episodes of pain were a new dimension of the illness and one that we were still learning about, but there was always the chance that Jimmy might die, very suddenly, during a period of pain. Pendlebury had warned us that anything might happen including sudden death. The morphine doses were being increased all the time, but still hadn't matched the degree of pain to be controlled.

The pain passed that evening, and Jimmy suddenly became very talkative and euphoric as I lay in our bed with him. It was the first night that he had moved into our bedroom to sleep. It seemed the natural place for him to be, as close as he could be to us all night, where we could love and comfort him just as we had when he was a baby. The double bed gave him more space to stretch out and our bigger bedroom gave us more room to nurse him during the day.

But this did mean that only one of us could sleep comfortably with Jimmy, and we were resigned to being separated again just at a time when we most needed each other. From that night on, we took it in turns to sleep with Jimmy, though he took the final decision as to who it should be. For the first week or two, it was often Paul, but as Jimmy's needs increased during the night, it was me that he requested. Paul slept very heavily and was notoriously difficult to rouse, and Jimmy usually needed attention every couple of hours.

Jimmy and I talked for three hours that first night. Our conversations about Heaven with Lewis had led Jimmy to the understanding that he was going there very soon, and I agreed that I thought he was.

Instead of feeling frightened, he became very excited at the prospect of getting there before us, and said he would ask God to help him to build a model railway for Paul, which would be ready and waiting for when Paul arrived. There were a few problems on his mind regarding time and separation, but we resolved most of them together.

From midnight until three, he chatted on, sometimes excited, sometimes agitated. It was time for him to complete unfinished business and to say all the important things that he wanted to tell me before it was time to say goodbye. We talked about how much we loved each other and he said there were no words possible, or numbers big enough, to express his love. We hugged and cuddled and cried together.

At last he said: 'When I go to Heaven, that's if I am going to Heaven, if I do actually go before you, I want Martin to have all my toys. People do that, don't they, say who can have their things? Well, I want Martin to have my toys if I go to Heaven first.'

In spite of all our attempts to direct Jimmy's anger away from poor Martin, we never really reunited the brothers in those last weeks. Martin longed to show Jimmy how much he loved him, and how much he cared that Jimmy was dying. Jimmy's continuing rejection hurt him deeply, and one day he said: 'Jimmy did love me before he was ill, didn't he? When he was my playmate, he did love me then?'

It was a great relief to be able to tell Martin Jimmy's exact words in bequeathing his toys to him. Martin was very proud. He had been very undemanding of Jimmy, and only wanted a little love and affection. In return he would have given Jimmy a lifetime of loyalty and support.

Jimmy and I dropped off to sleep about four o'clock. His pain returned just after ten next morning and it was so sudden and severe he shouted and cried. The morphine had little effect, and his fear made the pain worse. It was impossible to roll him over, sit him up, and give him the extra spoonful of morphine that he needed.

The pain continued longer than ever before. When Ian came on his daily visit, we agreed there must be something more we could do and he went away to phone Pendlebury and ask their advice about pain control.

The advice, such as it was, sounded brisk and impatient. Dying children in hospital were given their slow-acting morphine twice a day, and if they suffered a pain breakthrough, they were given paracetamol.

The presence of pain was treated very casually; what had we expected anyway, they asked. Jimmy was dying of cancer. Nobody had ever promised it would be pain-free.

After this, I never turned to the hospital for help again, although the Liaison Sister, Alison, rang every few days. She had been enormously helpful to us in the past, visiting us at home several times, always completely honest in the answers that she gave to our questions. Her strength and warm friendship had been greatly appreciated.

But I felt so guilty, talking to her about Jimmy's death behind his back, hoping he hadn't heard the phone ring. I found it very difficult and stressful to communicate in case I let go, lost control, and couldn't then return to Jimmy's bedside at the end of the conversation. There was little she could do from a distance of ninety miles in a situation which was, tragically, already resolved; and the unsympathetic response that Saturday from whoever dealt with our call about Jimmy's pain left its mark. I felt hurt and humiliated, pushed out in the cold.

Fortunately we had plenty of support and medical help at home; many parents in similar circumstances might not be so fortunate, and for them, the hospital would remain the only source of expert advice for the care of the dying child. Perhaps the problem is that hospitals are not so much unwilling to help at this stage, but unable to do so without creating a new structure in which their care would extend to the terminally ill at home. I am quite certain this could be done, whatever the distance involved, using the experienced help of local hospices to help bridge the gap between hospital and home. It is a desolate feeling when treatment has to end and the hospital support that families have relied upon for months is withdrawn. There is an urgent need for that support to continue both at the time and throughout death and bereavement, and steps must be taken to ensure that support is available for every family involved, throughout the country.

How much better for Jimmy if he had died that first weekend of pain. He had prepared himself, told us the important things he wanted us to know, settled his affairs on earth and looked forward to his journey to Heaven.

We were so unaccustomed to seeing him in bad pain that we didn't think he could stand it for long, and we expected him to die within a day or so. But nobody had realized how strong his young body remained, and how long it could coexist with advanced leukaemia.

✳

# EIGHT

# A Life Ending

The next weeks were slow and agonizing for both Jimmy and all who loved him, and his quality life was over. There was only suffering left. Nothing was keeping him alive except his vigorous young body's refusal to give up, and his strong little heart continued to beat at a furious pace, day after day, as everything else deteriorated.

'I wish I was dead, it's got to be a better deal than this,' he said several times. 'How long am I going to have to put up with this?' In Christian terms, he was ready to leave on his journey to Heaven, but nobody came to fetch him.

It was the final irony and, if God had any hand in it, I was angry that He cared so little for our child. Was it not enough that he should die so young of a horrible disease without suffering a prolonged and painful death weeks after his quality of life had come to an end? Was this the work of a merciful God who loves little children?

No child should be sent home from hospital to die without at least half a dozen practical items to ensure the quality of his care and comfort. Whilst the District Nursing Service can provide many of them, a check-list of these requirements should be co-ordinated, collected, and ready for use, before the need becomes urgent. Hospitals should never forget that although home is usually the best place for a dying child, parents who can face nursing a terminally ill child are, in fact, not only saving the hospital a lot of money, but sparing staff the distress of watching a child die on the ward. The specialists and clinic doctors remain jointly responsible with the GP for that child until the moment he or she dies and parents who nurse children at home deserve the very best support and consideration possible from the hospital, much as they helped and supported us when things were going well before Jimmy's relapse.

A syringe driver for continuous medicine dose should be lent for use at home. We relied on borrowing one from John's practice, and he drove a round trip of over fifty miles to obtain it. Every child needs an oscillating electric fan to alleviate the sweating which often occurs in advanced leukaemia; we were lucky once again in our friends, and Lewis lent us his own fan. Mouthcare sponges and glycerine for cracked lips came from the local hospital via John, and a special mattress from CancerCare. The district nurse provided a bed pan, urine bottle and incontinence sheets, but it took us over a week to assemble all the necessary items. Jimmy's hospital could have suggested the things he would need, and much time would have been saved.

Jimmy now dozed most of each day, drifting in and out of sleep, and he never sat up. It hurt his swollen stomach too much, and he lay semiconscious, usually on his back, rarely speaking. The need for entertainment had passed and he couldn't concentrate long enough to listen to a book being read, or a tape. We tried to play music softly in the background, but the noise irritated him.

Pass the Pigs lay on the bedside table, with a digital travelling clock and a drawing of a champion pig, both given to him by Lewis's daughter, Becky, who had only met him for a moment or two, but wanted desperately to help. The fan was placed a small distance from his bed so that the cool air wouldn't chill him, and his friends kept him well supplied with his favourite freesias. A little novelty key ring with two hearts floating in glitter was always by his bed. They had hypnotic significance, along with Bernadette's back door key, and she hoped the sight of them might trigger his mind to exercise the mental pain control she had taught him.

The first few days he was bedridden, we never left his bedside. Somebody was always sitting with him. But as the weeks passed, this became impractical and we relaxed our vigilance and let him rest alone, which he sometimes preferred. Every morning except Sunday, Karen drove twenty miles to help in the house. She never asked if we needed her help; she simply decided, in her quiet but firm way, that we did, and announced that she would come every day to do the shopping and household chores, cooking, looking after Christy and helping to nurse Jimmy.

She moved about so quietly, we hardly knew she was there. She never intruded and yet she was always ready to help carry Jimmy or wash him, when two pairs of hands were better than one. She too had to watch Jimmy's pathetic deterioration, and hear him cry out with his pain, helpless as we were to make it better. She never ran away and never let him down; no commitment to 'seeing it through', such as she made in the Christie's car park the year before, could ever have been more faithfully or lovingly fulfilled.

Each day Lewis would visit at least once, often twice, and he always came in the evening to say a night prayer with Jimmy and often to read to Martin, or bath him, or help dry the dishes or do anything at all that needed to be done. He understood how impossible it was for us to communicate at all with a God that could allow our child to suffer so much, and he never sought to change our attitudes or try and put the case for God, much as an ambassador might do to excuse his badly behaved country. It was very comforting that somebody should be praying so hard when we could not pray at all.

There was a fundamental difference in the way that we saw things. I imagined our family like a ship at sea, which had run into a violent storm, and lost a man overboard. The storm would pass, and the ship would have to sail on, leaving the drowned man behind. Lewis's Christian version of my metaphor was subtly different. The crew member was ill, he said, so an RAF Rescue helicopter had come and air-lifted him to safety, straight to the destination the ship was heading for, and Jimmy would be waiting for us there when our ship docked.

I had very little time to play with Christy, or even to look after him, so each evening he went home with Jean about five o'clock, and stayed until she or David brought him home late in the evening. He certainly didn't miss out on the attention he needed when he was with them. All the family loved him, as they had loved both Jimmy and Martin as babies, and he was fed and bathed and cuddled and cared for while we looked after Jimmy without Christy's crying to break the peace. Although there was little anyone could do for Jimmy any more, by taking care of practicalities David and Jean left us more time to be with him. They helped unquestioningly, no matter what the request, and fulfilled their commitment to Jimmy as his godparents in the most practical and complete way possible.

It was snowing one Thursday morning when Jimmy suddenly decided that he wanted to get up and get dressed. He was so weak, it would have been almost impossible and we both knew it. I suspected he had ulterior motives and the truth was soon revealed. For reasons we will never understand, Jimmy suddenly and desperately wanted to own a stopwatch. He might have used it in the attic to time engines on his model railway; or it might have been attractive to him because of all the complicated technology he could have played with. But whatever the reason, he decided he would get up, put warm clothes on and travel in his buggy to the video shop where he knew they sold stopwatches.

The first problem was that Jimmy was already too weak to walk even as far as the bathroom any more, let alone sit up. After much disappointed crying, the only compromise he would accept was that Paul would go and buy him one. The stopwatch duly arrived and he held it in his hand, clutched tightly under the duvet, for two days and nights before allowing us to put it on his bedside table with his other treasures.

Jimmy ate very little during his last month. As his tummy became more swollen and uncomfortable, eating tended to spark off the pain again. However, he loved being fed tiny teaspoonfuls of crushed ice lolly, though only Walls' Calypso would do.

At times he would eat half a lolly every hour or so, night and day, to refresh his mouth. The only other food he ate was chocolate cake, made by his favourite chocolate cake maker, our friend Christina. Jimmy loved tiny, thin slices of cake fed to him in crumbs, which he often requested every hour through the night. By this time, he couldn't distinguish night from day, but it didn't matter; it was worth being woken hourly to stumble in the darkness to the kitchen for another slice and a mug of weak, warm coffee which he sucked through a straw, just to see his pleasure.

Keeping his thin little body free of bedsores meant washing him thoroughly every day, especially as he often suffered from sudden hot sweats. During the first three weeks, we carried him very gently into the bathroom, laid him down on a sheepskin rug, and lifted him into the bath, taking care to keep his body stretched out straight. He couldn't sit up or lean over for more than a few seconds or the pain in his spleen would start; jolting his tummy was the worst thing we could do.

Jimmy grumbled gently at first about having a bath and being moved, but as he suffered more and more pain, his gentle grumbling turned to real fear. Sometimes Karen and I carried and bathed him together, other days Paul would come and help us, while Karen changed his sheet and duvet cover and cleaned the room. He was self-conscious at first about being carried and bathed in this way, but within a week or two, he was so sleepy, he would doze as we laid him down on the rug to dry him.

He had developed eczema on the back of his neck which itched and worried him. When the rash became infected, it added to his general discomfort and made him very upset. An antibiotic cream eventually healed it, leaving no soreness, but then I realized that the pain he complained of in his neck was not eczema. Several of his joints had become painful, and his shoulders and neck hurt whenever we moved him even a tiny fraction. In advanced stages of leukaemia, the leukaemia cells finally reach the joints, causing severe pain, and we guessed that Jimmy was now at this stage. Watching each slow stage of deterioration, it seemed so strange not to be doing anything to halt the decline. We noted each downhill step, powerless to stop it.

Jimmy's morphine dose was increasing gradually, to keep one move ahead of his pain, and a sort of weekly pattern had been established. First, there would be a pain breakthrough bigger than usual, and the morphine dose was increased. Then for the next three days, Jimmy would be very sleepy and frail, hardly aware of anyone around him, preferring just to doze all day and night. His breathing was often shallow and irregular, especially in the evening, and on several occasions we had both mistakenly thought he was dying. Sometimes his breathing would stop altogether and then restart. It would have been very peaceful if his death had taken place one quiet evening as we sat round the bed, reading or resting, the curtains drawn back to a clear night sky outside, and the freesias that we always kept by the bed filling the room with their sweetness.

Sometimes he would become a little confused, but never for very long. His dreams became entangled with real life and he would request strange things, or become agitated that we were going to take him back to hospital. He dreaded this more than death, which never frightened him at all. His voice when he shouted 'Mum!' was still very strong, but when this became weaker, he would sometimes ring a little bell we left by the bed.

One morning, when he had been bedridden about three weeks, we were warned to expect a visit from a doctor who would be coming to assess our claim for Attendance Allowance on Jimmy's behalf. A prior claim relating to the first six months of his illness had been rejected, and the DSS had no record of it. We were fully entitled to this financial help, and it would help replace my lost income, since I had been forced to give up my weekly newspaper column and reporting job when Jimmy relapsed.

The DSS medical assessment for Attendance Allowance then in

operation usually lasted well over an hour, we heard. The questions asked were thorough and personal, and a medical examination of the person requiring care had to be made. Considering that the claim involved a terminally ill child, we expected a degree of sensitivity and understanding of the problems we were dealing with.

A phone call warned us that the assessor was on his way and would have little time to spare. But we were unwilling to change Jimmy's routine, and the unfamiliar doctor arrived just as we were carrying Jimmy down the passage to his bath, which was already run. We had taken Jimmy's clothing off in bed, and he was naked, ready to be lifted into the water.

As he walked through the front door, the doctor announced that he only had ten minutes to spare. I explained that Jimmy was about to be bathed, but it would only take a few minutes to get him comfortably back in bed. Could he wait a few minutes? He said no, suggesting that he could ask questions in the bathroom as we worked.

This was out of the question. Jimmy had all the dignity and self-consciousness of any eight-year-old, and would be most upset to be bathed in the presence of a stranger. The doctor replied that he had 'dozens of these things' to do before five that afternoon, and he couldn't wait. Either the interview took place immediately, or he would have to go.

Realizing that the next assessment might be weeks away, there was little choice but to leave Jimmy back in bed, putting his comfort second to the convenience of the doctor. The forms were completed within minutes and the questions asked with what appeared to us a complete absence of compassion or sensitivity to the difficult circumstances.

Why couldn't Jimmy go to the toilet on his own? (Because he was too weak to walk or even sit on the toilet seat.) Why couldn't he sit on the toilet? (Because the poor little soul was so thin and weak, he would have slipped down inside the toilet seat, and holding him upright round his middle caused pain.) And so it went on.

The examination took place next. The doctor walked into the room, stood some distance from the bed and stared at Jimmy, who had slipped back into his normal comatose state.

'Does he always sleep like that?' asked the doctor. I explained that his illness caused characteristic sleepiness.

'Lost weight, has he?' I could hardly believe my ears as we stood looking at the emaciated body of my poor little love. I said I hadn't weighed him lately, but it was likely he was losing weight. Jimmy's eyes were shut, and though he was weak, there was nothing wrong with his hearing. The 'examination' took place as though the little boy on the bed didn't exist, or had already died. I felt stunned.

Within a quarter of an hour, the entire assessment was over, and the doctor moved towards the door. A request for advice on how best to follow up the original claim was met with 'You'll have to find that out yourself,' which was said over his shoulder as he left the house.

Had the assessment really been about Jimmy's welfare and our problems as carers? Few of us find it easy to ask for State help, especially when we do what we have to do for love of another person. This man's shortage of time to sit down and listen to us in our distress made it feel mercenary to claim the aid which was rightfully ours.

Those people who came to our home in the weeks that Jimmy was dying brought love and peace and support, making the atmosphere gentle and almost sacred with their goodness. The presence of this unsympathetic stranger had temporarily polluted the almost tangible spirit of loving strength.

The time came when Jimmy could no longer bear the pain of being carried into the bath, so he was washed in bed. Often it was done in the quiet of the afternoon, before Martin returned from school and while Christy was having his rest. Sometimes Jimmy hardly stirred at all until the job was nearly finished, but I had to turn him on his side to change the sheet underneath, and wash his back, which usually gave him the chance to register a quiet protest.

The only way it was possible to touch him was to give him an extra dose of morphine before starting. It was quite horrible sometimes to think that anything I had done might have added to his pain, but keeping him clean reduced the risk of bedsores, and the extra pain they would have caused.

I was used to his gentle protest whenever he had a wash, but I didn't want anyone else to misunderstand it, and feel hurt, especially if they were only trying to help him. It was all so very uncharacteristic, part of his sick psyche. I wanted to protect him so much that Karen was the only person who shared this intimate care of him. The effects of the morphine sometimes produced some startlingly bad language from him, often quite as imaginative as it was shocking, which made us want to laugh and cry at the same time. The power to shock was just about the only power he had left.

There really is only one way to remain able to function at all, nursing a dying child, and that is to suppress the reality of the horror and normalize the agonizing experience. A degree of brutalization is essential just in order to touch a body which suffers pain, and when it is the body which was conceived, born, nursed, loved and cherished by the carer, it becomes even more impossible to stand back and think about what is really happening. Every hour of every day belongs in a 'now' mode, and it is inadvisable to look back or forwards. It is an experience of doing, not thinking or being done to.

The disadvantage of this method of mental and physical survival is that as the weeks after death pass and life begins to return to normal, the aspects of dying, including the physical deterioration and slow crumbling of this fine and beautiful child become as horrifying as once they seemed normal. His death, now, in retrospect, seems unbelievable; yet at the time it was expected and unsurprising.

February became March as week followed week. We could hardly believe that this agony was lasting so long. It seemed so unfair that he should suffer and die at all, but even more unjust that the suffering should be so prolonged.

Paul's birthday fell one Saturday, but Jimmy was too tired and remote from us to understand anything as trivial and irrelevant as a birthday. There was absolutely no point in showing him the cake with the candles lit, when he might not even open his eyes long enough to see anything. And if he did understand what he was missing, that in itself might have made him miserable.

However, celebrating was important for the other two children. Jimmy was dying, but Martin and Christy were both very much alive and needing the comfort and reassurance that things such as a birthday give children.

I only left the house about four or five times during those last six weeks, and only when somebody Jimmy knew very well was there. My absences were never more than an hour, just to breathe some fresh air and take some exercise, and fortunately he never woke and asked for me, so he never knew I wasn't there. He still relied on my 'healing hands' to rub his pain better, and it was important I never let him down, or he would lose faith in my power to comfort him.

Whenever the pain slipped out of control, Jimmy became very

frightened and would whimper: 'Oh no, it's coming back, it's coming, the pain's starting,' and would grab at my hand and press it down firmly over his swollen spleen. I had to press down like this sometimes for an hour without moving, and even a change of hands terrified him in case it let the pain return.

These periods of pain breakthrough occurred about once a day and were distressing for us all. To counter them, he had an extra spoon of morphine immediately, but that was already too late. The medicine took a quarter of an hour to work, and sitting him up to swallow it sometimes increased the pain.

On several occasions, he told us: 'This is no good. How long is it going on? I wish I was dead. It would be better than this.'

The only thing that made it bearable to witness such distress was being able to help relieve his pain with my hand. As a little boy, he had always felt very sad that the skin on my hands was rough and dry, and he had a special affection for their ugly soreness. He took great comfort now in feeling their familiar roughness.

As the weeks went by, we wondered if Jimmy might have forgotten that he was dying. It was a month since we had confirmed that he was on his way to Heaven, but it hadn't happened. He knew he was very ill, but did he think he might get better? We thought we ought to find out what was going on in his mind.

Bernadette was the only person who could ask him; he was used to talking to her, so she agreed to try and assess what he thought about his illness. He had no need to protect her from the truth, as he might have done his parents. The chance came and she sat and talked gently to him. Did he think he would get better, she asked. His reply was no, he knew he wouldn't get better. There was no need to remind him he was dying, and no need for us to dwell on it.

Ironically, there were days when he looked as though he might be getting better. There would be more colour in his face, and his eyes would look a little brighter. Contact with Pendlebury, after their earlier rebuff, was only occasional and through Alison, the Liaison Sister, the hospital seemed surprised that Jimmy could still be alive.

His condition hardly ever changed, except just after an increase in his morphine. He dozed in and out of consciousness, he was too weary to communicate, he couldn't sit up or walk, but he could still ask for a drink or an ice lolly, or know that Tinker was sitting on his window sill.

As I nursed him day by day, I began to have very real doubts that passive caring was enough. Was he really dying? Supposing he had gone into some miraculous remission – shouldn't I stop aiding and abetting his death by doing nothing, and start fighting again? Were we watching a preventable death?

Ian shared our feelings, and it was a decision we all reached that we couldn't carry on any further without a blood test to establish what was really happening inside Jimmy's body.

The hospital Liaison Sister just happened to be visiting the town, to collect a cheque for nearly £45,000, the proceeds of the Rotary Club's appeal which Jimmy had launched only twelve months before, riding round so proudly and hopefully on his new bike for the television cameras.

When she came to see us at home, Alison agreed that a blood test was called for, but gave us little hope it would reveal any change. Even if Jimmy had gone into a late remission, nobody would be willing to treat him. But his tenacity and struggle to hold on to life left us always with a tiny spark of hope in our hearts, and we had to know for certain that there was nothing we could do, even at this late stage, to save his life.

The blood test next day proved a virtual impossibility, and after a quarter of an hour, with assistance from the district nurse, the health visitor and Alison, Ian was about to give up when he suddenly found a vein which supplied sufficient blood to test. Jimmy had screamed and shouted, and we all hated the distress we had caused him. Jimmy's anger was focused on Ian.

'Get out of here, and don't come back ever,' Jimmy shouted at him.

Next morning when Ian arrived as usual to see Jimmy, neither of us expected Jimmy to remember his outburst the day before. We were wrong, and as Ian walked in, a cross little voice pinpointed his presence immediately.

'I thought I told you to get out,' Jimmy persisted. 'I told you to get out and not come back.'

It was part of Ian's special skill and personal courage when dealing with children that he knew just how best to ignore Jimmy's anger and carry on as usual; Jimmy's feelings were directed at the doctor, any doctor, and all doctors, not Ian personally. He felt they had failed him by not making him better, and then, when they still went on doing nasty things with needles to him and still didn't make him better, he had every justification in feeling bitter and very annoyed.

We were too realistic about leukaemia to expect Jimmy's blood test to show a miracle had taken place, and that the disease was diminishing. Nevertheless, the results were shattering and dealt a final blow to all hope. Jimmy's blood consisted of 98 per cent immature blast cells and his haemaglobin was barely three, a quarter of what it would be in a healthy child. The only 'miracle', if there was one at all, was that poor Jimmy could be alive at all, and that his overworked heart carried on pounding at such a rate all the time.

Without further delay, it was decided that Jimmy should be free of the bother of having to wake up to take tablets or spoonfuls of morphine, and instead his dose should be delivered continuously into his skin using a syringe driver. This small, convenient device, which works on batteries, pumps a set amount of painkiller throughout the day and night. The needle doesn't have to be in a vein, and the syringe usually only needs refilling once a day.

The use of the syringe driver had probably been delayed by my own ignorance about it. Without any basic information or preparation about it from Pendlebury, I feared it as the very last step towards un-consciousness and death, and I thought its presence would cause Jimmy distress. Instead, the steady and continual pain control gave Jimmy fewer pain breakthroughs, and when they did occur, it was very simple to speed the drip up for quick relief.

The pump driver flashed and bleeped occasionally, and we told Jimmy it was like his lighthouse, guarding him night and day. The benefit to him was immeasurable, and to us, too. For the first time in a month, neither of us had to wake several times by alarm clock in the night to sit Jimmy up and spoon medicine into his mouth. The baby was still waking for feeds at midnight and four, but that was bearable as long as there were periods of sleep between, undisturbed by Jimmy's morphine doses.

The most unpleasant, uncomfortable thing we had to do for Jimmy was to give him an enema at least once a week, to help keep his bowel unobstructed. If he had become constipated, his swollen bowel would have put pressure on his painful tummy everywhere.

He hated enema day, and once threw his slipper at the poor district nurse, and called her a 'shit-bag'. Being unable to sit on the toilet seat, he preferred his old blue potty placed on the floor rather than a bed pan, and we lifted him out of bed, sat him on it usually for over half an hour, supporting him from behind and under his arms. Memories of his pride as a toddler, learning to keep himself dry and clean using that same potty, were never far away as we held him up, his poor head hanging down with exhaustion, deprived of his dignity as he tried so hard to do what was required of him. Fortunately for a child as careful and clean as Jimmy was, he remained in control of both bladder and bowels all the time and never needed incontinence pads or sheets in bed.

During the following week after the introduction of the syringe driver, Jimmy started to vomit every time he had a small drink. It was two weeks since he had been able to eat at all, and now he couldn't drink. With great patience and perseverance, he took tiny sips to try and satisfy his thirst, and when the fluid came straight back up, he just kept trying. Sometimes, on the third or fourth attempt he would succeed, and the drink would stay down. He never gave up or even complained. He just said, 'Why do I have all the bad luck?' and tried again.

Various drugs were tried, but to no avail. The amount of strange, rusty-looking vomit was far in excess of what he was drinking, but the sickness could have been due to any one of half a dozen different causes in a body which was slowly breaking down. We hoped Jimmy would not become aware and frightened of any sudden physical changes, although he had noticed his sight was very poor.

The sickness stopped for a day, then began again. Jimmy was so desperate for a drink, he would suck little sponges dipped in Coca-Cola, repeating his tiny sips again and again. His refusal to give up was very courageous and he never grumbled about the constant, unpleasant vomiting.

On Friday afternoon, I heard him shout, and found him trying to rip the syringe driver out. I replaced it quite easily, checked it was working, and sat listening to a dream he was having. He seemed to be in his classroom at school, and was playing the parts of both the teacher and a naughty boy. It was the silly boy who had been responsible for pulling out the syringe driver, and the teacher told him off, then started to collect the pencils.

'Now, come on, children, stop that silliness and gather up those lead pencils,' he ordered with real authority. It was one of the few times we were aware of fantasy and reality becoming entwined in his mind. His mind hardly ever wandered and he always knew who we were.

That morning, Jimmy's bowel felt distended and it had been decided that another enema was necessary, to relieve pressure. But in the hours that passed after Ian's visit, a marked deterioration in Jimmy's general condition was visible. His face looked grey and his saliva seemed sticky, making it more and more difficult as the day went on for him to speak clearly. Instinct told me that an enema would be unnecessary, but a district nurse came to carry out the task, and together we washed him and tried to make him comfortable.

In spite of kind offers by the district nursing services, we had managed to nurse our own son at home by choice quite without help, except for giving him the weekly enema. Most families nursing a terminally ill child probably need more help than we did, and for them there is no substitute for special paediatric-trained oncology nurses. Millions of pounds are being raised to train Macmillan paediatric nurses, a service which the NHS are committed to taking over and funding once it is established. But with only two nurses available in each of the seventeen regional health districts, the service will be far from adequate. On average, two, sometimes three, children die of cancer each month from Pendlebury's North-West catchment area alone.

During that last Friday, staff at the hospice over thirty miles away had suggested a certain drug to control Jimmy's sickness, and Paul had arranged to collect it from John, who had acquired it for him.

Jimmy slept peacefully, not waking to talk to me at all, and when Paul had returned with the drug, Ian called about ten that evening to put it in Jimmy's syringe driver. We discussed how we would know if Jimmy was really dying; Ian told us it was something we would simply know at the time and that it might be sometime during the night ahead.

The prospect of Jimmy dying within a few hours produced two conflicting emotions. One was despair that he should be leaving us; the other was relief that his long ordeal of suffering would finally end.

The new antisickness drug brought immediate relief. Before midnight, Jimmy was able to enjoy a proper drink uninterrupted by vomiting. It was such a pleasure to him, that he had another few sips of Coke, and then a little more. Then he slept.

We settled down as usual, Paul with Christy in the room next door while I lay very still next to Jimmy, so as not to disturb him. I fell asleep at about half-past twelve, but woke at three when Jimmy's breathing became noisy and laboured. Despite the effort, he was not in any distress. I got up and rolled back the duvet because he was so hot. I gave him a bottle in case he wanted to wee, but nothing happened.

He pointed at the duvet. 'I'm cold, pull the cover up,' he muttered. I obeyed his request, and went to wake Paul to warn him how bad Jimmy's breathing sounded. When I returned, Jimmy had changed positions and rolled right across the bed, with his head and chest over my side.

It was the first time in weeks it had been possible to hold him so closely in my arms without fear of hurting him. It was such a wonderful feeling of relief to have him back where he belonged. I curled up against him and encircled his body with my arms, keeping my left hand directly over his pounding heart which bumped up and down under my fingers. He continued to breathe with difficulty, very rapidly, so I talked to him quietly and gently just as I had when he was a baby being rocked to sleep, until he dozed again.

I held him closely and loved him with all my love as the minutes ticked by. Then, just after half-past four, his respiration slowed down to a quiet, peaceful rhythm. I guessed that this change must be significant. His breathing continued, slow, unhurried and relaxed while I talked gently as before and thanked him for the love and joy his life had brought us. There was no fear or pain, only love, as his life ended. The heart beneath my hand gave a final beat and stopped and I knew that Jimmy had died, curled up within my arms, as close to me as the baby he had once been, warm and quiet within my womb.

# NINE

✳

# Afterwards

Jimmy was as beautiful in that first hour of death as he had ever been. The sense of his being was strongly present in the room; the expression on his face was a familiar one, alert, interested and slightly quizzical, as if he were just about to ask a question.

A few moments after he died, I left him to wake Paul, who took him in his arms and loved him and wept, and then we roused Martin to make his farewell. Martin's flow of love, rejected for so long, reached his big brother at last. He climbed into bed with Jimmy and hugged and kissed him as he had tried to do so many times before.

As we gathered round Jimmy's body to grieve together, alone and privately for a while before letting in the outside world, there was already great relief that his death should have taken place in the midst of such closeness and love. How differently we would have felt if Jimmy had died without warning while a meal was being prepared, or a nappy changed, or the phone answered, with nobody close by to be with him as he left us. There could have been no gentler, more perfect a death, as close to us in his life's very last moment as his first.

There was no unfinished business, no loose ends to interfere with the purity of grief and the long process of mourning, which had already begun for us six months before as we heard the news of Jimmy's catastrophic relapse.

Paul's farewell to Jimmy had been in the form of a personal message, the significance of which he knew Jimmy would understand. Weeks before, Jimmy had promised that as soon as he reached Heaven, he would start work on the new model railway layout. With God to help him do the difficult bits, the track would be ready by the time Paul joined him. So it wasn't necessary for Paul to say goodbye the night before Jimmy died and perhaps frighten him by doing so. Instead, he reminded him to get the track set up and ready as planned. Jimmy nodded and understood.

Ian came as soon as we rang, about half an hour after Jimmy died, to certify the death and issue the certificate, and the undertaker arrived at six o'clock. It was already light that last morning in March and the dawn was fine and sunny, like a summer's day.

We left Jimmy's body lying in our bed and settled in the big room to make the necessary arrangements. Martin immediately retreated into the safe, familiar world that he had shared with Jimmy of Thomas the Tank Engine videos, and it made a curious, surreal background to the formalities that had to be discussed with the kind and sympathetic undertaker. Jimmy had never grown out of Thomas the Tank Engine, and to hear the familiar sentences and sound effects made it almost beyond belief that we could be sitting, talking about Jimmy's funeral, within a few feet of where he would have been sitting, watching, attentive and happy.

The undertaker did not want to take Jimmy out of the house to the chapel of rest without putting him in a coffin first, but he had no coffin small enough. A special child-sized coffin would have to be fetched that day, so Jimmy's body would have to stay in the house until evening, he said.

It was not as we would have wished. Having made such complete and perfect farewells, we were quite ready to let Jimmy's body leave the house in the quiet of early morning while his beauty remained intact; although his physical presence would have left us, his spirit would remain with us in the house throughout the day.

Paul waited until eight, and then began to ring our closest friends to tell them Jimmy had died. With great courage and strength, he conveyed the message many times and listened with patience and fortitude as people struggled to express their sorrow.

Martin replaced Jimmy immediately as the person for whom we had the greatest concern. His memories of Jimmy would eventually become linked with the fleeting fragments he could recall from the day on which Jimmy died, and we did not want that day to be frightening and sad.

So we kept to the plans for a walk and a picnic with Karen and John, Becky and Jonathan that we had already made for Martin earlier in the week. Saturday was very fine all day, a March day to remember for its blue skies and brilliance. Once again, we stretched that original commitment to its limits, and Karen and John were with us as always to 'see it through, whatever', which they did.

This day, which had begun with an ending in the quietness of dawn, seemed to stretch on for ever, hour after hour, like our lives stretching ahead, empty without Jimmy.

As each hour passed, Jimmy's body looked less and less like his vital, living self. The fine delicate features of his face stiffened into the grotesque, his body became cold and white, like marble. Within two hours, his beauty had faded, and his face was empty of his spirit.

Lewis had been unable to be with Jimmy during the last few days because of a slipped disc, and was lying in bed at the Vicarage; although we missed him very much, his certain and confident message of Heaven was as freshly in Jimmy's mind as though it had just been spoken, and Lewis's work as pastor had been completed when Jimmy was still alert enough to understand.

Paul and I both wanted to spend some moments with Lewis, so we left Jimmy's body in Karen's loving care, to go across to the Vicarage. The funeral, in the Parish Church, was to take place three days later, on Tuesday afternoon. Wednesday was Martin's sixth birthday, and it was very important to leave his special day unmarked by Jimmy's death.

Friends came and went throughout the day, some wishing to see Jimmy's body and make their own personal farewells. Sadly, the condition of his body deteriorated as each hour passed, and he looked less and less beautiful, and nothing like the child he had once been. It was a great relief when the undertaker arrived with the coffin at about seven that evening. Having no experience of death before, my lasting impression of Jimmy through the following weeks was the image of him that I saw at the very end, not the fine, robust-looking child he had once been.

He was placed in his coffin in the clothes he had been wearing at the time of his death, which included his favourite Greenpeace tee shirt depicting the *Rainbow Warrior*, which seemed a fitting shroud for a little boy who loved to remember the day he had actually been on board the ship and danced with the crew.

As the undertaker prepared to close the coffin, Martin ran into their room, and grabbed several soft toys, including the purple teddy bear Jimmy had bought in Skipton, and a funny little dog called Towser, still labelled round the neck with a Christie's hospital tag inscribed 'My name is Towser and I belong to Jimmy'. He dropped them both into the coffin. Jimmy's Ra-ra, which was two little pieces of cot sheet material sewn together, which he had recently named Adam and Eve, were placed in his hand, just where he liked it to be as he sucked his thumb, and the coffin lid was closed after we had kissed him for the last time.

The coffin was carried slowly out, down the alley and into the street where the hearse was waiting. We followed behind and waved goodbye.

The need for Paul and me to be together that night, and every night, was so urgent that we started immediately to convert Jimmy's bed and room back into our own. If we hadn't returned that night and reclaimed the only place where we could be quiet and private in the house, it might have been weeks before we could have faced the sad task of cleaning and tidying Jimmy away. But Jimmy was part of us both, and our bed was always his home. His death had been so gentle that it was part of life itself, and there was neither fear nor distaste at lying down to sleep in the place where Jimmy had died. On the contrary, it brought us closer together and remains a peaceful little shrine in his memory.

On Sunday afternoon, we learned the very first lesson in living with death and separation. We climbed a small fell overlooking Thirlmere and soon realized that wherever we go, and whatever we do in the foreseeable future will be dominated by memories of doing it before, when Jimmy was with us. This particular walk was very significant. The last time we had attempted it was only three weeks before Jimmy's cancer was diagnosed. He had been tired and very irritable in the hot sunshine, and we had accused him of allowing his selfishness to spoil everyone's day. Although we apologised later for our impatience, the walk will never be a happy, carefree expedition again.

Yet the afternoon brought a message of hope too. I left the family and climbed high above them until I had put all suffering below me. I was left with nothing but the tranquillity and beauty of the landscape around. Despite everything that had happened, it was with a sense of surprise that I recognized the feeling of happiness emanating from the grandeur of the scene in front of me. Guilt that anything could be pleasant without Jimmy was quickly banished, leaving a capacity for joy and happiness quite untouched by his death which I hope is such a part of me that it will last all my life.

Monday was a busy day ordering flowers for the funeral, arranging the practical details and preparing for the arrival of our families. In the afternoon we went to the Registrar's house to register the death, so that we could hand over the certificate of burial to the undertaker, and the funeral could take place the next day.

The kind part-time Registrar had a guest house, with a room at the rear for registration business. She was open only twice a week for all the births and deaths in the district, and by the time we arrived, ten minutes before she was due to open, a queue of bereaved relatives and proud new parents had already formed in the garden. The weather was cold and wet and there was nowhere to wait but outside. However, knowing the circumstances, she soon showed us into the lounge and allowed us to wait in comfort. On many similar occasions, we were shown small personal kindnesses which often helped to relieve the stress of public duties.

Completing all the documentation was a solemn and austere formality. Jimmy's short life, expressed on official paper, seemed so pathetic in contrast to the excitement and pride we shared when we had registered the birth of this first child eight years before, after eleven years of waiting.

My family arrived and with food and wine on the big table as usual, it could have been just another long-drawn-out family meal. Nobody really knew how best to react or behave. Was cheerfulness called for, or should we all be silent and very serious? The very normality of the family meal brought its own tensions; being alone and silent would have been so much less stressful.

We woke up next day, the day of the funeral, to a mixture of snow-storms, blue skies and sunshine. Mike and Sheila, Paul's brother and sister-in-law, arrived with their daughters, and we made a buffet lunch for everyone.

Martin looked so smart and dignified in his funeral clothes. He wore new black trousers and shoes, Jimmy's white shirt, and a black tie and a smart black velour top located in a bag of jumble. Christy wore his dummy tied on a black ribbon and pinned to his chest, so there was no danger of his losing it in church as he was nursed by Karen and Jean.

Paul was dressed in dark navy; funerals are just as important family landmarks as weddings, yet no photographs are ever taken. But I longed to take Paul's picture looking so sombre and controlled. I wore black, and my old black cape that Jimmy knew so well and used to snuggle in and wrap round himself when he came running to meet me after nursery school.

The funeral was due to start at two o'clock. The hearse arrived a quarter of an hour before, with one large funeral car to take the four of us with Granny Anna and Cate. The others were to meet us outside church to form the funeral procession. The town was very subdued, with several shops shut out of respect for Jimmy. There was almost no traffic anywhere and as we made our slow way to the Parish Church, we could see why. Police motorcyclists had stopped the traffic, and it was silently queueing as the cortège drove by. Then, as the hearse entered by the short road into the churchyard, a policeman in full uniform, boots polished, head high and eyes forward, saluted the coffin. It would have been the proudest moment for Jimmy; instead it was Martin's, and he nearly fell off his folding seat in the old car with sheer delight and excitement that people should think so much of his brother.

I had fully expected to cry all the way through the funeral service, and especially during the hymns we had chosen, which were all Jimmy's favourites. My dread had been that we wouldn't be able to control our emotions in front of so many people. But these fears turned out to be groundless.

As we entered the church, Paul and I behind the coffin, with Martin between us and the baby in my arms, a wonderful feeling of calm control took over and we walked with pride for Jimmy, especially when we saw how many people had packed into the big church, leaving standing room only, in honour of our son. I felt completely surrounded by love and comfort and what I feared would be the biggest ordeal of my life became instead a celebration of Jimmy's life, and the great good that he had brought his community and every one of us who knew and loved him.

The theme of the service was centred on life's journey from birth to death, from Christmas to Calvary, and the certain hope that Christians have in Easter and the resurrection, with its message of strength and hope. Lewis, still in pain from his slipped disc, saved the congregation from becoming too emotional with his firm and confident delivery and many of those present found it one of the most uplifting occasions they had ever attended. There were tears, but none so distressing that they prevented us from singing the hymns or joining in the prayers.

The readings included a short chapter from *The Prophet* on the subject of parents and their children. Kahlil Gibran's book of secular wisdom was written in 1924; the prophet is about to leave his people, and before he sails away they ask him to discuss a wide number of topics including justice, love, marriage and children. It was only five days before Jimmy died that I first read *The Prophet* and quickly learnt that my new discovery had been other people's bedside bible for years. The chapter on children, and how parents must always allow them to be themselves and not extensions of ourselves, fitted in so perfectly with our ideals of parenting that it made a perfect reading for the funeral.

The words spoken during the service were positive, strong and hopeful even to nonbelievers. The hymns Jimmy would have chosen began with 'All Things Bright and Beautiful', and continued with 'One More Step Along the World I Go', a particular favourite, and ended with a rousing, exultant version of 'Sing Hosanna'.

As we looked at his pathetically small coffin standing alone and isolated in the front of the church, we sang for him, and the sound we made engulfed the little box and the lofty church all around, drowning the occasional sobs we heard from behind. In the end it was the organ playing the solemn Adagio which Jimmy loved so much from Mozart's Clarinet Concerto which proved the greatest challenge to everyone's emotional control.

Martin lost his battle and cried, wiping his eyes on his velour sleeve and burying his head in my coat. But I thought of Jimmy's own vision of the world spinning in space as the music slowly progressed, and remembered the night as we walked in the dark along the track from the lighthouse when we looked up at the stars and tried to understand the vastness of the universe.

The coffin was borne down the aisle by the pallbearers, and we walked behind, almost unaware of so many people watching us, thinking only about Jimmy's last journey. A large black and white photograph of Jimmy, showing his sweet and gentle smile, watched us as we walked out of church. As the long procession followed through the churchyard, the sun shone and the only noise to be heard was the sound of playtime at Jimmy's school, a few yards away the other side of the hedge.

However uplifting and comforting a funeral can be, nothing can soften the austere reality of the grave, the yawning hole waiting to receive its new occupant. The young children watching must have found it almost inconceivable that we were going to put Jimmy in a box in a hole in the ground, and then throw soil on top of him.

Raw grief replaced love and comfort as the coffin was lowered down with ropes, and everybody cried except Christy, who chose that moment to have a little chat with Karen in best baby language. Instead of throwing a handful of soil on the coffin below, I tossed Jimmy a little bunch of rosemary for remembrance, and I looked up and round me as I stepped back to see a circle of faces wet with tears, some cast down and others turned to the sky in a wild sort of grief. It was a time of private, permitted grief for both men and women, and nobody sought to comfort anybody else until the procession left the graveside.

The formality of Jimmy's funeral service and burial had temporarily isolated his closest family from the love and support that reached out and touched us at all other times. But now this period of isolation was over, and people were waiting with arms outstretched to comfort us. Martin saw Miss Thompson and ran to her with great relief.

'I'm so glad it's you,' he said. 'I was feeling so sad seeing Jimmy being put in the ground, but now I feel all right because you're here.'

We left Jimmy in his lonely open grave and led the way to a nearby hotel where we had arranged to provide tea for all those who wanted it. Eighty people came, and it took two hours to speak to everyone there and receive every individual message of comfort and love. The sadness of Jimmy's death was strangely modified at the genuine pleasure we felt in seeing so many close friends who had travelled long distances to be with us that day.

At last the public performance was over, leaving Paul and me free to return to the churchyard, where the grave had been filled in and covered with wreaths and bouquets of flowers.

The churchyard must be one of the loveliest anywhere in the country, surrounded by hills, with the imposing Victorian church and its tall steeple overlooking it. Even the graves of those who died years ago are carefully tended by their families, the grass is cut frequently and flowers bring splashes of colour to the predominant green and grey. The churchyard is never empty. There is always someone there, quietly honouring the dead in a sacred place of great peace.

The snow showers had stopped, and the April evening was very cold and clear. We wondered if the expected frost would damage all the flowers and plants, and we thought of Jimmy beneath the earth. His body was not lonely and isolated, left out in the cold as I had feared; instead it was warm and protected forever from all further harm and hurt. He lies uphill slightly, with his head facing Loughrigg Fell, and when I visit the grave, I like to kneel by his side, one hand flat on the grass as though he is lying once more in our bed and I am holding his hand.

The day should have finished then and we longed for silence. But families have to be fed, and the usual family reunion seemed to be taking place an hour later as everyone sat round the big table. Before long there were jokes being told, even laughter and witty conversation. Nobody really knew how to behave or what to do, Jimmy's loss was so great. So in their nervousness they acted normally.

The children were astonished at the way the adults were acting. 'I can't believe it, listen to them!' his cousin Jonathan cried. 'Don't they know that Jimmy's *dead*?' he demanded.

Later that evening, when the party had broken up, Paul and I listened to the tape-recording of Jimmy's voice Paul had made six weeks before, talking about all the experiences he had enjoyed during the past six months.

Next day was Martin's birthday and with all his cousins still here, he was saved from feeling lonely. In the afternoon, when they had left for home, he went on a voyage of discovery through Jimmy's toys, which he had inherited.

Everything had to be taken out of each box. Jimmy used to label the various components of each item and he put things away and kept his treasures neatly and tidily. Martin pulled them out and spread things round him on the floor but then his attention would wander to the next novelty, leaving all the tiny parts to get trodden on or mislaid. Once they had been examined, we explained to Martin how it was necessary to put them all away until he was older and would appreciate them better.

On Saturday, four days after the funeral, the house echoed to the shouts of nine small boys running riot, racing up and down, and enjoying Martin's party. It was important not to cancel Martin's party for at least two reasons. One was that the party represented the family's ability to carry on normally, something Martin needed to be reassured about; and the other was to banish any fears his friends might have felt coming to the house where Jimmy had died.

There is little to be said further about 'afterwards' except that continual, raw grief gives way to a deeper depression, even a general gloom about the state of the world, the planet and man's inhumanity to man. After two months, the continual thoughts about Jimmy became reduced to frequent ones, then gradually lessened a little more. Grief becomes a way of life to be lived through like pain of any sort; but during periods of relief, things can change for the worse again at any time, and take you right back to the beginning, like landing on a snake in snakes and ladders. The only advantage that a painful, prolonged dying has over sudden death to those left bereaved is that it allows time to adjust to loss and separation, and the process of mourning starts far sooner and may even be gentler and more gradual.

Letters and cards came by every post, and every single expression of grief was appreciated and treasured.

There were personal letters of condolence from such diverse sources as the DSS and the British Rail drivers who fixed it for Jimmy to drive a train. There were letters from people we had never heard of, but who knew about Jimmy and had suffered with us over the months as the news of him became more hopeless.

The only people close to us in our family tragedy who failed completely to acknowledge Jimmy's suffering, bravery and death were those who had cared for him at Pendlebury. As each day went by without so much as a short note, we became more hurt and disillusioned by their confusing silence, the very people who had promised the family such support in happier days before Jimmy became yet another failure. They were the people who had witnessed at first-hand Jimmy's tough and cheerful determination, and it was their words of comfort which would have been of the greatest significance to us. Yet Jimmy seemed to represent nothing more to them ultimately than a case history, a number, and a file of test results and notes.

Six weeks after Jimmy's funeral, there was exactly £900 in donations to share between leukaemia research at Pendlebury, and Greenpeace. A letter expressing our sadness at their deliberate omission was sent with the money. It elicited a reply from the consultant who was sorry we had felt neglected, he said, but many parents liked to be left completely alone after the death of a loved one. Jimmy's attitude was always a 'refreshment' to the staff, and he thanked us for our courage through the difficult months. The words were genuine and kind; it would have been most gratifying to have received such a letter without any prompting.

The letter was followed up a month later by a meeting with the consultant, during which I was able to ask many questions, make serious criticisms openly and frankly, and contribute suggestions about various ways in which the quality of their service to the children and parents might be improved. The consultant had come from Pendlebury to meet Karen and me in a hotel, away from bad memories, and he listened patiently as we questioned the ethics of selecting treatment protocols by computer, and the way in which families are handled if treatment fails and they have to take their child home to die with little or no support from the hospital. But the most important question as to why Jimmy relapsed and died so unexpectedly remained unanswered because nobody, as yet, knows.

What of life now? What sorrows leave most pain?

It is the hole in our lives his leaving has caused which will never be filled by anything or anyone else. It is the notion of loss; not only our loss, but Jimmy's own loss of himself, the loss of a life with such promise and potential. It is the rest of our lives, stretching for years ahead without Jimmy. It is the slow realization that life has changed for ever and will never be the same again; and that happiness will never be complete and perfect because Jimmy died.

Every day brings poignant reminders of Jimmy as a baby, a toddler, going to school or playing. We pass gates he swung on, steps he tumbled down, trees that he climbed, streams he splashed in. A pair of size 13 football boots, worn once only, still coated with dried mud, sits in a PE bag marked with his name in the cupboard.

Jimmy's notebook fell open at a page which read: 'The Thing I Would Most Like To Do . . . is drive a car, I would like a Citroen silvergrey. I would like to get to places where I cannot go by myself. I would drive it fast and slow. I always put my seat belt on. Then I start up the engine and whizz away.'

At the time he wrote that with such hope, already terminally ill, I wrote: 'Betrayal. I talk about his dying, his death and the future without him with everybody but him. I secretly take the cordless phone to whisper. I feel so dishonest. I know he knows, but how much does he understand? Then, finally, I feel as if I am aiding and abetting in his death, as if, instead of fighting for him, I am gently leading him by the hand towards dying, which I seem to want him to do, because I know he cannot escape. He must wonder what I am doing. How strange to collude in his death. I feel split in two. I want him to live, but not as he is now; so I want him to die to relieve his suffering, and I want death to happen before he becomes aware and terrified of physical failings and death itself. I have never told him a lie or been dishonest with him before.'

No diary was kept during his illness, nothing written down except that short confession. The writing and record-keeping began after his death.

This is how the sadness felt in the first week after his burial:

'Crushing sadness . . . like a huge rough rock pressing up against me so I feel as if I am choking. Ache all the time with the absence and loss. People keep recalling his sweet smile. The grandfather clock ticks steadily on and each tick and tock carries time further away from when Jimmy and I were last together. I love him completely. This new beginning without him has made me understand that my whole life now will be forever sad. This is a great shock to someone like me who has always been happy and contented.

'One of the worst things is school and his friends. I wonder what he would have been learning today. A year ago it was unthinkable that he should be dead now. Suffered, fought and died in six months. Unthinkable and unbelievable.

'I miss his busy-ness, the way he ran from room to room as he set something up he wanted to do. I miss his eight-year-old wisdom, his impatience with his mother. I miss his perfect body, his skin, his sweet smell, the gap between his big toes, his face, the mole on his neck, his fine hair so soft to stroke. "Oh Mum!" he'd sigh with embarrassment.'

There is no message of hope to other parents who face the loss of a child or grieve a sudden death. Each loss is individual, no two bereaved parents will ever share the same emotions. Only two small crumbs of comfort have emerged from our experiences of loss so far.

The first concerns isolation. Some parents see the loss of a child as so enormous that it isolates them from other people who have not had that experience and could not possibly imagine how terrible it is. Platitudes expressed by people whose whole families seem to have led charmed lives, untouched by sorrow, are especially tiresome to respond to.

But, far from isolating us, Jimmy's death has united me with many people who have suffered a similar loss, maybe years before, who do not normally talk of it any more publicly. Then there are the countless thousands bereaved by holocaust and war, or by disease. Look in any English churchyard; sudden, nameless illnesses carried off almost every child in some families and my grief now unites with the suffering of millions of parents through the ages who have all experienced the sadness of outliving a child or children.

One enduring lesson which Pendlebury taught us so well at the very start was to waste no time before creating quality of life, in case that life should be short. We followed their advice; and all those who acted as we did to make a last year or few months or weeks worthwhile have the great satisfaction and comfort of knowing that a life of only eight years or less may be more greatly enriched with quality than a life which meanders aimlessly through eighty years.

As I grow older, Jimmy will always lie in his quiet country churchyard, forever aged eight; it is so strange to be the mother of a child who will never grow up. Meanwhile, each member of the family goes about the process of mourning in a different way and now we are learning to allow for each other's differences. Leukaemia lays waste bodies, but it need not kill love too, and separate families.

Jimmy is dead and nothing can bring him back. It is hard to find anything positive that will ever emerge from such a tragedy of waste and pain, but perhaps by describing our experiences, we can all do better for other children, particularly those dying, and encourage our research scientists never to give up seeking a full understanding of cancer and its causes in adults and children. The key to discovering cause, cure and prevention may well be money to finance research. It may, even now, lie within our grasp, just for the price of a couple of fighter jets or a stretch of new motorway.

A month after Jimmy's death, we wrote this article about him for all the people living in our town.

# AT REST AT LAST

As everyone knows, our eight-year-old son Jimmy, one of this town's three child cancer victims, finally lost his tenacious grip on life on 31 March. Last October the doctors said he might last until Christmas. At the beginning of January, they gave him three weeks. But he fought with such strength that it was another three months before death finally took him from us.

It was during last autumn that we knew that we were going to lose our son and we decided not to waste his last precious months. There were treats and gifts galore. Few boys his age have flown a plane, been to meet Father Christmas in Sweden, fired a shell from a Chieftain tank or driven the London express at 110 m.p.h. Jimmy did all those things and more, despite his illness.

To those who arranged all these treats and gifts, we are truly grateful.

They enabled us to make the end of his life as full as we possibly could. To those who cared for him professionally, enabling him to die with dignity at home, go our thanks for dedication beyond the call of duty. Our gratitude extends still more to those endlessly kind people of this community who have prayed, visited, child-minded, cooked, baked, or simply shown by quiet deed or word that they wanted to ease our pain.

Jimmy's and the other childrens' illness has, in the words of many, united us all in a way few events have done for years. The magnificent response to the Rotarians' appeal for the Royal Manchester Children's Hospital involved nearly every club, group and institution in the village.

It is human nature, when faced with an outrage such as the lingering death of an innocent child, to look for explanations and to try to salvage something positive from the experience, so that tragedy may have some meaning and be not in vain.

For anyone searching for an appropriate response, it might help to know how Jimmy felt about himself and his world.

He often asked us what caused leukaemia. Although the question could not be answered, he was quite justified in believing that the cause was some obscure toxic agent in our environment. He was also aware how research depends on charity. He was particularly angry that governments spend millions of pounds on the low-flying jets he heard over our home and nothing at all on trying to find out what was slowly killing him.

During his seventh year he became aware, as many children are, that there are a lot of nasty things going on in our world. He knew about pollution of air, seas and rivers, overintensive agriculture, the doubts about nuclear safety and the threat posed by the motor car and the probable consequences of the 'greenhouse effect'. He once said, as the terrible truth about his relapse began to dawn on him, that as long as we went to Heaven with him, he wouldn't mind dying because the world was not such a wonderful place after all. Coming from a child who should have had everything to live for, that should shock us.

Jimmy recognized the greed and selfishness of man in the Western world. Perhaps anyone else who shares his vision might like to help one of the organizations working to change our nasty planet-killing habits, a gesture he would have appreciated.

Jimmy quite naturally formed an unspoken bond with his fellow sufferers. With scarcely any complaint, he suffered alongside them for twenty months the pain of the crude and toxic treatment, the infections, the sickness and the unending burden of hardly ever feeling well and strong. For many children this courage and endurance come to nothing, and like Jimmy, they die. Because research into child cancer relies entirely on charity, and because this research directly affects the prospects of a cure, for the sake of Jimmy's friends still fighting on, we urge people to continue to raise money for Royal Manchester Children's Hospital.

Jimmy had good friends at home, many of them adults, and he loved the village. He liked nothing better than to play in the park, paddle in the becks, or visit the shops. He particularly loved his school, and longed to be well enough to go back and be an ordinary boy with his friends again. If his illness truly has united us it would be fitting, in his memory, if this unity could be made to last so that the village could work as one to promote and defend its real wellbeing, which lies in strong community bonds and a proper concern by all for its environment and its problems.

We would like to thank all those of the various denominations who have prayed so long for the life of our son, and for our family. We hope that they will permit Jimmy's grieving parents the thought that, as God helps those who help themselves, we must all act, as well as pray, to make a healthier world where innocent children do not die from cancer . . .

# TEN

## Moving On . . .

The February sun is shining out of a cloudless sky today, its brightness exaggerating the bareness of the trees as I walk round the park. Wheeling Christy in his buggy, I retrace my footsteps along those same paths where Jimmy played for the very last time two years ago. The wind seems colder today – otherwise it feels as though time stands still in this place.

But the feeling is no more than a passing whim. Time has moved on, slowly and clumsily, clogged with the details of everyday events; so many, in fact, that it seems odd that the practical necessity of committing so many of them to memory never reduces the sharpness of the recent past or blurs any detail of Jimmy's illness and death. Whatever the time, wherever the place, the mind links present to past at the slightest trigger of a familiar sound or smell or sight. The link can be the merest suggestion – the face of a pale child; the smell of freesias or the fleeting glimpse of a little boy with blond hair dashing by on a red bicycle . . .

This last chapter of Jimmy's book is not about him at all, but about us, a brief history of adjustment and survival which is still unfolding. It would be quite untrue to say that we have come through as the people that we once were, and that adjustment to loss enables us to carry on as before. Losing Jimmy has marked us for ever. The experience has become part of our very beings and we are changed people. But the knack of survival lies in accepting this change and sadness as essential parts of ourselves now, leaving enough spare capacity to be filled again with the sheer enjoyment and pleasure of living, even though Jimmy cannot be part of it any more.

In the last few weeks of his life, we travelled side by side with Jimmy and approached death together. In the quiet moment that it came, we were forced to part and he went on alone, leaving us to retreat from the brink.

Over the next year, that journey of despair and futility which life had become slowly reverted to a more familiar pattern of comparative banality, broken occasionally by the ups and downs of the sublime or the ridiculous.

For however much we mourned Jimmy's loss, we could not prevent ourselves slowly responding once again to the ordinary and trivial, as life subsided from the extraordinary back into some recognizable routine. Yet the brevity of Jimmy's existence had emphasized how fragile is our attachment to this world. Life offers us all just one chance, and even that can be foreshortened at any time. Jimmy's illness taught us not to defer or cancel any opportunities that arose; and, subsequently, the year that followed was one of adventure and change rather than passive, unproductive grief.

Jimmy's death left us at first with surprising recklessness and lack of caution. The experience of watching him die had robbed us of perspective and made us feel that nothing else would ever really matter again. We took risks, and even exposed ourselves to danger and debt. Past events had proved that caution and carefulness could do little to change fate, so why fight the predestination over which we had no control – the predestination, maybe genetic, maybe environmental, perhaps both, that had decided that Jimmy should develop cancer in the first place, and that all his efforts to survive should be to no avail? In the months that followed, we frequently abandoned common sense and good advice, allowing instinct to dictate our decisions. There was usually just one criterion involved – if it felt right, we did it.

Easter fell just a fortnight after Jimmy's death. It was cold, wet and very windy, and the promise of resurrection from the dead seemed remote as I visited every day the small mound of newly dug soil which marked Jimmy's grave. The visit was becoming a daily obligation little short of an obsessive ritual. As sure as the bears would get me if I stepped on a crack in the pavement, so guilt and punishment would follow if I failed to visit the grave daily.

By going away for Easter, this compulsive and impractical daily ritual could be broken – if only I could leave Jimmy behind, alone and unvisited, and remain at peace with myself. So we spent Easter in Rippendon with Maureen and Roger and the children; five days went by without visiting the churchyard and the obligation was lifted, like a bad spell broken. The visits after we returned became voluntary acts of will, performed when the time felt right rather than a self-imposed daily punishment.

An overwhelming weariness and isolation dominated those first weeks and months without Jimmy. Friends who were unable to control the tears as they walked into the house stayed away and assumed we would prefer to be left alone at times when we needed them most. Some who did come required the comfort and reassurance that little about us had changed, and that life had returned to normal, re-assurances we could not give.

Other people's problems at that time seemed so infinitely banal, it was hard to be sympathetic. Worries about children were particularly tiresome and trivial to hear; unless the problem was terminal, there seemed nothing much to worry about. Our experiences had carried us outside the normal sphere of life, and for some time it was impossible to recover any sensible perspectives. Even close friends admitted feeling that they were unable to reach or comfort us, as though we were somehow beyond ordinary contact, exalted by some sort of super-suffering.

We were all physically tired with little left to give, and Christy's round-the-clock needs were difficult to satisfy. He was such a beautiful baby, people would stop to admire his stunning blue eyes and murmur platitudes about how lucky we were to have him, and how some things are meant to be – not that they meant Christy was intended as a replacement for Jimmy, they would add hurriedly.

I longed to sleep undisturbed for days, a possibility about as likely as pigs flying. I resented the way the children's everyday needs continually separated me from my grief and prevented me from feeling it fully. When my resentment reached its peak one day, I held Christy close to me, protecting him, as I stamped my feet repeatedly on the floor and visualized the anger like an electrical charge travelling safely out of my body as though earthed. The relief was so great, I could then carry on the feeding and changing, washing and ironing, shopping and cooking. To spend time alone was selfish and impractical, because the family urgently needed to be together to reaffirm our stability and security in the face of Jimmy's absence. In retrospect it is plain to see that the obligation to keep some sort of family routine running for Martin and Christy undoubtedly prevented our grief from over-whelming us completely.

A strange incident occurred about this time which, under normal circumstances, might easily have been laughed off or made the subject of a dinner-table anecdote. Instead, something that might have been relatively insignificant grew, in our grief, into what seemed a frightening and inexplicable form of persecution.

A couple of months after the funeral, I rang Greenpeace to ask in what particular way they planned to spend our donation. They told me that some of it would be used in their work at Sellafield, and after ten minutes' conversation, some of it about monitoring background radiation near the nuclear re-processing plant, the call was suddenly cut off, and I heard a voice saying, 'We are checking, we are checking . . .' over and over again. Greenpeace rang back and were not at all surprised by the incident. Their calls had been cut off in this way before, my contact told me, and we talked about phone tapping.

I listened at first with disbelief and decided that years of campaigning against the dirty habits of greedy multinationals and the killing of whales had left Greenpeace with mild paranoia – until about six weeks later, when a local call was suddenly cut off at home and a phantom voice echoed down the line with the same words as before, 'We are checking, we are checking . . .'

We, too, checked, and by ringing from our business line to our home number and cutting the call as it connected, we would pick up this same voice. It was our turn to feel paranoid. The repeated phrase could have been nothing more than a check by telephone engineers. Yet no fault had been reported on either of our lines, and there was no evidence of any BT work in progress locally. We quickly developed a very strong hunch that our phone was being tapped.

Why this should be, when neither of us had ever been involved with anything remotely subversive, we failed to see. Yet there was the voice, whenever we chose to activate it. In the absence of a more obvious explanation, we jumped to the conclusion that it had to be our recent dealings with Greenpeace which had made us of interest to some faceless guardians of national security.

It was only eight weeks since we had buried our son, and the idea that somebody somewhere regarded us as potential troublemakers simply because we had donated money to, among other projects, helping Greenpeace's work at Sellafield was deeply hurtful. We were angry and indignant, and we occasionally expressed this outrage by calling up the voice and shouting at its detached and disconnected tones in the hope of frightening our 'listener' as much as it was scaring us.

The mystery surrounding the origins of the voice will perhaps never be solved, just as we will probably never know whether it was our exaggerated emotions at the time that invested an innocent fault on the line with a sinister and haunting significance which pursued us throughout the following six weeks; at this point the strange voice disappeared as suddenly as it had arrived, and has not been heard since.

Spring merged into summer, with weeks of hot and sunny weather. Christy, at nearly a year old, was still so small and weak that he needed regular physiotherapy sessions at home to strengthen his shaky little limbs. By being strapped firmly to a special chair with a low table, he had finally developed enough control and muscle power to sit up alone without constantly keeling over sideways. His character revealed stamina and stubbornness alike, but his wide grin, so like Jimmy's, that made even his eyes smile, endeared him to all and exposed the impish sense of humour that he also shared with his lost brother.

Each Thursday morning Karen appeared, quiet but purposeful, and in the course of the morning she would clean and look after Christy while reducing the washing and ironing to neat piles of clean clothes. No gift was more precious to me than a couple of hours of freedom, alone. The flat would look neat and clean on my return, but Karen was more than just a fairy godmother – she had become a genuine one, too: it was Jimmy himself who had finally decided on the appointment of proper godparents for Christy. As Christy's oldest brother, he had taken the matter very seriously; just a few weeks before he died, he chose John and Karen as suitable candidates and asked each one of them individually if they would consider his request. He was genuinely delighted when they both agreed.

Venturing back into the world after months of isolation with Jimmy was particularly hard. Wherever we went, whatever we did at first left us as outsiders and misfits. It was far too soon to become part of village life again. Acquaintances weren't ready for relationships to resume as before, and nor were we. Day after day I stood alone outside school waiting to collect Martin, as other mothers avoided contact. Our presence often imposed a strain on others, and just the sight of us made people silent and sad, reminding them of Jimmy and the vulnerability of their own children.

Thoughts of Jimmy at this time were still dominated by his illness and dying. The vision of his empty little shell, devoid of life and spirit as he lay on our bed in the hours after his death haunted me, but the memories were too distressing to share with anyone else, not even

Paul. We grieved apart, rarely in unison. Some of my worst days were his better ones, which was all to the good – the fitter of us was then able to carry on caring for the children allowing the other a little relaxation from the strain of keeping family life running cheerfully.

The name of a social worker who had some experience with bereavement counselling had been passed to me while Jimmy was still alive. My original concern had been to ensure that Martin would not become frightened of death or terrified of life so she kindly lent me some rather fey little books about the animal world, hoping that Martin would relate Jimmy's death to them. But the storybook notion of an elderly, weary badger hibernating and not waking up seemed to be in the natural order of things whereas the gradual, sometimes painful dying of one's big brother in the room next door was hardly comparable, and I found I could not use the literature.

After Jimmy's death, we qualified to join Pendlebury's monthly club for bereaved parents, but the evening meetings were at the hospital ninety miles from home and neither of us felt it would be helpful to return to the old building, which held so many bad memories.

Yet there was within me a great need to open my heart to somebody who would not suffer pain from talking about Jimmy. So I contacted the social worker I had already seen and we started to meet. I regarded these sessions as my little treat, a tiny bit of self-indulgence every six weeks or so. I talked and she listened. I liked her very much and I felt we had much in common – age, children, background. She too had suffered a family bereavement the year before. She quickly became more friend than counsellor the few times we met, and the value of her company lay in the fact that sometimes she could be detached enough to look at things from an angle I hadn't thought of. When she walked out of the door, she carried some of my burden away with her, and I knew the extra load would not be too heavy for her to bear.

I had understood her visits were at my request – her previous work had been with the elderly and she was seeking wider experience of bereavement in young people so I felt we were of mutual use to each other. I trusted her as a friend; then one day I confided some trivial but private thought which was troubling me. 'I can say it to you, because at least I know it will go no further,' I told her confidently. She was honest enough to reply that if ever I said anything at all worrying, she would have to report back to her Team Leader.

With a shock, I realized that my voluntary move into the boundaries of Social Services had labelled us officially as clients. People I had never met could make us the subject of case conferences and take important decisions about our family based solely on my confidences to a new friend. Suddenly I felt very frightened; with wild visions of dawn raids by social workers who would come to take the children to some place of safety, I disclosed nothing personal again and gently withdrew from the situation, explaining that I had outgrown the need for our occasional meetings.

Nothing could have been further from the truth. But with Big Brother watching me, my confidence was so shaken and I felt so hurt by the lack of confidentiality that I could no longer talk openly. Privately I was yearning for somebody who would listen but not be obliged to report my feelings to anyone in authority, someone whose duty to comfort and counsel was not a statutory one. It was almost a year later before I discovered the help we could have received from Compassionate Friends, the organization which exists solely to help families like our own. Although I had no wish to attend meetings, the library service supplied books each month which described exactly the feelings that we were experiencing, what problems to expect, and how to deal with them. It was amazing to discover how much we had in common with so many other parents. My only regret was that we had taken so long to make contact.

Throughout the hottest weeks of the summer, I climbed the attic ladder each evening to write Jimmy's story. Dust had collected on the model railway track, now standing abandoned and disused. Occasionally Paul cleaned the engines and track just to keep it in running order, but it was a joyless task. Martin expressed no interest whatsoever, and the very sight of the layout must have caused him pain. Yet Jimmy's powerful presence was still trapped under the eaves, like each day's stifling heat, and it seemed a fitting mausoleum in which to sit writing his biography.

Writing about him became an obligation, a debt of honour that I owed him. Once I had completed the book, I knew I would then feel free to let go of him and move on in pace with time because I had made him immortal in words which would never fade as pictures might. The task was wholly absorbing; I hardly noticed the time, and wrote into the early hours for days and weeks, although the attic was stuffy and uncomfortable. I cried as I wrote, and cried again as I read and re-read. I resented interruptions, or any events which threatened to separate me from *Jimmy* each evening. He was with me most vividly throughout, and as the book drew to a close three months later, I was prepared to leave him safely within its pages.

There was a great temptation that year to skip the town's traditional Rushbearing procession in July. The year before, Jimmy and I had trudged round the hot, dusty procession route through the streets together, me pregnant and he weary with chemotherapy. At the time, we were still confident of Jimmy's 60 per cent chance of cure, and looking forward with excitement to the birth of a normal healthy baby. Only a year later, Christy had arrived and almost died and Jimmy was gone forever. Now, as Martin stood alone and partnerless, his rushes wilting in the heat, I wondered whether we should have gone quietly away for the weekend. We were out of place at joyful occasions and as misfits our presence blighted the enjoyment of others.

But to run away would be to postpone the ordeal of the first Rushbearing without Jimmy, and that particular bridge would then be there to cross next year. So we stayed to face it, supported by friends who wept with us as the crowded Parish Church echoed once again to 'Sing Hosanna'. We decorated Jimmy's grave with Martin's rush-bearing and joined other parents at the children's sports, where only twelve months before we had watched with such pride as Jimmy battled against the unpleasant side effects of his treatment to come first in the egg and spoon race.

The grey Lakeland slate headstone for Jimmy's grave had been ordered, and the wording composed by Paul. At the top of the small stone was to be an engraving of a kingfisher to remind us of Jimmy's favourite bird, so elusive that he never succeeded in seeing one in its natural habitat. His cousin Jonathan supplied a drawing to work from, and the bird was to be set against a background of water and fells. The epitaph reads: 'James Thomas Renouf, A Most Precious Son and Brother, Died March 31st 1990, aged 8 years. Only his loss is greater than ours.'

We both looked forward to the day when the soil had settled sufficiently for the stone to be put in place as a proper mark of our son's little space. But when the stone was eventually cemented in, the finality of this pathetic little tribute distressed us more than ever. Nothing could be more pitiful or inadequate than an epitaph for an eight-year-old.

The summer term ended and Martin's long school holidays began.

He enjoyed school because routine there remained unchanged, whilst home during Jimmy's illness was often confusing and unsafe in comparison. His cousin Jonathan arrived to stay and Martin immediately slotted into Jimmy's role as family artist, drawing and painting for hours with Jonny. Martin was looking forward eagerly to Christy's first birthday. A celebration was called for.

For the first time since Jimmy's death four months before, the whole family had something worth celebrating – Christy's survival, and his personal victory over illness and death. Most of that victory lay in the skilled use of the most advanced medical technology available and the ceaseless monitoring that was performed every second during innumerable crises; but we were proud of Christy's spirit and stamina that contributed so much to his survival, and his first birthday deserved the very best celebration we could manage.

His party was held in the park. Forty friends came to share the picnic tea with at least four hundred wasps on a sunny Saturday afternoon. Christy sat unsupported on a rug, legs stuck proudly out in front of him, presiding with great pleasure over his presents. After tea the more energetic guests divided into two football teams and held an impromptu match while the wasps claimed the remains of the cake. It was a happy day and we were pleased that the mood of celebration had come naturally, without force or strain.

Sometimes, we felt, it was other people who dictated how we should behave, or what we should do. We ourselves were becoming adept at mourning and so accustomed to grieving that small fragments of ordinary, everyday life began to coexist comfortably within the huge sadness. Perhaps onlookers were surprised; sometimes ill at ease in our company, they were uncomfortable and bewildered by the growing frequency of laughter and apparent normality in everyday life.

Not so Cate, who was neither shocked nor bewildered by the jokes and wild laughter; as we sat out in her garden late into the sultry evenings that hot August she and our cousin Julia giggled together just as we had in childhood. In terms of relief and release, laughing was indistinguishable from crying and with nobody to watch or disapprove, I felt like a lifer on weekend parole.

Visiting Cate in Poole for the first time without Jimmy was similar to the first Rushbearing without him. The longer we put it off, the harder it would be. Cate's house seemed so neat and clean and cool when we arrived – and so empty without Jimmy. Perhaps it was because we were gradually adjusting to his absence at home that we noticed it more elsewhere without time spent adjusting. I visualized this emptiness like some big black hole in space; one false move and gravity would be lost, dragging me into the dark vortex where all control would vanish. Though at the brink occasionally, I never tumbled over the edge into that vortex of breakdown I feared so much.

The weather was exceptionally oppressive that week and the heat was so intense that we waited until early evening before throwing ourselves into the sea each day for a cooling swim. In some ways, it was a most enjoyable week, and in others it was painfully sad for us all. Grief and grieving can cause considerable intensification of feelings and experiences; the sad ones become sadder still, but the moments of genuine happiness and enjoyment can be equally intense.

An important decision awaited me at home. Returning to work at any level was the last thing I was contemplating. I had given up my job as a district reporter and correspondent on the weekly paper with great relief, and I vowed I would never return. Yet writing *Jimmy* had given discipline and shape to my life, and I had enjoyed the distraction of working to a set pattern each day.

About two years previously, a well-known Lakeland family had asked me to consider writing a biography of their grandfather, the painter Alfred Heaton Cooper. Alfred, who died in 1929, was the head of this remarkable family of painters which continues today through his son and grandson. The family wanted to commission a biography of Alfred, whose landscapes illustrated a score of travel guides in the early 1900s. I refused their first request in 1988, but now they asked again and I agreed, on condition I could work independently, without pressure from anybody.

I began to read avidly about Alfred's contemporaries and major influences, and to visit places where he lived and painted before he came to the Lake District. There were few letters and only scraps of a journal to work from. But fortunately the 150 sketch books that he left were inscribed with date and place as fully as any appointments diary, and using them, we could trace the story of his life. He wrote and illustrated a guidebook about Norway, the birthplace of his wife, which became his adopted second home; I dreamed of fjords and salmon racks and trolls as I sat up in the attic cataloguing and compiling.

Gradually the character of this distant but pleasant and affable man, who lies dead in the same churchyard as Jimmy, began to invade my mind. The visions of Jimmy shifted slightly aside to let Alfred settle comfortably in my head. I tried to see the world through his eyes, and to assess landscapes as Alfred would have done. Alfred's temporary presence in my consciousness gave me less time to feel pain for Jimmy's absence; and on sad days I could escape into Alfred's world and find peace and relief as I imagined a Norwegian glacier at sunset, or enjoyed the details of his domestic life at home as I discovered more and more about the man.

Living somebody else's life instead of my own was such a relief that I decided to extend the practice even further and audition for the next play to be performed by the local amateur dramatic group. The play was a contemporary comedy and the rehearsals promised to be funnier and more farcical than any of the intended jokes.

The very best thing about acting was the freedom it allowed to laugh and fool about without restraint, or disrespect for Jimmy. As the person who laughed, I was acting within a stage character where frivolity was entirely permissible; then, two hours later, I would return regretfully to the pain of my own reality. The stress of the actual performances was, however, far from fun. Control of life remained so brittle that it left no room whatsoever for extra stress.

Grief not only penetrates and destroys concentration and memory. It also makes ordinary troubles seem almost intolerable. 'Not this – and Jimmy too!' was our common reaction to anything going wrong. It was even worse if somebody was actually responsible for an avoidable mistake and could be blamed; the person or body in question became the subject of intense anger and resentment. Having been unable to blame anyone for our son's illness and death, it was as though a large residue of stored-up anger lay waiting now to be directed at life's ordinary irritations and frustrations.

The night the dishwasher exploded was a good example of this. Late one evening, while Paul was out and the children in bed and asleep, I switched on the machine. There was a flash, two loud explosions and flames shot out from behind the panelling, narrowly missing my skirt as I jumped back in terror. Fortunately the two exposed wires which had touched bare metal and sparked off the fire burnt themselves out, leaving the machine intact but the entire room covered in a greasy soot.

I was very angry – it was a classic 'Not this – and Jimmy too' situation. Close questioning of the service engineer revealed a design fault that the manufacturers had known about, but failed to correct. Months later, an angry campaign of letters and publicity paid off and the BBC's *Watchdog* programme uncovered dozens of identical cases. We had been lucky. Another family had lost their home in a similar fire. The manufacturers refused to operate a recall at first, then were finally forced to. But there was a small element of paranoia in my intense anger; it was nothing less than a personal assault that this large firm cared so little for our safety. The company knew some time before that their product was seriously faulty and deliberately chose to continue to expose families like our own to danger rather than risk the bad publicity and poor sales that a recall might cause.

But why did these bad things keep happening to us? It was sheer bad luck, people told us. Sooner or later, they said, it will be somebody else's turn.

But it was my turn again one day in autumn when I noticed I couldn't bend one knee while bathing Christy. Within a day, one tiny little throbbing point spread its red heat up my thigh and down to my ankle; for two weeks the infection fought a winning battle against antibiotics until there was nothing left to do but adopt a more unsophisticated approach to the swollen mess.

The local casualty department was busy that Monday afternoon as I waited among bent fingers and dislocated shoulders.

'Well – shift yer bum onto that bed,' was the doctor's bored greeting, as he looked at me through dull eyes. He was grubby and disgruntled, perhaps very tired; and what he did next virtually without local anaesthetic would have won him the title of Torturer General of the Year outright in any Inquisition contest. 'Oh God – you're not going to faint on me,' he complained peevishly. Three hours later, and my leg still felt as if it was being stuck with red-hot pokers. My fragile control snapped. Already battered and damaged enough, I felt as though I had been personally assaulted, even violated. 'Not this – and Jimmy too!' I wailed. The poor man's face took up its position in my store of bad memories, and I could hardly look at him each time he checked the progress of the abscess he had excised.

A quick recovery was essential because we had less than a month to go before we were due to fly out to Zimbabwe for a three-week holiday as guests at the British High Commission. The invitation came from Kieran and Joan, Diplomatic Service friends we had not seen for years, and we readily accepted their kind offer of hospitality. Paul and Kieran had known one another since teenage years. Kieran's marriage to Joan, the four children that followed and their ascent up the Diplomatic ladder via several foreign postings prevented us from seeing them often, and our last visit had been to New York, exactly ten years before, when Kieran had been a First Secretary at the UN. His latest posting to Harare was as British High Commissioner, and Joan's colourful letters made Zimbabwe sound both very beautiful and exciting.

The visit had first been considered after Jimmy's relapse but he was already too ill to feel much enthusiasm and he told us sadly that he thought it would be too much for him. We knew he was right. The visit exposed us to the risk that his condition might suddenly deteriorate, and the idea of his dying in Africa, so far from the comfort and support of home, was inconceivable. We postponed the trip rather than abandoned it, resolving to take Martin one day.

In the end, it was Jimmy himself, indirectly, who made the visit possible. For weeks the DSS withheld his Attendance Allowance, which meant that he was unable to benefit personally from the money during his lifetime. Then, some time after his death, a large backdated cheque arrived. Instinct told us to spend the money on something spectacular and we decided that it would pay for our African adventure.

As our departure date drew nearer, I became more and more unhappy about the trip. I felt insecure and unprotected – if we could lose one child and almost lose another in the relative safety of a country like Britain, anything at all could happen to threaten us in Africa. There were snakes and AIDS, malaria and bilharzia, accidents and acts of God to consider. How could we spend so much time nursing Christy to health and then expose him to all manner of avoidable danger?

But Paul's excitement and pleasure at the forthcoming holiday were so refreshing to see that I couldn't possibly tell him my true feelings about it and risk spoiling his anticipation. Many, many times since Jimmy's death I had watched him sit or lie silently on the sofa for hours at a time, saying nothing and looking at the wall. Now he pored over the gruelling itineraries that Kieran had worked out for us while my dreams of lazy days spent doing little more than watching a flame tree bloom by the limpid blue waters of a shady pool slowly faded.

We phoned Harare for final instructions, counting each £10 minute; it seemed an eternity before a respectful voice informed us that Kieran was 'at tennis' and could not be disturbed. Only a fortnight later we, too, were at tennis while silver was laid gently on damask for lunch to be served under the fragrant frangipani; and there, just as in my dream, the flame tree blooms, its orange flowers reflected in the crystal waters of the beautiful swimming pool.

We had arrived after an overnight flight like crumpled refugees, baby and sleepy child in tow; Kieran was there on the tarmac to greet us in the early morning, a tall, distinguished diplomatic figure wearing the uniform of high colonial office – his battered panama hat. The Union Jack, raised each morning at dawn, fluttered in the breeze outside the Residence as Joan and the house staff waited on the verandah by the front door to greet us as we arrived. Bacon and eggs were served in the dining room half an hour later as we sat under the watchful gaze of a British monarch's portrait. Emerging as though from a distant nightmare, I looked out to the gardens and thought I could see Heaven beyond the elegantly festooned curtains which hung like sculptured scrolls round the tall windows.

This glimpse of Paradise did nothing to control fears about the local fauna and it was some days before the Gaboon viper by the pool was reduced in size to the harmless lizard it was in reality. Slowly we all relaxed.

The itinerary that Kieran and Joan had planned and arranged, which took us on a week's tour round Zimbabwe, seemed exhausting just to contemplate. They both understood how weary we were and how paralysed and vulnerable we might feel as new arrivals in a country so far from home. However, our time was short, and they had decided that this mustn't prevent us from going to see the things that make Zimbabwe such a beautiful country.

'Look,' Joan said in her forthright way, 'we didn't know Jimmy; and we can't even pretend to understand what it must have been like. We weren't there; but we can give you something else while you're here. This is a wonderful country, and you can experience some of its beauty and excitement, and let yourselves enjoy it, if only you'll leave the memories behind for a while and allow it to happen. Make the most of your time here away from it all – it's up to you.'

Gradually, day by day, the tensions eased. Pain and loss seemed so far away from the jacaranda and sweet frangipani trees. We relished each tiny detail of life in the house without guilt. It was elegant, sometimes grand as the occasion demanded, but it always remained essentially a family home where Jemima, the bull terrier, left muddy paw prints on the carpet, and there was laughter in the kitchen. Theodora, the housekeeper, acted as Christy's nanny while we played tennis or swam or slept. He shuffled about on his bottom on the kitchen floor as the house staff cherished their new white baby; outside, Limited, the gardener, mowed the acres of lawn with Martin as passenger in the grass-catcher.

We loved life in the house, but Martin became more and more subdued and angry as time went on. 'All this – and no Jimmy to share it with,' was his message to us all. No amount of cajoling and special treats lightened his depression. His conversation, normally so lively, was reduced to monosyllabic grunts; he refused to eat, rejecting all his favourites so carefully prepared for him. Instead he splashed in the pool or buried his head in Asterix books. At the time his behaviour seemed incomprehensible. We had hoped so much that this visit would furnish him with wonderful and exciting memories to help balance the bad ones. Looking back we can see why he rejected us and all the attempts we made to please him. Nothing, not even Zimbabwe, could compensate him for losing Jimmy or console his loneliness.

Within a few days of our arrival, we prepared to set off in a borrowed car equipped with emergency tinned food, large floppy sunhats, anti-mosquito bands and a set of instructions. Two of us were missing; Jimmy, as he always will be, and Christy, who was to stay with Joan and Kieran for a week. The decision had already been made without consultation, at the highest level, by Joan; it wasn't safe to take Christy to the malarial places we were to visit, and plans for his welfare had already been laid. I tried to feel guilty at leaving him, but I couldn't. The decision had been taken out of my hands. 'Make the most of it', Joan advised, so I did. Christy shed not a tear all week for us; he was far too busy entertaining his new friends in the kitchen and basking in all the loving attention that his gracious hosts gave him.

During the week away, we travelled over a thousand miles on smooth, tarmac roads empty of almost all traffic. All Martin's anger and resentment disappeared once we were alone; life on the road was no longer very comfortable or luxurious, but required careful thought and quick-wittedness, and he rose admirably to the challenge. We stayed in simple lodges, visiting several National Parks, and there we watched, in the wild, the animals that Jimmy would so dearly have loved to see. There were giraffes and elephants, white rhinos, buffalos, antelope, monkeys, hippos, crocodiles, lions and many more. News of the drought now affecting this wonderful country fills us with great fear for its warm and friendly people.

No day went by without moments of despair and hopelessness as we longed for Jimmy's presence and tried to imagine his comments and reactions to everything we encountered.

Travelling as we did alone demanded concentration, especially when dealing with unplanned events. On one occasion, it was how best to break open the securely locked car to retrieve the ignition keys inside – without shade, drink or a telephone nearer than twenty dirt-tracked miles away. That particular problem was solved with a piece of bent wire by four friendly locals who appeared from nowhere.

Several times we rode the bush trail on horseback to get closer to the animals; this seemed enormously exciting until my horse threw me onto rocky ground downwind of a herd of buffalo. Remounting for an hour's jarring ride back was the only way to reach safety. Bumping along in the burning sun, I thought of Jimmy dying and found it equally absurd that we were now in southern Africa on horseback watching giraffes grazing. The sense of unreality at times made the events of the past year seem increasingly like a disjointed dream.

We took the Flight of the Angels over Victoria Falls in a perilous little single-engine plane; we sipped champagne on a glorified raft up the Zambezi River at sunset as the hippos yawned dangerously near the rocking boat. Accommodation was in a lodge on the banks of the river where the bushpigs took dustbaths by the back porch and a lion lurked occasionally at night behind the washing line. Early one morning we awoke to hear a JCB at work outside the window. Mystified, we pulled back the shutters, and came face to trunk with a large elephant, busy uprooting a tree by the window.

The adventures that we had were sometimes quite risky. Jimmy's quiet passing had left no fear of death, so perfect was its love and peace. But suddenly it occurred to us that accidental death might be very different. Then all fear reappeared. Ferocious Zimbabwean thunderstorms were terrifying, bumpy and turbulent air flights caused cold sweats, and the sudden storm that almost upturned our little boat on Lake Kariba left me lying face downwards on the heaving deck praying for deliverance from the crocodiles and hippos lurking below.

We returned from the week's trip to find all was well with Christy; and much relieved, we slept soundly in comfortable beds that night. Next morning we woke to the sound of his little voice, chuckling as

he played in his room just down the passage; but the chatter turned
suddenly to hysterical screaming and within seconds I was running to
him, dreading what I would find. Joan was already plunging his arm
in cold water as I arrived on the scene but even she had not been quick
enough to save his skin. It hung off his hand and arm in shreds where
he had plunged them into a cup of hot tea. We couldn't believe the
damage that so little liquid could do; ironically it was one of the
commonest household accidents that had turned out to be far more
dangerous to him than a hungry lion or any of the more exotic dangers
that we had anticipated.

The doctor was out jogging and took an hour to answer our call
for help. All we could do was to hold Christy's arm and hand in cold
water while he screamed incessantly. My imagination ran wildly ahead
as I planned our repatriation, Christy's fight for life and his inevitable
death. It was completely beyond my comprehension that he might
survive; since Jimmy's illness, all accidents and illness had become
terminal in my mind. Nothing else was important enough to bother
about.

The doctor's delayed arrival actually did no harm, because the long
wait in cold water turned out to be the most effective way of
minimizing Christy's bad scalding. The doctor reassured us all immediately that the burn was only superficial; we had prevented serious
damage with the cold water, he said, and the fact that Christy was still
bawling so vigorously was a good sign. I had dreaded taking him to
hospital because of the danger of AIDS; however, he was treated at
the doctor's surgery in exactly the same way as in any British casualty
department. His arm was encased in bandages impregnated with an
antibiotic cooling paste and we were told that within three weeks there
would be hardly a mark to show for his accident. The doctor insisted
that we were suffering more than Christy.

He was right, but I didn't believe him at the time, even though
Christy spent a happy day with no sign or pain of distress. Recalling
our fears for Jimmy, I waited for the first signs of the infection which
I thought would kill Christy. Not even the spectacular, melodic Shona
sung Mass we attended at the Catholic Cathedral next morning offered
any solace; and with little faith at that time in religion or Western
medicine, I decided in my panic and disbelief to find a witch doctor,
for an alternative opinion.

My resolve was only half serious – but finding a witch doctor was easier than I had imagined. That afternoon, while wandering round a showpiece Shona village just outside Harare, a tall man wearing a big black cape covered in stars and moons approached us and inquired what was wrong with our baby. He told us he was the medicine man, and had noticed Christy's bandages. Zimbabweans love and cherish all babies, and the sight of an injured one was too much for him to ignore. We told him about the accident and asked him what we should do. His remedy was simple – we should ignore Western doctors and instead mix egg white with Stork margarine and some soot, and smear the potion over the burn. He sold us some powder for about 20p, which he delivered in a screwed up newspaper; we took it back with us, but the housekeeper had no time for witch doctors and threw it away in disgust, so the remedy escaped further analysis.

Sunday being the staff's day off, teatime was by popular choice a simple occasion at the kitchen table. I could hear laughter below as the toast was burnt and the eggs boiled but I stayed in our room alone, to think about the implications of everything that had happened, and explore my pessimism.

Paul was extremely irritated by my depression and pessimism over Christy's accident. Shaken by his unsympathetic attitude, I recognized that this fatalism was beginning to darken not only my life, but everybody else's around me. I had become trapped in Jimmy's terminal mode, and it had to be left behind. I joined the laughter downstairs with new resolve.

Christy's amazing recovery helped me in my effort to be optimistic. Three weeks later, with his bandages removed, the pale but almost unscarred little hand and arm proved as nothing else could that hope can be rewarded.

The tennis, the swimming, the sheer exhilaration of being with friends in a beautiful place made Zimbabwe almost impossible to leave. The holiday was filled with contrasts – from the vision of sunrise turning Victoria Falls the palest pink to the tipsy Booze Cruise down the Zambezi as the sun hung like a ball of fire over the dense bush; from the grandeur of a Diplomatic Ball to the simplicity of the village where hundreds flocked to see Kieran and Joan switch on the first solar-powered electric light at the simple clinic. There, two nurses cared for a population of twenty thousand, scattered over forty miles of bushland.

Joan's warmth and wit, married to Kieran's intellectual energy and drive, ensured there was never a dull moment; and because our little family was anonymous, nobody had any expectations of our behaviour. We could laugh or cry whenever we wanted, and it was very difficult to leave such freedom and return home to cold, grey England in winter.

We left Harare in a buoyant mood, hoping we would be able to raise the air fare again and return as soon as possible. We even considered starting a new life in this remarkable country, but the practicalities were too daunting.

Our African euphoria slowly drained away as Christmas approached – another first without Jimmy. The strain of carrying on the old traditions made Christmas a tense, unhappy time as it will be for many years; yet without the obligation on us to make a children's Christmas-time for Martin and Christy, the festive season would have been even bleaker. What of those parents who lose an only child? We thought of them frequently; and we remembered the families we had met whose lives had been devastated by diseases like cystic fibrosis; some of them faced losing more than one child. Our sadness seemed nothing in comparison.

Martin and I met up one afternoon with Karen, Becky and Jonathan and we decorated Jimmy's grave with flowers and holly. Martin had brought a can of Jimmy's glitter spray to add some sparkle to our arrangements. When, with great indignation, he and Jonny found a heap of dog muck on a grave, Martin grabbed the can and dashed round, spraying all the offending piles he could find with Christmas glitter. 'There – that's better,' he said with satisfaction, and went home to write a letter of complaint to the church magazine.

New Year was nothing to celebrate; the division of years separated us even further from the time we looked back on with such longing, when Jimmy was still with us. Entering another year forced us further apart from Jimmy.

Occasionally we dreamed of moving to a house with a garden. Caring for a garden seemed the ideal thing to help promote our own regeneration, but the likelihood of this ever happening lessened as the recession deepened by the day. Consequently it became a subject to be avoided for fear that it might cause growing discontent that couldn't be satisfied. The property pages of the local paper were discarded each week, unread.

It was more than a bit of a shock, therefore, to find ourselves standing on the upstairs landing of a perfectly strange house one Friday afternoon, making a cash offer for a property that we had only heard about three hours previously. It was a four-bedroomed house, built solidly in 1905, with spacious cellars, wood panelling, and moulded ceilings. Outside was a sloping terraced garden with rockeries and lawn picturesquely set with a backdrop of fields and fells. Previous owners had cared for it so well, it was the sort of garden that passers-by stop to admire.

The house, as it happened, was directly opposite Granny Anna's flat, and ideal for helping her whenever necessary. But within hours of Bracklyn appearing on the property market, it attracted interest from dozens of potential buyers, especially elderly people who appreciated the solitude and close proximity to the village.

We knew, the minute we set foot in the house, that we wanted to live in it. But was it too soon to move after Jimmy's death – too soon to leave him behind?

'You know, Jimmy doesn't exist any more,' Martin had informed me with authority one morning while we walked to school. As I composed a reply, a slow smile spread across his freckly face. 'But his spirit is there, in all our hearts, for all of us who love him,' he added triumphantly. As Paul and I stood on the landing that Friday at Bracklyn, we knew how much Jimmy would have approved. It was an ideal place for his spirit to live on in our hearts, and would provide Martin and Christy with the best possible opportunity for a happier childhood than they had already experienced.

There were minor snags to overcome – finding an instant cash buyer for our own property; and competing against a string of older, wealthier buyers offering more money than we could afford for Bracklyn.

Several times during the previous three years, we had been approached by a neighbouring business interested in acquiring our building. One phone call confirmed they would buy immediately, and a price was agreed two days later. Our own offer for Bracklyn, however, was inadequate; others were willing to go much higher to acquire such a popular house. But the two elderly lady owners, who had known us for some years, wanted to see their house as our family home. We increased our offer and it was accepted.

Nothing could have been simpler. Our spirits rocketed as Bracklyn became the symbol of the renewal and rebuilding of our lives. With a darkroom in the cellar, Paul would work from home without the massive overheads from the old studio. Within days, documents began to travel between the solicitors, and moving day was to be within six weeks.

Then without warning, on Valentine's Day, our buyer withdrew, claiming he was unable to finance the purchase. The dream disintegrated.

Life hit new depths of misery that day. The climax of grief and disappointment, hopelessness and anger was a noisy one. Paul was alarmed at my uncharacteristic outburst, but the force of it persuaded him how important it was not to give up, at least without trying. So we told nobody of the situation and began to mount a rescue plan for our dream.

It was, undoubtedly, the force of my anger that drove us on. Even our best attempts at making a new beginning seemed doomed to failure, through no fault of our own; but such injustice exploded in a storm of righteous anger which made it somewhat easier to beg bank managers for a loan. Yet the answer was the same wherever we tried: we were in the wrong place at the wrong time, asking the impossible.

Undeterred, we refused to admit defeat. Then, one day, there was a bank not only willing to listen but actually impressed enough with our audacity, not to mention tenacity, to spend an afternoon visiting the site. With enormous support from several sources, a deal was finally negotiated and we were offered a bridging loan backed by capital from a kind benefactor. In real terms, it gave us two years at Bracklyn while selling our old home. If all failed, we would simply re-sell Bracklyn and move back.

Acquiring Bracklyn this way sometimes seemed a reckless gamble, and at other times a calculated risk. It certainly would not have been our course of action if life had remained as ordinary and conventional as it had been before Jimmy became ill. But our lives had become extraordinary, even existential, and we looked no further than the present to snatch what share of happiness we considered was due to us.

Just before we moved, we celebrated Paul's fiftieth birthday with a party which lasted all day. Although Jimmy's absence was felt by all most keenly, it no longer dominated the occasion as it would have done just months before, and the party restored confidence in our ability to entertain and give pleasure to the eighty guests who came to share our special day, and who took their lead from us that it was all right to smile, even laugh again.

The first anniversary of Jimmy's death fell on Easter Sunday. No single gesture that day could possibly express our feelings, nor could any single act summarize or symbolize his loss or our own. Attending morning service at the Parish Church seemed like a suitable act of thanks to all there who supported us so staunchly; the service was very long, but the spontaneous displays of love and sympathy from everybody nearby who remembered the date were very moving.

The Gorrigans came over to join us in the afternoon and although none of our plans for a walk together worked out, it was very comforting to be together with people who needed no explanations, people who were standing at our side during the very worst of times.

However we had chosen to spend Jimmy's anniversary, the sadness that such a day brings is beyond consolation. Nothing is adequate to express the love that we still have for our beautiful child, or what his loss has meant to us. Anniversaries are not uplifting or proud days, as we learnt that first year. Easier, instead, to allow the melancholy and indulge the grief without repression, knowing that the intensity of the day will pass.

Moving day, three weeks later, would have been a triumphant act of hope for a better future without the spectre of debt and uncertainty which shadowed it. A sense of unreality accompanied the move; could this really be us embarking on a course of such supreme madness?

Yet within days, it felt as though we had lived at Bracklyn for years. Our favourite portrait of Jimmy hung on the stairs, and his gentle little face watched us as we moved round the house. It was as though he was there, within the family, but without his illness. Bracklyn held no memories of sadness or anguish, and his quiet, unspoken presence was safe within its warmth and solidity.

Yet with the uncertainty that lay ahead, the house could not be regarded as home. Instead, I thought of it as a superb holiday home, taken on a long lease, to be enjoyed one day at a time.

Paul made the garden productive immediately with good crops of raspberries, sweetcorn, cabbage, beans, lettuce and herbs. The garden is colourful throughout the year and Jimmy's grave had never seen such varieties of flowers and blossom as we now gathered for him from the new garden.

The phone rang one day in June, and a researcher from BBC1's *Songs of Praise* requested a meeting. I assumed, as a local reporter, it was for information for the programme that they were planning in our town. Instead, I was asked to appear in it, talking about Jimmy and whether it was possible to reconcile the concept of a merciful God with a world in which innocent children suffer and die.

I told them I couldn't be hypocritical in any way, and that what I would say might upset many devout churchgoers. There would be no bogus religious enlightenment or conversion born of noble suffering. The producers said that was fine by them. *Songs of Praise* wanted to tackle difficult issues in an honest way, and my testament, whatever it was, would be respected and not manipulated by clever editing.

The interview, with presenter Martin Bashir, took place in the garden. A voice that I couldn't believe was my own talked about Jimmy's last few months, the love which surrounded us all and our relationship with a God who allowed little children to suffer. Such a God of love and compassion seemed to be an absurdity, a contradiction in terms; and the only visible facet of His goodness I could recognize lay in the love that others gave us.

We talked of grief and guilt; and of allowing happiness and joy to creep back into shattered lives. I expressed great optimism in the future of our family and chose 'Sing Hosanna' as an appropriate way to summarize that hope. It was to be sung at an outdoor service later in summer, in celebration of Jimmy's eight loving years, and in recognition of the bravery of all children undergoing chemotherapy and radiotherapy in their fight against cancer.

The interview ended and we looked round. The entire crew of eleven were deeply moved by our conversation and the experience of filming the interview drew us together as though they had all known Jimmy personally.

The outdoor service took place one rain-soaked Saturday. It was as difficult to face the camera then as it had been easy before. For most committed believers taking part, the three-hour recording was an outward and joyful expression of their faith, but for me it was hard to feel any commitment to the words of hope and trust as rain drenched us all. Yet the public performance of the triumphant 'Sing Hosanna' had to match the message of hope already recorded in the garden at Bracklyn – but this time the tears were choking, and no sound would come. That rawest of grief was eventually shared with an audience of seven million, and the messages and letters that followed the broadcast from others proved how many people share our incomprehension at the mysterious ways in which God works.

With summer ending, and no sign of a resolution to the problem of keeping Bracklyn, Paul closed the unsold studio building to reduce overheads and started to work entirely from the new house. To compensate for any drop in income this might cause, we agreed to share the bread-winning between us. The first step towards this was a return to the columns of the local paper, a job which I had vowed I would never do again just the year before. Requiring, as it does, a certain boldness to tackle issues often within the public eye, it was not the sort of job for somebody wishing to find solitude and anonymity; however, just a year made a big difference to attitudes and feelings, and it was much easier to return to the old routine than anticipated. Another lesson was learned – to avoid the finality of 'never'. Who can be that certain of anything?

However, the income from the newspaper alone was inadequate and I decided to work part-time and send Christy to nursery each morning. Nine years at home with small children since Jimmy's birth had been a long stretch; and the sadness and disillusionment caused by Jimmy's death made me less of an imaginative and energetic mother than I used to be. Christy, especially, deserved all the ingenuity and patience possible to help his slow progress, and the weary, depressed woman I might have become by staying permanently at home was by no means the best person to provide exclusively for his needs.

I wrote a couple of letters applying for local jobs without much enthusiasm, not really knowing what to do. Then, queueing in the post office one day, I saw Irene, who together with her husband, Paul, runs a busy printing works and a couple of stationery shops. Paul and Irene had been our friends for nearly ten years.

'Come and work for us,' she said impulsively. 'Why not?'

After careful thought I decided there was no good reason why not. So, with Christy booked in at nursery, I started work. My job involved an enormous variety of tasks connected with every possible aspect of printing. There was no time to think of anything except the job in hand, and I returned at the end of that first morning incredulous that anybody should actually want to pay me for enjoying myself. The greatest novelty lay in the fact that four hours had passed without a nappy in sight – and nobody had been sick down my skirt.

Despite proud feelings at helping to contribute to our family finances, it took time to readjust to our new roles, sharing domestic chores and working routines. Early mornings have always been notoriously bad times for missing Jimmy – but with a job to get to, no time for contemplation and an obligation to be efficient and pleasant, it became very much easier to live through the bad days. The sheer variety of the work involved, together with Paul and Irene's good sense, compatibility and quick humour made working hours a safe but lively part of each day.

As each week went by, we knew our days at Bracklyn were numbered. Then, out of the blue, our original buyer returned with a much-reduced offer, but one we couldn't afford to reject. His offer would still clear our debts, and secure Bracklyn for life. We accepted. The next six weeks were so fraught with legal wrangles, the deal almost fell through several times. But our gamble finally paid off and we sold the old studio and flat and bought Bracklyn outright on the last day of October.

Leaving the flat for the very last time was more of a wrench than could possibly have been imagined. It was unthinkable that we would never return to the place that meant so much to Jimmy. To leave it for ever was almost like deserting Jimmy, leaving him behind.

But in one way that was precisely what had to be done; however difficult. This final farewell needed a ritual to accompany it, some outward gesture; if Jimmy's dying were to be left within its walls, then so too should his laughter and some relic of our love for him.

The weather that morning added Gothic melodrama to the farewell. A grey darkness fell as day broke, and the wind battered the windows with rain. With bunches of freesias and sprays of greenery, we made several beautiful arrangements and stuck them in empty milk bottles. The idea of the bottles had been Cate's contribution – she remembered how such a small absurdity would have tickled Jimmy's sense of humour.

Each display of flowers was left with a card and message round the studio, darkrooms and flat upstairs. The scent of freesias filled the old building.

The final visit to our bedroom was very happy. I stood in the place where Jimmy and I had curled up together as he died in my arms, and the room was a warm, soft cocoon in which the memory of his love was imprinted for eternity. Then I gathered up his spirit and took it, within mine, to be with us always at Bracklyn in peace and safety. There was just one final, private note to leave behind. It is hidden so well that only a demolition gang will ever find it.

New Year's Eve that year was a celebration for the first time since Jimmy became ill; suddenly it seemed worthwhile to look forward to the future rather than longingly to the past, and at last we laughed again as Becky, Jonathan and Martin entertained us in the familiar way, as they had done so often with Jimmy before. But we celebrated midnight now instead of mourning it, facing the future with renewed energy.

How neat it would be if our story were to have a 'happy ever after' ending. But happiness and contentment are such fragile commodities, we cannot presume to protect them from future breakage; it only takes a second's chance or circumstance, and life's former certainties lie in fragments.

We are gradually reassembling those broken fragments, but although the pieces don't quite fit together as they used to, and there are gaps where others have been lost for ever, the finished object is becoming recognizable again, flawed but still beautiful.

Life now is a little like my dance/exercise class. 'Smile!' the teacher shouted at us as I stretched and kicked self-consciously during the first session, only months after Jimmy's death. 'Smile!' she ordered, but I failed to see why I should have to smile when I felt so bad. Some weeks later, I couldn't fight it any longer as I bounced about with the energy and rhythm of dancing. 'Smile if it hurts!' she shouted. The command wasn't necessary. The sheer joy of living was so irresistible that the smile had already come spontaneously.

'Christy won't ever be sad,' Martin said recently, with some envy. Having been younger, then middle child and now elder, Martin's understanding of life is impressively wide and philosophical, and his patience and love for a demanding little brother is unstinting and generous.

Christy will need that strength and support in order to overcome the minor brain damage caused by his illness after birth, which leaves him clumsy and unsteady on his wobbly little legs, and his speech equally wobbly and indistinct. But his bright, happy, and sociable disposition has survived the saddest of years, miraculously intact. It is wonderful to see the other two children from our town who shared Jimmy's 1988 diagnosis of cancer so fit and well now, indistinguishable from other children. But for them, the checkups and clinics will continue long into the future, and the fear of seeing a child from clinic days suddenly relapsed and back in Borchardt Ward never goes away.

Jimmy's illness and death influenced both those he knew, and many he never met. The fund-raising for his hospital at Pendlebury continues sporadically, with gestures both great and small. A concert in memory of Jimmy, both organized and performed by Sonja and two others in our Parish Church, raised over £1,000 in one evening, money which we gave to Pendlebury specifically to improve the care of dying children. Local Rotarians raised £45,000 in one year alone, as a major contribution to the cost of building new parent accommodation attached to the children's cancer ward. Others make individual efforts in his memory by running marathons or holding coffee mornings; and this year his family and closest friends have presented his school with the Jimmy Renouf Memorial Trophy, to be awarded annually for service to others.

'Why – why did you write this?' one tearful friend demanded as she handed me back the manuscript of *Jimmy*. Three weeks later, a suitable answer emerged.

By an extremely circuitous route a dog-eared copy of *Jimmy* reached the trustees of the Sir John Fisher Trust. After reading the book, they donated £100,000 to CancerCare at Lancaster, to open a new education centre committed to training staff in helping families affected by cancer, whether the victims be children or parents. A further £5,000 annually will provide specialist training to help children like Jimmy, who face terminal illness, by providing a suitable experienced nurse to work with the families. May CancerCare's initiative inspire similar projects all over Britain.

It would be exciting to wake up one morning and hear that some astounding research breakthrough had uncovered the cause and prevention of childhood cancers. Like all parents of sick children, we want to know most urgently why it was our child in thousands that was susceptible, and whether there was anything anyone could have done to prevent it.

When Jimmy was ill, we heard of many research studies into causes of leukaemia and effectiveness of treatment; but it was disappointing that the scientists never came to ask us what we considered were fundamental questions about our family, its genetic make-up, its general health and the background in which we lived.

It is therefore the most encouraging news since Jimmy died to hear from Dr Richard Stevens, the Consultant Haematologist/Oncologist at Pendlebury, that these questions are to be routinely asked of each family whenever a child is diagnosed with leukaemia in the next five years. Perhaps the longed-for breakthrough will emerge from among thousands of pieces of information so painstakingly collected.

The five-year project is one of the largest studies ever undertaken, and it will try to plot the patterns, geographical distribution and genetics of childhood malignancy throughout the UK.

In practical terms, this means that every new case will be investigated on five different counts: the incidence of natural or man-made radiation, including X-rays and background radon gases either during pregnancy or after birth; exposure to potentially hazardous chemicals; radiation at work which could cause damage to the father's sperm cells before the birth of the child; the influence of electromagnetic fields generated by powerlines, underground cables and household electrical appliances; and infection in early childhood, especially exposure to viral infections, which might lead to leukaemia.

We will always feel the closest affinity with every child who sets out from diagnosis day on the long road towards recovery within Pendlebury's old walls. We were delighted to hear from Dr Stevens how much parents appreciate the new accommodation just below the ward, which our town worked so hard to help finance. But what of new research?

Needless to say, the amount of this vital work possible is directly linked to the amount of charity money available to fund it. This not only reflects the priority that governments place on such work, but the public too. Doctors and administrators are left juggling with limited funds.

As Dr Stevens describes: 'Whilst the national organizations for co-ordinating the treatment of childhood cancer – for example, the Medical Research Council and the UK Children's Cancer Study Group – act as a forum for the children's cancer specialists in the UK, we are still very dependent on charitable monies for research and even basic medical care. Half of our middle-grade oncology doctors at RMCH are paid for out of "soft" money, both locally and nationally funded. Within a state health care system this is not the ideal or fairest situation but is basically no different from the majority of countries throughout the world. If the general public feel a need and desire to help support childhood cancer then it is our responsibility to try and use that money to the best advantage, be it for research, hospital facilities, or home support systems.'

There are several projects that Manchester are particularly involved with: one is to try and assess more accurately 'good' and 'bad' risk children at diagnosis so that treatment can be tailored more to the nature of their disease. There are also studies into the effects of treatment in long-term survivors, and the measurement of metabolism and weight loss of children from diagnosis through treatment, as well as the analysis of the genetics of solid tumours.

Treating children is one thing – but knowing when to stop is vitally important to future health, and researchers are looking very closely at something called Minimal Residual Disease, which is detecting the very last cancer cell which may be present in a child who otherwise appears to be in remission.

In practical terms, the care of the family is essential in the wellbeing of each sick child, and the two Macmillan paediatric nurses specially trained since Jimmy's death are now working in the community to try to help co-ordinate local hospital and GP practice health care needs. Several adult hospices in the North-West have agreed to admit children on request, but most families like our own prefer to keep children at home.

So much more still needs to be done to provide better home support for dying children. It is almost impossible to imagine how only two nurses can possibly provide for each individual family living within the Greater Manchester, Lancashire and South Cumbrian area.

'This is difficult, as the needs vary greatly from family to family and district to district,' Dr Stevens comments. 'For example, some local hospitals and district nurses have much greater freedom for administering intravenous drugs and narcotics than others. Likewise many practices will see only a very occasional child with terminal malignancy and therefore it is almost impossible to maintain local expertise – hence the need for specialist nurses working out of a regional centre.'

In the time since Jimmy died, hundreds of child cancer patients have succeeded in leaving drips and drugs behind for ever; others have failed and already died, or will do so soon. Maybe this book will encourage us all to work even harder towards finding the cause of this mystifying disease. By publishing Jimmy's story, my simple hope is that the love he engendered in so many people will spread even further to many more.

# If You Want To Help

If Jimmy's story has moved or saddened you, perhaps you feel that you would like to make a personal gesture to help other children with cancer. Several of the following charities contributed in various ways, either directly or indirectly, to helping Jimmy and his family; a donation to any one of them will help other families survive the tragedy of childhood cancer.

CANCER RELIEF MACMILLAN FUND
FOR PAEDIATRIC NURSES,
Anchor House,
15-19 Britten Street,
London SW3 3TZ

The greater the number of specialist paediatric nurses this charity can train, the more help there will be for families caring for a very sick or dying child at home. (A percentage of the royalties from this book will be donated to Macmillan.)

LEUKAEMIA RESEARCH FUND,
43 Great Ormond Street,
London WC1N 3JJ.

One of Britain's biggest cancer charities which researches the causes not only of leukaemia but also of myeloma, Hodgkin's disease and other lymphomas. There are 17,000 people of all ages stricken by these cancers each year.

LEUKAEMIA RESEARCH AT
ROYAL MANCHESTER CHILDREN'S HOSPITAL,
Hospital Road,
Pendlebury,
Manchester M27 1HA.

Donations to Jimmy's hospital will bring immediate help to children currently undergoing chemotherapy and bone marrow transplants.

CHILDREN'S CANCER RESEARCH FUND,
9 Langham Road,
Bowdon,
Altrincham,
Cheshire WA14 2HT

This charity was founded in 1992 specifically to fund vital research based on The Royal Manchester Children's Hospital's unique database of information on child cancer cases dating back forty years – money is urgently needed to fund this important work.

THE MALCOLM SARGENT CANCER FUND FOR
CHILDREN,
14 Abingdon Road,
London W8 6AF

This charity exists to relieve the extra financial pressures imposed by cancer on families; throughout Jimmy's illness, the fund helped pay the cost of transport between home and hospital both for Jimmy's treatment and clinic appointments and to ensure his family could afford to visit him daily when he was an in-patient, despite the 180-mile round trip. Cash is also provided to help families pay bills for necessities such as extra heating at home.

CLIC (CANCER AND LEUKAEMIA IN CHILDHOOD)
CLIC House,
11-12 Fremantle Square,
Cotham,
Bristol BS6 5TL.

CLIC helps children and families in the south-west of England, but other areas have been so impressed by its work and the inspiration of its founder, Dr Bob Woodward, that similar support groups may follow in other centres.

THE COMPASSIONATE FRIENDS
6 Denmark Street,
Bristol BS1 5DQ.

The grief which a family suffers when a child dies is often best understood by others who have already experienced this devastating loss; Compassionate Friends is an international organization of bereaved parents offering friendship and understanding to other bereaved parents. A network of local groups operates throughout the country, and TCF also have a newsletter, and a most valuable library service.

If you would like to offer practical help at a local level, inquire at your local hospice, children's hospice or hospital – many large centres run support groups which help provide holidays, parties, treats and respite care for very sick children and their families.

# Children

## AND THE

# Spirit World

A BOOK

FOR

BEREAVED

FAMILIES

## Linda Williamson

PIATKUS

First published in 1997 by
Judy Piatkus (Publishers) Ltd
5 Windmill Street, London W1P 1HF

A catalogue record for this book is available
from the British Library
ISBN 0–7499–1773–3

Edited by Kelly Davies

Set in 11/14 Monophoto Times
by RefineCatch Limited, Bungay, Suffolk
Printed & bound in Great Britain by
Mackays of Chatham PLC